Service Learning in Higher Education

Elaine Clanton Harpine

Service Learning in Higher Education

From Pedagogy to Practice

Springer

Elaine Clanton Harpine
Group-Centered Learning, LLC
Corpus Christi, TX, USA

ISBN 978-3-031-51377-0 ISBN 978-3-031-51378-7 (eBook)
https://doi.org/10.1007/978-3-031-51378-7

This Springer imprint is published by the registered company Springer Nature Switzerland AG
The registered company address is: Gewerbestrasse 11, 6330 Cham, Switzerland

Paper in this product is recyclable

To my loving husband, Bill, for your never-failing devotion, my dear friend and editor, Judy Jones, for encouraging me to write this book, and to every university student and child who worked with me using academic service-learning and the Camp Sharigan Project.

Preface

Twenty-two university students gathered nervously, watching the clock, waiting for a school bus to pull up and deposit thirty children, first through third graders, onto the front porch of the after-school facility, ready to enter Camp Sharigan. The university students had been working for weeks to make sure everything was ready. In class, they had explored and discussed the theories that would help them work with at-risk students. They explored chapter after chapter in their textbook linking such concepts as intrinsic and extrinsic motivation, cognition and experiential learning, personal needs versus social needs, self-determination and self-efficacy, self-centeredness versus moral values, controlling emotions, and the list could go on. Why were these university students so determined to read every page of their textbook? They wanted to be ready to help thirty children who were failing in school, children who had given up, saw no hope, children surrounded by poverty. The university students knew that they only had one week (two hours a day, for five days) in which to change these children's lives forever. A university service-learning classroom project had become more than just an assignment or requirement on the syllabus. These students were warriors, and they were going out to do battle with reading failure.

Academic service-learning encompasses college campuses in countries all around the world. Perhaps more than four million students participate in service-learning projects every year. Over 1000 universities offer service-learning, just in the United States.

Academic service-learning is a teaching-learning methodology that encourages experiential learning and classroom engagement. Service-learning is more than just community service. Academic service-learning always links directly with the course being taught.

Academic service-learning offers a unique learning experience that brings the university classroom in contact with the real world, making theories and concepts relevant to life today and tomorrow. The university classroom is no longer about taking notes and listening to lectures. The classroom takes on new life, a new level of importance.

Service-learning includes action, learning, and reflection—tying service and course content together for a deeper understanding and application of the course. Indeed, research has shown that students better understand course content and consequently do better on their exams after real-world, hands-on application through service-learning projects.

What Is Needed to Teach a Service-Learning Course?

Many say they would like to use service-learning, but they simply "do not have the time." This book provides a step-by-step manual for those who would like to add academic service-learning to their course curriculum but have no idea where to begin. This book tells exactly how to add service-learning to a university course while making it easy to use service-learning.

In addition, for faculty members who already incorporate service-learning into their university classrooms, this book offers new ideas and techniques for improving experiential learning and student engagement. Therefore, this book will serve the needs of first-time faculty who are new to academic service-learning as well as those who have been using service-learning for years.

This book also can serve as a text or manual for workshops and conferences teaching how to design courses in service-learning. Each chapter ends with questions to help in planning the course, a troubleshooting checklist, a planning guide sheet, and a case study example. The case study example shows exactly how service-learning was used to teach the theories and information in a university course. The example runs throughout the entire book to give a complete picture for how service learning can be interwoven into classroom course content.

What Are the Advantages of Using This Book?

Many books on service-learning are collections of essays about service-learning or compilations of presentations from a conference or convention. In contrast, this book shows how to implement service-learning in the classroom. It gives everything needed to be successful with academic service-learning.

If you are teaching a variety of classes, you can easily combine the efforts of your students into one service-learning project. You do not necessarily need to do a separate project for each class that you teach. This book shows you how.

One semester, I was teaching a graduate level group therapy class and a graduate course on human growth and development. Both classes employed an academic service-learning pedagogy. The two classes worked together beautifully, even though they never met until the first day of *Camp Sharigan* with the children.

Service-learning is a wonderful way to bring students from different disciplines together. Working together as a team in a community setting is advantageous for all students involved.

So, What Are You Waiting For?

If you're looking for a way to bring real-world experiences into your classroom, then academic service-learning is for you. If you're looking for a way to encourage your students to improve their problem-solving skills, their critical thinking, and their ability to analyze information, this book can help you bring those skills into your classroom. If you would like to help your students learn to interact and empathize with the needs of others, then academic service-learning can encourage your students to develop cross-cultural understanding and civic participation.

Most of all, if you are looking for a way to turn your university course into a learning laboratory where students get excited just to come and learn, then welcome to academic service-learning. Academic service-learning is a teaching method that will encourage students to read their textbook and want to learn more about the theories and principles being taught in class. It also helps improve test scores. The benefits are endless to you the teacher, the student, the community, and the university.

Academic service-learning has expanded to encompass almost every department and discipline at the university, undergraduate and graduate level. Service-learning is no longer just in the behavioral sciences. Engineers, business majors, law enforcement, nursing, environmental studies, computers, music, art, public relations, and education are all taking advantage of academic service-learning courses. Academic service-learning fits the needs of every discipline.

Chapter 1 explains how to get started developing the pedagogy for teaching an academic service-learning course. Service-learning should begin with looking at the goals and objectives of the course. Chapter 2 discusses the research and theories supporting the teaching methods used with academic service-learning as well as how to increase student engagement in the university classroom. Chapter 3 describes how to select a service-learning project. Selecting an academic service-learning project is more than just deciding on a community work site. Chapter 3 gives issues and questions to consider. Chapter 4 talks about how students learn best in the college classroom. Chapter 5 focuses on how to create an intrinsically motivating learning environment. Chapter 6 gives step-by-step details on linking service and learning in a course. Chapter 6 stresses connecting the course content and textbook with the service project. This is vital because academic service-learning is more than just tacking a service project onto the end of the semester. Academic service-learning must be built into the course. Chapter 7 discusses reflection activities and how to measure the effectiveness of learning in the classroom as well as at the service project. Chapter 8 tells how to write an academic service-learning syllabus. Chapter 9 discusses leadership development and how to incorporate change in the classroom and at the community worksite. Chapter 10 gives details for preparing students to work in a community setting. Chapter 10 considers the impact of academic service-learning on the students, the university, and the community. Chapter 10 also gives suggestions for ways that you can share your experience with others on campus and in the community.

Where many books provide an array of essays talking about service-learning, this book explains the step-by-step process for implementing academic service-learning into the college curriculum. This easy-to-use, hands-on guide contains everything needed to implement academic service-learning in any classroom.

Welcome to academic service-learning. I think that you will find it a productive and wonderful way to bring a university classroom to life and to help students learn more than they ever thought possible.

Group-Centered Learning, LLC
Corpus Christi, TX, USA

Elaine Clanton Harpine

About the Author

Elaine Clanton Harpine, Ph.D., is a motivational psychologist specializing in group-centered motivational program design. She has 50 years' experience designing and conducting motivational prevention programs for children and youth. She earned her doctorate in Educational Psychology, Counseling from the University of Illinois, Urbana-Champaign. She received the 2022 Albert Nelson Marquis Lifetime Achievement Award for her work with inner city children and youth.

Dr. Clanton Harpine has published 19 nonfiction books:

- *Why Can't We Teach Children to Read? Oh, but Wait, We Can, A Step-by-Step Plan for Teaching Your Child to Read* (2022).
- *After-School Programming and Intrinsic Motivation: Teaching At-Risk Students to Read* (2019)— 2020 top publication in quality education by Springer Nature.
- *Teaching At-Risk Students to Read: The Camp Sharigan Method* (2016).
- *Group-Centered Prevention in Mental Health: Theory, Training, and Practice* (2015).
- *After-School Prevention Programs for At-Risk Students: Promoting Engagement and Academic Success* (2013).
- *Prevention Groups* (2013).
- *Group-Centered Prevention Programs for At-Risk Students* (2011).
- *Group Interventions in Schools: Promoting Mental Health for At-Risk Children and Youth* (2008).

Also, her book *No Experience Necessary!* received an Award of Excellence from Group Publishing in 1995. Other children's books include:

- *Come Follow Me* (2001–2003)—two volume set.
- a three-volume family series completed in 2003.
- a youth book in 1989.

She has published numerous articles for teenagers on peer pressure, coping with failure, alcohol abuse, parents, suicide, and more recently, articles on using group-centered interventions in the schools. Other writing includes:

- *Erasing Failure in the Classroom*, Vol. 1.
- *Camp Sharigan* program (2nd *ed.*, 2016), Vol. 2.
- *Vowel Clustering* (2010).
- *Reading Orienteering Club* (2017), Vol 2.

Her research for eighteen years focused on using group-centered interventions with at-risk readers. Dr. Clanton Harpine designed *Camp Sharigan*, a motivational reading program. She also designed the *Reading Orienteering Club* after-school prevention program for at-risk children. She has published her research with these programs in psychological journals and reported it at the American Psychological Association's conventions. She is the past editor for the "Prevention Corner" column in *The Group Psychologist*. She was selected for inclusion in *Who's Who of American Women* for her work with children in inner-city neighborhoods and at-risk communities.

Acknowledgments

I wish to express my appreciation to my husband, Bill, for his love and support throughout the entire project and for his patience and helpful comments on the text. I also want to thank Judy Jones, my editor and friend, for her support and help in the development of this book. A very special thank you goes to all of the university students, children, youth, community volunteers, parents, teachers, and university faculty with whom I have had the pleasure of working throughout the years with academic service-learning and the *Camp Sharigan Project*. Always remember, we can teach children to read, and if you teach children to read, you can change the world.

Contents

Chapter 1
Yes, I Want to Use Academic Service-Learning: Where Do I Begin?

As we were reviewing the syllabus on the first day of class, one of my university students raised a hand and asked, "we don't really have to do this service ... do we?" I explained that, yes, we were all going to work on a service-learning project together. As I continued, I showed slides from Camp Sharigan, showing that we would be going out into the community to build a make-believe reading camp for children who were struggling in reading. From the other side of the room, another student spoke up and said, "this is going to be great. When do we start?"

So, yes, your class may greet you with a variety of responses, but you might also want to consider that, at the end of the semester, one student wrote on the class evaluation: "I didn't want to do the service-learning project, but I'm glad you made us do it. I learned so much from working with the children. I'm even going to change my major to do community work with children."

Service-learning should change the lives of the community in which you work. Academic service-learning can also change the lives of the students you teach. Academic service-learning opens a new door and invites students to participate in the learning process, not as passive listeners but as active partners in a learning community.

What Is Academic Service-Learning?

Academic service-learning is a teaching method that links academic curriculum to a community problem. Service and learning connect to help students better understand the course content's real-world application. Research shows that the benefits of academic service-learning are the same regardless of the size of the institution—community college, 4-year, private, or research university (Cronley et al. 2015; Sandy and Holland 2006; Taggart and Crisp 2011). Therefore, in this book, we will

E. Clanton Harpine, *Service Learning in Higher Education*,
https://doi.org/10.1007/978-3-031-51378-7_1

use the terms *university* and *college* interchangeably with academic service-learning.

Academic service-learning links learning and service together. Academic service-learning connects a professor's classroom learning goals with the community's needs, so the service project enhances the students' learning while improving the lives of those in the community. The service-learning project is integrated into the entire course. With academic service-learning, learning takes place in both the classroom and at the community worksite. Therefore, in this book, the word *classroom* is used to refer to how you teach in the actual college classroom. The word *worksite* refers to what the students learn at the community service site.

Academic service-learning produces stronger student outcomes. Academic service-learning produces higher grades and assessment scores (GPA, test scores, and knowledge learned), better retention and graduation rates, stronger student engagement, commitment, persistence, and improved self-efficacy (Bringle and Hatcher 2017; Eyler et al. 2001; Krsmanovic 2022; Vogelsang and Astin 2000; Warren and Sellnow 2010). With academic service-learning, service-learning becomes the method through which the professor teaches the course.

Academic service-learning courses integrate the service project into the course content. Today's employers are looking for college graduates with real world knowledge and experience, not just textbook facts (Arum and Roksa 2011). Academic service-learning provides a real-world experience. *It is this linking of service and learning that makes academic service-learning so successful.*

Why Is Academic Service-Learning More Beneficial Than Other Forms of Service?

The feature that makes academic service-learning stand out above all other forms of service and learning is *fully connecting the course material and the service project* (Howard 2001; Kuh et al. 2008; Warren and Sellnow 2021). Academic service-learning teaches students how to apply the course's content to real-life problems and encourages students to problem-solve to find solutions to those problems. A statistics class stated that they understood the course material better with the service-learning project because they had to apply what they had learned in class (Kamuche 2006). Academic service-learning helps the university, the students, the community, and the faculty because it connects directly to student engagement.

How do university students benefit from academic service-learning? University students participating in academic service-learning produce higher test scores and demonstrate stronger application of textbook content than students who did not participate in an academic service-learning course (Kamuche 2006; Warren 2012; Warren and Sellnow 2021). Other benefits include:

- Students learn how to apply what they are learning to real-world problems.
- Students strengthen their problem-solving skills and critical thinking abilities.

- Students develop teamwork and leadership skills.
- Students' communication and interpersonal skills improve.
- Students acquire a deeper understanding of different cultures and may even banish stereotypes.
- Students frequently demonstrate more interest in their course work.
- Students show a higher level of motivation and persistence.
- Students expand their awareness of the needs of others and sometimes may discover professional career opportunities to pursue after graduation.

Academic service-learning can be used with any course, in any field, at any university. Theatre, bookkeeping, economics, dental training, math, computer science, education, biology, psychology, communication, and online courses are using academic service-learning. Academic service-learning focuses on teaching techniques that engage students and help them learn.

How do university professors benefit from academic service-learning? Improving student engagement is a major topic of discussion among university professors. Professors obviously want to help their students learn. Students who are engaged in the learning process learn more (Bringle and Hatcher 2017).

Faculty are seeking ways to increase student engagement. Academic service-learning has proven to be an excellent method for increasing student engagement and academic success (Ash et al. 2005; Bringle and Hatcher 2017; Krsmanovic 2022). Learning in the college classroom improves and gains new significance when students participate in a high-quality academic service-learning course. Such a course encourages service in real-world settings that applies to what students are learning in class (Bringle et al. 2010). With academic service-learning, students demonstrate critical thinking, analytical reasoning, teamwork, and enthusiasm (Wang and Rodgers 2006).

Faculty need to create high quality learning environments to increase student engagement. Professors can create a high-quality academic service-learning environment by connecting service and learning. Academic service-learning becomes the teaching method (pedagogy) that helps students apply theory, textbook knowledge, and practical real-world application to the course they are studying. Students even reported increased motivation to learn course content because of their participation in academic service-learning (Hart and King 2007). Many faculty are turning to academic service-learning to improve student outcomes and engagement in the learning process.

How do universities benefit from academic service-learning? Universities are very interested in student engagement. Why? One reason is that student engagement has been shown to be one of the major predicators for student retention. More than 50% of college freshmen never finish college (Bringle et al. 2010). Universities are seeking ways to increase student outcomes as well as boost student retention (Bringle and Hatcher 2017). Research shows that academic service-learning increases student engagement, academic success, and retention (Bringle et al. 2010). Faculty and administrators have become more interested in academic service-learning because of the need to improve student engagement and retention (Kuh 2007).

Interest in service and learning is growing daily. Universities around the world are exploring which form of service offers the best advantages for students. Although academic service-learning shows strong evidence of success, the real difference lies in how instructors intertwine service and learning in their course material. Academic service-learning cannot just be added on at the end of the semester. It must become the way in which instructors teach the course. Academic service-learning starts on the first day of class and continues all the way through till the end.

Advantages of Using Academic Service-Learning as a Teaching Method

All universities and professors seek to improve academic success. Academic service-learning leads to academic success by enabling students to apply what they are reading in their textbook to the community site where they are working. When teaching goals are intertwined with service and academic content, student engagement, learning, and persistence improve (Bringle et al. 2010; Kuh et al. 2008).

Academic Service-Learning Teaches More than Mere Community Service

Although all community service helps to build civic mindedness and concern for others, mere community service is not listed as one of the "high impact practices" that improves student success, persistence, or performance in the university classroom (Kuh et al. 2008). Academic service-learning has shown more success in the college classroom than other forms of service and learning because of the way the course material and the service project intertwine (Howard 2001; Krsmanovic 2022). Teaching style correlates with student performance (test scores) and knowledge learned (Kamuche 2006).

Academic service-learning teaches engagement and success. As noted above, student engagement is crucial to student success. Student engagement is defined as the level of participation students have in the learning process (Bringle et al. 2010). Intellectual improvement and understanding of new concepts are influenced by how much effort a student puts forth. Motivation is a key ingredient. Student engagement is measured by how involved a student is with the course, how motivated the student is to learn, and how much persistence the student displays toward learning. Academic service-learning provides a teaching method that strengthens student engagement (Bringle and Hatcher 2017). Let's envision how this could be applied.

> To demonstrate the diversity of academic service-learning, let's create a university landscape architect course. The instructor could have students begin the semester learning the basic vocabulary from the text and studying planting design principles. The class could use

> in-class exercises and projects to practice these design principles. Then, students could plan their own landscape design. The design might be critiqued by experts and even community members. Student engagement always shows the most improvement when instructors challenge their students. In this case, student engagement would be high because students would be extremely motivated to apply the landscaping principles learned to create their own individual landscape design. The final step could be to create the design in the community.

Creating a design on paper is not the same as creating a design in the real world.

Putting the landscape design into practice is an essential part of the learning process (Nijhuis and Bobbink 2012).

Academic service-learning teaches that service and learning are equally important. Academic service-learning projects do not necessarily need to be complicated, but they must connect service and learning together. Let's look at an example of how this could be done in an English, history, sociology, urban studies, psychology, political science, economics, or communications course. If professors want their students to work in a soup kitchen, to make the service into an academic service-learning project, there must be a connection with the course being studied. In English, have students do a creative writing project based on the people they meet. In sociology, history, economics, or communication, for example, ask students to keep a reflection journal based on their observations. Instructors could even go one step further in class and have students' problem solve to look for possible solutions in the community—jobs, housing, medical support. As the students learn about the needs of others, they could apply course content to their experiences at the soup kitchen. This simple example can be applied to many courses. The idea is to make service a learning experience (Blaisdell 2005). Then, to adapt such learning to what is being taught in the classroom.

Academic service-learning teaches through active learning. Academic service-learning uses active learning instructional techniques directly connected to the course. Academic service-learning challenges students and faculty to create a collaborative teaching and learning structure in the classroom and at the community worksite.

Active learning emphasizes acquiring knowledge, skills, and values. Active learning instructional techniques help students become active learners through their classroom participation as well as their involvement at the community worksite. With academic service-learning, students volunteer in the community to help learn course information as well as to fill the community's needs (Wang and Rodgers 2006).

Students are not just passively watching and listening in the classroom. Academic service-learning shows students how to apply what they are reading in the textbook to real-life problems. Academic service-learning also encourages students to find solutions to those problems.

> A political science professor teaching a senior government course on human rights used research teams, real case studies of asylum seekers, additional readings, guest speakers, field visits to detention centers, and even mock trials in class to help students understand the needs of asylum seekers. (Dicklitch 2003)

Academic service-learning turned the classroom into a learning laboratory where students were challenging themselves to learn even more than the class requirements. We'll talk more about how to use active learning in Chapter 2. For now, we'll simply state that academic service-learning requires active learning to be successful.

What Is the Difference Between Community Service and Service-Learning?

On the first day of class, I always ask, "has anyone ever participated in service-learning?" Usually, several students eagerly announce that they have. Many students participate in community service projects in high school. Students may also have been involved in service-learning through other university classes. Therefore, they enter the college classroom with a notion of what working in the community means.

Is there a difference? However, service-learning and community service are not the same. Most researchers divide service in the community into three categories: community service, co-curricular service-learning, and academic service-learning. Community service and service-learning may be local, national, or international. The location or amount of volunteer time is not what defines the difference between community service and service-learning.

Community service is volunteering to help others. Volunteering is wonderful and volunteers learn as they work, but research does not show community service to enhance academic learning (Howard 2001). Classroom learning and university retention are secondary to the volunteer experience. With community service, the emphasis is on service in the community. For example, a university math class might hold a beach clean-up day. This is definitely needed, but, if there is no link back to what the students are studying, it is not an academic service-learning project.

Community service or service learning. One of the hardest steps for most people adopting an academic service-learning pedagogy is truly distinguishing between community service, co-curricular service-learning, and academic service-learning. One study found that of all the faculty surveyed, not one gave the same definition of service-learning (Resch and Schritteser 2021). It makes a big difference because, as we discussed earlier, only academic service-learning enhances academic outcomes and student retention (Howard 2001). Let's look at an example to illustrate the distinction.

> A professor required 10 hours of service. Students were responsible for finding their own work sites. At the end of the semester, students wrote a two-page reflection report describing their experiences. Is this an academic service-learning project?

No, because the course content is not integrated with the service project. Some professors merely send students out to volunteer in the community. Community service is great, but service-learning is more than just a tacked-on community project.

What is the contrast between academic service-learning and co-curricular service-learning? Co-curricular service-learning is usually related to the student's field of study, but not necessarily a specific course. Co-curricular service-learning strives to teach students skills from the service site that they can use later in their careers. Co-curricular service-learning can be a fabulous experience for students, but research has not shown co-curricular service-learning to increase student outcomes or retention as effectively as academic service-learning (Hart and King 2007). Let's look at how a co-curricular service-learning project could be converted to academic service-learning.

> If political science students set up a booth at a community event to register prospective voters, this would be an example of a co-curricular service-learning project. It is related to what they are studying and teaches leadership and organizational skills, but it is not part of the course curriculum. Yet, if the same professor used the service project on registering voters for an upcoming election to teach the rights of citizens, effects of gerrymandering, nation-wide political effects of non-voters, and whatever else was being covered and discussed in the course, then the voter registration service project could indeed become an academic service-learning project.

The difference lies in how the service project is integrated with the course content.

Co-curricular vs. academic service-learning. Let's look at the results when two professors decided to test the effectiveness of co-curricular vs. academic service-learning. The two university classes covered the same course content. Both classes provided one-on-one tutoring in literacy and included reflective assignments. The difference was that one class used traditional lecture with the reflective exercises and service-learning added on. The other class used active learning and worked together as a class analyzing and evaluating after each tutoring session, applying what they learned. The academic service-learning students wrote their reflections individually but then discussed the reflective assignments as a group. As one university student from the academic service-learning section said,

> The service-learning project has been a positive experience to me academically, … you really need to digest the material that we are presented with in order to use it correctly as a tutor. I also feel my mind set was changed, I was no longer learning something for a test, I had to learn it and know it or I may fail my student (Written reflection SL♯18, 11–15). (Hart and King 2007, 328)

The academic service-learning students in this study saw value in what they were doing in the community. They were helping others learn to read, but the real value for the university students came from the entire course experience. They learned more. They were able to connect theory and practice. The academic service-learning course had far more impact than the co-curricular course because the service project became authentic and grounded in what was being taught in the classroom. That does not mean that the students in the co-curricular class did not have a meaningful experience. It is just that the academic service-learning course produced much higher student engagement and academic achievement (Hart and King 2007).

Academic service-learning strengthens learning and engages students in the learning process. Students have shown improved problem-solving skills, critical thinking, application of knowledge, and higher levels of cognitive development (including remembering and decision making) when participating in academic service-learning courses (Barnett et al. 2009). The key is linking service and learning together.

Example of Academic Service-Learning

To illustrate how academic service-learning can be used in a university course, I will use examples from a course that I taught—psychology of motivation. Throughout the book, you will also see examples from the service-learning project that I used with this course—*Camp Sharigan* (Clanton Harpine 2024), a reading clinic for struggling and failing students. Using one single, ongoing case example throughout the book ties service and learning together and allows examination of specific teaching strategies.

Throughout the book, I will highlight the teaching techniques employed. The same teaching principles that I adopted for my course could be used by a professor teaching accounting, chemistry, English literature, communication, Chinese, sociology, law enforcement, environmental studies, math, physics, health science, journalism, nursing, or any other course taught at a university. The principles are the same.

Case example. One of the major goals in my psychology of motivation class was to teach my students how to create an intrinsically motivating learning environment. I wanted them to learn the difference between creating an actual motivational environment and just offering rewards or prizes.

Group work. One day, I divided the class into small groups. Each group was assigned to produce a five-step plan for developing a motivational environment for *Camp Sharigan*. When the small groups came back together as a total class, the critical thinking and analysis began. One group wanted to make signs. Someone else mentioned that the children could not read. Through discussion, problem-solving, and analyzing the needs of the children, the class decided on making signs with pictures to identify each workstation. The end result was signs attached to workstation pictures, colorful banners, and a designated work area for each station. This works well with *Camp Sharigan* because it is a make-believe camp with ten workstations where children work on a different task at each workstation. There are such stations as the Rainbow Bridge, Friendship Tree, Snake Pit, Lake Read, Mount Reading, Camp Cabins, and even a Stop Sign. The classroom assignment also worked well for my instructional goals because the textbook assignment for that day was identifying personal motivational needs. The students had to think of what the children needed to be able to work at *Camp Sharigan* as well as what would be fun, exciting, and motivating. They used their textbook to identify these needs. As one student said, "I hated reading when I was in school. If we're going to get these kids excited about reading, it has to be fun. Yes, I know we need to teach them to read, but we have to get them interested first."

Teaching through discussion. This led to discussions of overcoming failure and disappointment—two topics from the textbook. *Camp Sharigan* brought the textbook theories and information to life and made them suddenly seem like more than just words on a page. The concepts being discussed in the textbook were the exact problems the students were facing in creating an intrinsically motivating environment.

Creating an Academic Service-Learning Teaching Method in a University Course

Converting a course to academic service-learning does not take away from the content of what should be taught in the course. It also does not make the course less rigorous. It does create a wonderful learning atmosphere that helps university students learn more than they ever imagined.

How could a course be changed to incorporate academic service-learning? To show how we could convert a community service project to academic service-learning, let's look at a university art class. Some might claim art to be an unlikely course for academic service-learning. It's actually perfect. Let's create an example.

Community service project. There is an international organization called "Empty Bowls" that focuses on raising money to feed the hungry. A community-minded art instructor who wanted to teach students how to make clay bowls might have students make bowls to sell and raise money in order to make a donation. This could be a wonderful, worthwhile community service project, but there is no connection between service and what is being taught in the course.

Change. In contrast, if the professor connected the course goal of making clay bowls to an assignment to organize a student art fair, a simple service project could be transformed into an academic service-learning course. Students could make a clay bowl for an art show. Each student could select a different country where hunger prevails. Students could also research to discover what type of clay bowls are made and used in that country. The students could create an original painting on their bowls depicting the countries they have chosen. The students could also work in groups and teams to organize an art show at which they could sell their pottery to raise money for the "Empty Bowls" charity. The teacher might also have students make a video to advertise the upcoming art show and show how the students created their bowls.

Benefits. With such an academic service-learning approach, the students would learn much more than just how to make a clay bowl. Students would learn all of the details in class for shaping, painting, and glazing pottery. They would also be learning how artists sell the products they produce. This would now be an academic service-learning taught class because students would be learning (1) the principles of making a clay bowl, (2) the history of pottery in different countries, (3) how to create an original piece of art to paint on their bowl, (4) how to organize and direct an art show for selling pottery, and (5) how to help others in need by raising money to feed the hungry.

Academic service-learning strengthens classroom learning. Any course can be converted to an academic service-learning approach. With academic service-learning, the service project begins the first day of class and becomes the teaching technique that helps students understand the course's theories and concepts.

Where Do I Begin?

A university education should help in preparing students for a career and a successful, happy life. How will your course contribute? What exactly, at the end of the semester, do you want your students to have learned from your course?

Set course goals. Course goals list what students should know and understand from the class by the end of the course. As Grant Wiggins and Jay McTighe (2005) explain in their book *Understanding by Design*, "look at the big picture." Teaching is about transferring what you know to your students. How will you make this transfer happen? As Wiggins and McTighe say, "work backwards."

What do you want students to learn? At this point, some may be saying, "Shouldn't I think about what kind of service project I want my students to do before I think about course goals?" No. We always want to think about the course first. Academic service-learning is built upon course content. It's like building a house. A builder cannot put on the roof before building the foundation and structure. Academic service-learning is course-driven; therefore, start with the course content.

Think about what you want to teach the students. Wiggins and McTighe (2005) suggest that you ask a series of questions to get started:

What do you want students to remember?

How will you help students learn this information?

How will you know when students have learned the information?

Case Example

Let's look at how I applied these three questions to my own course.

Question #1: What do you want students to remember? In my psychology of motivation class, I wanted my students to know and understand the difference between intrinsic (internal) and extrinsic (rewards) motivation. I wanted my students to know and understand that intrinsic motivation is much more powerful than extrinsic motivation. I wanted my students to understand the "cost" of using extrinsic motivators, especially since in school most of my students had been inundated by extrinsic rewards. Students needed to be able to identify and use intrinsic motivation during our service project at *Camp Sharigan*.

Teaching techniques. To help students understand these points, the course included research studies, class problem-solving exercises, group discussions, and the *Camp Sharigan* service-learning project. Each student completed an observation report from *Camp Sharigan* in which they identified the intrinsic motivators and explained the results of those intrinsic motivators. The observation assignment asked specific questions that students had to answer from their experience at *Camp Sharigan*. Again, they had to link textbook material with real-world activities.

Teaching critical thinking. Opinions never counted in my class unless research facts supported them. Students were instructed to use their textbook.

Question #2: How will you help students learn this information? I not only wanted my students to learn how to create an intrinsic environment for *Camp Sharigan*, but also to *experience an intrinsically motivating classroom environment*.

Teaching techniques. Since intrinsic motivation is more effective in the classroom than extrinsic (Ryan and Deci 2008), I wanted to design classroom experiences that would encourage positive self identify, erase negativity, eliminate competition, encourage self-efficacy (belief that a student can learn), strive for balance between choice and control, and always strive for positive change. An academic service-learning course helps students develop intrinsic motivation to master the course content. We will say more about intrinsic motivation in Chapter 5.

Teaching intrinsic motivation. Intrinsic motivation is essential in an academic service-learning classroom. Intrinsic motivation is that internal desire to explore and learn (Reeve et al. 2003). Motivation explains why we act and behave in a certain way (Reeve et al. 2007), but motivation can be positive or negative. Indeed, "A prize, an award, and even money, which are all extrinsic, may bribe someone into performing a certain action, but compliance is not true motivation" (Clanton Harpine 2015, 87). Neither is fear. Grades are a form of extrinsic motivation. In contrast, real motivation must come from within the person.

Creating a motivational classroom. We can create a motivational classroom, but we cannot motivate students. We must give students the tools to motivate themselves (Deci and Ryan 2012). It is intrinsic rather than extrinsic motivation that generates persistence (the will to try and keep trying) (Cerasoli et al. 2014). So, I needed to create motivational strategies that would help my students attain the learning goals set for the course. Research shows that intrinsic motivational strategies lead to better test scores, retention of textbook material, and overall learning outcomes (Ryan and Deci 2008). Intrinsic motivation is important for student engagement and for student satisfaction.

Question #3: How will you know when students have learned the information? My hope was that, as my students went out into the world, they would apply what they learned. They could use intrinsic motivation rather than extrinsic rewards with their families, their work, or in all situations involving motivation.

Teaching techniques. An essay exam gave my students an opportunity to explain the theories they had learned from the textbook. Students also completed an observation report in which they answered specific questions concerning intrinsic and extrinsic motivation, for which they had to cite examples from *Camp Sharigan*. They completed a research paper on motivation. One of the reflective exercises asked students to draw a comparison between the intrinsic motivational learning environment that we created for *Camp Sharigan* and the motivational learning environment used in our classroom. Motivation is one of the keys to improving student engagement.

Teaching transference to the real world. We all want to teach information but useable information. Understanding a theory or concept and being able to apply it is different than just knowing facts. I wanted my students to know how damaging extrinsic motivation could be. They needed to see, from a week of working with failing students at *Camp Sharigan*, the difference when we used intrinsic rather extrinsic motivation with the children. Academic service-learning can bring this level of learning to the college classroom. Service-learning, when service and learning are linked, can bring student engagement as well as critical thinking to any college classroom and course. By the end of the course, the students had a working knowledge of intrinsic motivation and could apply it in a real-world setting.

Summary

Academic service-learning introduces university students to hands-on learning experiences (learning by doing), real-world problem solving, group discussion and decision making, observing change in action, as well as reflecting on what has been learned. Academic service-learning strengthens student engagement and success in the university classroom. Research shows that students learn more and score higher on end-of-the-semester tests through courses taught using academic service-learning. Academic service-learning enables students to apply what they are reading in their textbook to the community site where they are working. Research documents that academic service-learning improves students' mental wellness, allows students to develop and test their leadership skills, improves communication, increases community awareness, and improves academic performance in the classroom, even with test scores.

Building an Academic Service-Learning Pedagogy

Questions to Help in Course Planning

1. What are your course goals? Establish at least three course goals.
2. How will you strengthen student engagement?
3. How will you measure learning and knowledge gained throughout the course?

Troubleshooting Checklist

1. What accommodations will you make for diversity?
2. What kind of classroom will you be teaching in? Yes, it is possible to do academic service-learning in a lecture hall. Not easy, but possible. If assigned a lecture hall, can you request a room change? If not, how will you accommodate?
3. How do you encourage acceptance and kindness to others during your class?

Planning Guide Sheet

1. Set 3 or more course goals.
2. List at least 5 things that you can do to help create an intrinsically motivating environment in your classroom.
3. List 5 ways that you can encourage student engagement in your course.

Case Example

In accordance with Wiggins and McTighe (2005), I set six class goals for my psychology of motivation class.

To challenge students to discover the complexities of motivation for self and for others.
To change student opinions about motivation.
To increase positive student engagement in the course.
To rebuild and/or improve each student's self-efficacy about their ability to learn and succeed at the university.
To create an intrinsically motivational learning environment in my classroom and teach students how to apply intrinsic motivation in the real world.
To demonstrate the benefits of working in a cohesive group atmosphere in our classroom and at *Camp Sharigan*.

References

Arum, R., & Roksa, J. (2011). *Academically adrift: Limited learning on college campuses*. Chicago: University of Chicago press.
Ash, S. L., Clayton, P. H., & Atkinson, M. P. (2005). Integrating reflection and assessment to capture and improve student learning. *Michigan Journal of Community Service Learning, 11*, 49-60.
Barnett, M., Silver, P. T., & Grund, T. S. (2009). Implementing service-learning pedagogy: A case example. *Journal of Higher Education Outreach and Engagement, 13*, 117-134.
Blaisdell, B. (2005). The soup kitchen writing workshop. *English Today, 21*, 50-54. https://doi.org/10.1017/S0266078405003111
Bringle, R. G., & Hatcher, J. A. (2017). Innovative practices in service-learning and curricular engagement. *New Directions for Higher Education, 147*, 37-46. https://doi.org/10.1002/he.356
Bringle, R. G., Hatcher, J. A., & Muthiah, R. N. (2010). The role of service-learning on the retention of first-year students to second year. *Michigan Journal of Community Service Learning, 16*, 38-49.
Cerasoli, C. P., Nicklin, J. M., & Ford, M. T. (2014). Intrinsic motivation and extrinsic incentives jointly predict performance: A 40-year meta-analysis. *Psychological Bulletin, 140*, 980-1008. https://doi.org/10.1037/a0035661
Clanton Harpine, E. (2015). *Group-centered prevention in mental health: Theory, training, and practice*. New York: Springer.

Clanton Harpine, E. (2024). *Camp Sharigan: A ready-to-use group-centered intervention for grades 1-3* (3rd ed.). Corpus Christi, TX: Group-Centered Learning.

Cronley, C., Madden, E., & Davis, J. B. (2015). Making service-learning partnerships work: Listening and responding to community partners, *Journal of Community Practice, 23*, 274-289. https://doi.org/10.1080/10705422.2015.1027801

Deci, E. L., & Ryan, R. M. (2012). Self-determination theory. In P. A. M. V. Lange, A. W. Kruglanski & E. T. Higgins (Eds.), *Handbook of theories of social psychology* (Vol. 1, pp. 416-437). Thousand Oaks, CA: Sage.

Dicklitch, S. (2003). Real service = real learning: Making political science relevant through service-learning. *Political Science and Politics, 36,* 773-776. https://doi.org/10.1017/S1049096503003111

Eyler, J., Giles, D. E. Jr., Stenson, T., & Gray, C. (2001). At a glance: Summary and annotated bibliography of recent service-learning research in higher education (3rd ed.). San Diego: Learn & Serve America National Service-Learning Clearinghouse.

Hart, S. M., & King, J. R. (2007). Service learning and literacy tutoring: Academic impact on pre-service teachers. *Teaching and Teacher Education, 23,* 323-328. https://doi.org/10.1016/j.tate.2006.12.004

Howard, J. T. (2001). *Service-Learning Course Design Workbook*. Ann Arbor, MI: OCSL Press.

Kamuche, Felix U. (2006). Service learning and student performance. *Academic Exchange Quarterly, 10*, 187-192.

Krsmanovic, M. (2022). Fostering service-learning and leadership development through first-year seminar courses. *Journal of Service-Learning in Higher Education, 15,* 54-70.

Kuh, G. D. (2007). Success in college. In P. Lingenfelter (Ed.), *More student success: A systemic solution*. Boulder, CO: State Higher Education Executive Officers.

Kuh, G. D., Cruce, T. M., Shoup, R., & Kinzie, J. (2008). Unmasking the effects of student engagement on first-year college grades and persistence. *Journal of Higher Education, 79,* 540-563. https://doi.org/10.1353/jhe.0.0019

Nijhuis, S., & Bobbink, I. (2012). Design-related research in landscape architecture. *Journal of Design Research, 10*, 239-257. https://doi.org/10.1504/JDR.2012.051172

Reeve, J., Nix, G., & Hamm, D. (2003). The experience of self-determination in intrinsic motivation and the conundrum of choice. *Journal of Educational Psychology, 95,* 347-392. https://doi.org/10.1037/0022-0663.95.2.375

Reeve, J., Ryan, R. M., Deci, E. L., & Jang, H. (2007). Understanding and promoting autonomous self-regulation: A self-determination theory perspective. In D. Schunk and B. Zimmerman (Eds.). *Motivation and self-regulated learning: Theory, research, practice* (pp. 223-244). Mahwah, NJ: Lawrence Erlbaum Associates Publishing.

Resch, K., & Schrittesser, I. (2021). Using the service-learning approach to bridge the gap between theory and practice in teacher education. *International Journal of Inclusive Education, 20,* 136-151. https://doi.org/10.1080/13603116.2021.1882053

Ryan, R. M., & Deci, E. L. (2008). Self-determination theory and the role of basic psychological needs and personality and the organization of behavior. In O. P. John, R. W. Robbins, & L. A. Pervin (Eds.). *Handbook of personality: Theory and research* (pp. 654-678). NY: The Guilford Press.

Sandy, M., & Holland, B. A. (2006). Different worlds and common ground: Community partner perspectives on campus–community partnerships. *Michigan Journal of Community Service Learning, 13*, 30–43.

Taggart, A., & Crisp, G. (2011). Service learning at community colleges: Synthesis, critique, and recommendations for future research. *Journal of College Reading & Learning, 42*, 24-44.

Vogelgesang, L. J., & Astin, A. W. (2000). Comparing the effects of service-learning and community service. *Michigan Journal of Community Service Learning,* 7, 25-34.

Wang, Y., & Rodgers, R. (2006). Impact of service-learning and social justice education on college students' cognitive development. *NASPA Journal, 43*, 316-337.

Warren, J. L. (2012). Does service-learning increase student learning?: A meta-analysis. *Michigan Journal of Community Service Learning, 18,* 56-61.
Warren, J. L., & Sellnow, T. L. (2010). Learning through service: The contributions of service learning to the communication discipline. In D. L. Fassett & J. T. Warren (Eds.), *Handbook of communication and instruction* (pp. 129-145). Thousand Oaks, CA: Sage Publications.
Warren, J. L., & Sellnow, D. D. (2021). Increasing learning while serving the community: Student engagement as the key to learning in a basic public speaking course. *Journal of Higher Education Outreach and Engagement, 25,* 25-35.
Wiggins, G., & McTighe, J. (2005). *Understanding by Design*, 2nd ed. Alexandria, VA: Association for Supervision and Curriculum Development.

Chapter 2
The Advantages of Using Academic Service-Learning in a University Classroom: What Does the Research Say?

Sometimes students start the semester a little resentful that I do not use traditional lecturing. As one student said, "it's your job to teach me the book; I don't need to read it." Yet, by the end of the semester, I frequently receive such comments on the end of the course evaluation as, "I didn't like it when you made us talk [group problem solving discussions], but I wanted to help the kids. I read the book and worked hard in class. I learned more in this class than any other."

Academic service-learning empowers students, increases their desire to learn, and enables students to apply what they are learning in class to the real world. When students perceive that a course is purposeful and useful, they become more engaged with the learning process. They are more motivated to learn and, as a result, learn more (Warren and Sellnow 2010). So, never be afraid to try something new. Academic service-learning, for some, is new and puzzling, but it is built on a rock-solid foundation of research. Academic service-learning uses active learning instructional techniques and stresses student engagement with real-world problems. Creating realistic challenges for students is one of the keys to student success.

Academic Service-Learning Pedagogy

Throughout this book, we will be discussing how to build an academic service-learning pedagogy for a university course. We will use the word *pedagogy* to mean the method used for teaching the class. For academic service-learning, pedagogy will also extend to the service worksite because service and learning are linked.

The original version of the chapter has been revised. A correction to this chapter can be found at https://doi.org/10.1007/978-3-031-51378-7_11

E. Clanton Harpine, *Service Learning in Higher Education*,
https://doi.org/10.1007/978-3-031-51378-7_2

Which comes first, service or the course? Many think that academic service-learning starts when you arrive at the community worksite. Wrong. Academic service-learning begins on the first day of class inside the classroom before you ever even go into the community. Academic service-learning ties service and learning together.

Academic service-learning provides students with real-world application and a better understanding of course content. Academic service-learning enables students to improve their problem-solving skills, critical thinking, application of knowledge, and higher levels of cognitive development (including remembering and decision making) (Barnett et al. 2009). This is why an academic service-learning pedagogy is such a strong teaching method. Academic service-learning allows students to put theory into practice (Forsberg et al. 2019).

The service project is interwoven into the course being taught. It's like building a house, the builder cannot put the roof on first. The builder must begin by building a solid foundation. Then, build up to the roof. The same is true with academic service-learning. The pedagogy or method used for teaching the class is the foundation upon which academic service-learning is built. Active learning is the supporting substructure underlying academic service-learning.

What Is Active Learning?

The battle about how to be a more effective teacher has been raging for centuries. There are almost as many theories as there are teachers, but one finding that has remained constant over the years is that students learn better when they are actively engaged in what they are learning (Angelo 1995; Bleske-Rechek 2001; Deslauriers and Wieman 2011; Deslauriers et al. 2019; Dewey, 1933; Eddy and Hogan 2014; Freeman et al. 2014; Haak et al. 2011; Hake 1998; McKeachie 1987; Shields and Gredler 2003; Sukacke et al. 2022; Theobald et al. 2020).

Active learning means action. Active learning goes by many names, but the main concept is that active learning enables students to interact with the theories and information that they are learning rather than passively sitting and listening to a lecture. Active learning instructional methods are interwoven into the very framework and design of academic service-learning.

Academic service-learning needs active learning to be successful. Since we are building an academic service-learning course we must use active learning as the foundation. Why? As research has shown, active learning instructional techniques produce higher student outcomes (GPA, test scores, and knowledge learned), better retention and graduation rates, stronger student engagement in the classroom, deeper understanding of the theories and knowledge being taught, improved self-efficacy, superior student commitment and persistence, excellent problem-solving skills, plus critical thinking, analytical reasoning, and the ability to apply the course's content to real-life problems (Bringle and Hatcher 2017; Deslauriers et al. 2019; Eyler et al. 2001; Freeman et al. 2014; Harton et al. 2002; Krsmanovic 2022; Vogelsang and Astin 2000; Wang and Rodgers 2006; Warren and Sellnow 2010). This is exactly what we are striving to achieve. With academic service-learning, we want more than just a community service project; we want the academic advantages.

Is the Teaching Method Important?

Yes, the teaching method that you use in the classroom is critical to the success of academic service-learning. The teaching pedagogy that you develop for your course will determine whether your academic service-learning course succeeds or not. Yet, even when faculty and students hear that students learn more through active learning, it is difficult for some faculty and students to believe that active learning instructional techniques are actually better (Sukacke et al. 2022). Indeed, researchers have found that both university faculty and students often resist switching to active learning instead of lecturing (Sukacke et al. 2022). However, if you wish to use an academic service-learning pedagogy and reap the benefits of academic service-learning, you must shift from traditional lecture to active learning. Academic service-learning cannot simply be tacked on to traditional lectures. Let's look at what the research tells us.

Which is more effective, active learning or traditional lecturing? Research has shown that instructors can cover the same amount of information through active learning as with lecturing (Deslauriers et al. 2019). Test scores are also higher with active learning (Deslauriers et al. 2019; Freeman et al. 2014; Harton et al. 2002). When students working together in groups were compared to students in traditional lecture sections, the classes that worked together in groups had the highest test scores (Williams 2011). Lectures are passive; they are not interactive. Even when professors allow questions, the questions are directed to the professor, not between class members. For interaction to lead to student engagement, it must involve everyone in the group or class. Let's look at some research studies testing these two methods.

Which is better? A study from Harvard (Deslauriers et al. 2019) tested the question of which is better—lecturing, or active learning? They compared "students' self-reported perception" of what they had learned with the actual test scores showing what they had learned. These were large enrollment typical lecture classes with random student assignment. One half of the students participated in classes taught using active learning instructional methods. The other half of the students participated in lecture classes taught by popular, highly rated instructors. All courses covered the same text and information. Instructors were able to cover just as much material in the active learning classes as the lecture professors. The only difference was active learning vs. traditional lecturing. According to the test scores from both groups, the active learning students learned more. On the self-perception reports, the students in the lecture classes believed that they had learned more when they actually had not. Why? As the researchers said, faculty and students are accustomed to and comfortable with lectures; they do not trust active learning (Deslauriers et al. 2019). Yet, for academic service-learning to succeed, faculty and students must switch to active learning.

Students need to be actively involved. Another research study demonstrated that, by encouraging students to become personally involved with the subject being studied (self-referencing) and by relating textbook material to everyday life, the students were able to produce higher scores on a test one week and even two weeks after the class material was presented (Hartlep and Forsyth 2000). Again, active learning makes it easier for students to become personally involved with course content. Research strongly supports that students learn more through a class taught with active learning rather than through lecturing (Stains et al. 2018).

Student engagement requires active participation. Just sitting and passively listening is not considered a form of student engagement, not even when you add question and answer sessions to traditional lecture. As a team of researchers demonstrated, active learning proved to be superior to even "interactive lectures." Test scores were higher and students who participated in the active learning sections said that they would not have been able to learn as much if it had not been for the active learning techniques that were used in class, and this was in a technical computer class (Kothiyal et al. 2014).

Lectures may also be harmful. Another study looked at 2000 classrooms, taught by 500 different professors, at 25 dissimilar United States universities. Researchers concluded that lectures do not help students learn; instead, they actually increase the likelihood of failure compared to active teaching methods (Stains et al. 2018). In still another study, a research team analyzed 225 classes. In each case, students improved on exams through active learning. Research documented that undergraduate students in classes using traditional lecturing were more likely to fail than students participating in active learning; classes using traditional lectures demonstrated a higher likelihood of failure—55% failed under lecturing (Freeman et al. 2014).

Are students really learning from lectures? From my own experience, I know that there is always a tendency for some to believe that students will only learn from lectures, even though research supports the opposite. Let's look at an example.

> One semester, another faculty member and I were both teaching the same course, with the same textbook, and covering the same material. I was using academic service-learning with *Camp Sharigan* (Clanton Harpine 2024). The other professor used traditional lecture with an added service requirement at my *Camp Sharigan* community project. I went to the class before the service project to present a slide presentation on *Camp Sharigan* to the students. The professor requested that I come near the end of the lecture so that I wouldn't interrupt. As I quietly slid in at the back of the lecture hall and waited, I noticed two students on their laptops sending messages on Facebook and several other students scrolling on their phones, while one student was even watching a movie with the sound turned off (reading the closed captions at the bottom of the page). Yes, I am certain there was a student somewhere in that room actually listening and taking notes. However, just because you give a dynamic lecture does not mean the students are listening or engaged in the learning process.

At the end of the semester, testing showed that students from the academic service-learning section outscored students from the lecture section.

Why do faculty and students distrust active learning? If active learning instructional techniques have been shown through research to be more effective than lecturing, why do so many faculty and students still distrust active learning? The best answer is tradition, combined with the fear of something new and different. Lectures have been the predominant teaching method at colleges since the beginning of university education. Some professors may be saying, "discussion just wouldn't work for my class. I have too much information to cover." But is that true?

A paradigm shift. Opinions are great, but the proof is in the test scores and the knowledge students gain. As one research team stated, faculty and students must make a "paradigm shift"—change their view of education and learning (Sukacke et al. 2022). The research team's conclusion was that active learning is definitely worth the change, but faculty and students must transform how they think and work together in the classroom, learn new skills, and develop new responsibilities (Sukacke et al. 2022).

An academic service-learning pedagogy cannot be built on lectures. The shift from lecture to active learning is essential for academic service-learning to be successful. Students learn more when they are personally involved in the learning process.

How do students feel about active teaching techniques? Some professors say that they are reluctant to switch from lecturing because they fear that teacher evaluations will suffer in active learning classes (Uttl et al. 2017). In my own courses, when asked if they preferred interactive (active learning) teaching methods or lecturing, students said:

> "Interactive, it gets people thinking."
> "It teaches me more, helps me understand."
> "Interactive, the traditional lecture is so boring and is used by almost all teachers, and it is usually never interesting."
> "Interactive because it makes you wanna go to class. Traditional lecture keeps me uninterested and wanting to go to sleep."

What are the Advantages of Using Academic Service-Learning?

Academic service-learning increases student engagement. Student engagement is essential for effective learning experiences at any university, and most universities encourage faculty to strengthen student engagement. Student engagement is measured by how involved the student is with what they are learning and the student's level of interaction in the classroom. Research has repeatedly shown that students who are actively engaged in the learning process learn more (Bringle and Hatcher 2017).

Academic service-learning encourages students to get involved in the learning process. Students do not automatically become engaged the minute they walk into the classroom. Students must be challenged to get involved. Academic service-learning helps students become more involved through classroom participation as well as their involvement at a service worksite. Active learning and academic service-learning work hand-in-hand together to build a strong teaching pedagogy. Students are not just passive bystanders; they are part of the learning process.

Academic service-learning encourages students to work together in groups. Working in groups and classroom discussions increases student engagement (Holtz 2004; McKeachie 1987; Williams and Williams 2011). Students act on the knowledge that they gain from class. Such action makes it easier to understand the information being taught rather than just memorization, which is typically forgotten a few months later.

Academic service-learning improves memory and recall. Learning-by-doing or the intentional hands-on use of the information being taught increases a student's ability to remember and recall knowledge learned (Steffens et al. 2015). Through active learning, students have the opportunity to work with the information they are learning from the textbook. When such learning is applied to a hands-on service opportunity, as with academic service-learning, students reap the benefits. These are skills needed not only for success in the university classroom, but also for careers and throughout life.

Academic service-learning and active teaching techniques improve test scores. Active learning instructional techniques, such as working together in teams or in small groups, have increased student performance on examinations (Harton et al. 2002; Latane 2002). A study of 477 university students over five semesters showed that students who participated in academic service-learning scored significantly higher on course exams than students who did not participate in a service-learning section of the course (Strage 2000). Written journal entries from students participating in the academic service-learning section of the course revealed that students were able to draw links between the course material and the service project. Their reflections and involvement of course content increased across the semester (Strage 2000). One of the reasons that academic service-learning courses improve test scores is active learning.

Academic service-learning prepares students for problem solving in real life. Problem-solving teaching techniques have been proven to improve the understanding of difficult textbook material (Shields and Gredler 2003), and when students are required to apply theories and concepts from the textbook to real-life situations, self-referencing (thinking about how the information being learned relates personally) strengthened the retention of the textbook material (Hartlep and Forsyth 2000). Such connections with the course content only happen when the service project and what is being taught in the classroom are interwoven together into a strong teaching pedagogical structure.

Academic service-learning teaches critical thinking. Critical thinking improves in the college classroom when teachers use interactive student discussions, teach problem-solving, and allow students to apply what is being learned to real-life situations (Angelo 1995). Academic service-learning provides this real-life experience. Group discussions and an emphasis on problem-solving have been shown to have the greatest impact on critical thinking (Astin 1992; Cooper 1995; McKeachie 1988). Organizing, planning, and solving problems associated with the service project enable students to apply critical thinking and problem-solving techniques taught in the classroom. Academic service-learning uses active learning to promote innovation, problem-solving, critical thinking, and to analyze the pros and cons of an issue. Active learning, especially small group activities, has been shown to be effective even in large university classes (Bleske-Rechek 2001).

Active learning instructional techniques also help underprivileged students. Active learning teaching techniques have proven to help first generation college students, students of color, and lower achieving students more than traditional lecture (Theobald et al. 2020). Problem-solving, active-learning, and higher-order cognitive skills, such as critical thinking exercises have proven to help reduce the achievement gap for disadvantaged students (Haak et al. 2011). As research shows, "... active learning reduced achievement gaps in examination scores by 33% and narrowed gaps in passing rates by 45%" (Theobald et al. 2020). Higher test scores and higher likelihood of retention are two reasons active learning is used with academic service-learning.

How to Build an Academic Service-Learning Active Learning Teaching Pedagogy

Now, we have established that active learning teaching techniques are more effective in the university classroom than traditional lecturing, that many students may be surprisingly eager to adopt active learning, and that active learning is essential if we want to be successful in creating an academic service-learning pedagogy. Our next objective is to show how to integrate active learning and academic service-learning.

Academic service-learning helps teach course content. Eliciting understanding is most professors' goal. Every professor faces the task of consolidating an almost-limitless amount of information into a one semester course, and professors usually have multiple courses. An academic service-learning pedagogy provides professors with a method for teaching this almost-limitless amount of information. When students see real-world connections with what they are reading in their textbooks or studying in class, they are more likely to become engaged in the learning process and thereby understand what is being taught. Using an academic service-learning style pedagogy or teaching method also provides differentiated learning opportunities to help all university students understand the course material better.

How can the service project be integrated into the course content? In my own classes, I used a problem-solution format. I gave the students problems related to the reading clinic that we were building. Since I refused to accept opinions, the students learned that they had to back up their ideas with researched facts. I emphasized that I wanted the answers contained in the textbook or peer reviewed journal articles. They searched through the text for answers. Then, in class, we applied those answers, and evaluated, analyzed, and pulled together the concepts that we needed to produce an intrinsically motivating reading clinic for children. Students even started bringing their textbooks to class and laying the book open on their desk. They became involved with the service project. They wanted to create the best possible camp for the children. Student engagement in class became remarkably high. Let's look at an example from my psychology of motivation class to illustrate how I used active learning.

Case example. I arrived a few minutes before the first day of class, arranged the desks in a large circle instead of rows, and placed a copy of the syllabus and a short description of *Camp Sharigan* on every desk. As one student later told me, "I knew this class was going to be different the minute I walked in the room."

Leadership and team building through working together on a service project. This was a junior-level psychology of motivation class. Our service project was to create a reading camp for failing first through third grade children. The step-by-step instructions (contained in the *Camp Sharigan* program packet) told the university students exactly what they needed to do to create this hands-on reading camp. Therefore, from the very beginning of the semester, the students learned leadership skills, team building, and group process and development. Such teaching techniques are important for all academic service-learning courses.

Group discussion and critical thinking. On the first day of class, after reviewing the syllabus, we jumped right into a discussion about how you can tell whether someone is motivated. Different students shared their thoughts on how to motivate others. Then, while sitting in the discussion circle, I dropped the bombshell that it is not possible to motivate another person.

Problem-solving. Controversial concepts, even on the first day, help students realize that they must think, analyze, research, and challenge many of their time-honored opinions.

Using service to teach about classroom motivation. Then, I pulled the service project into the class discussion and used *Camp Sharigan* to teach my university students about motivation. Even though these were junior-level students, they entered class with the preconceived idea that motivation is a bowl of candy sitting on the teacher's desk, earning points for an ice cream party at the end of the month, having a competition and handing out awards, or earning money for good grades in school. I needed to change those opinions before I could begin to teach about motivation.

Teaching students how to analyze and solve problems. So, I asked, "how are we going to create this *Camp Sharigan* for 30 children who are failing and have given up hope that there is any possibility of them ever learning to read? They need motivation, but since the textbook says that we cannot motivate another person, what are we going to do?" Naturally, the students started listing all sorts of rewards and prizes, but I stopped them and said, "that is not real motivation. True, we could use prizes, awards, candy, or even money, but what would the results be? In your textbook, such prizes and rewards are called 'gaining compliance.' As your textbook explains, bribes only work for a short time, and compliance is not really motivation. It's like giving in to someone, even though you don't want to, just to get the reward or prize they offer. We want true motivation that lasts a lifetime. True motivation comes from within the person. How are we going to achieve this with the children?"

Assignment from discussion that directly links with textbook. "Your first assignment will be to read your chapter and come to class ready to explain to me what the text says we should use instead of prizes and awards."

Using active learning. As you can see at this point, this one class session has used group discussion, problem-solving strategies, critical thinking, and group interaction. The students are thinking and analyzing the textbook material being discussed. They are not just passively sitting and listening. They are involved in the discussion. This exact technique can be used in any course. Business majors, pre-law students, artists, computer scientists, journalists, social workers, law enforcement majors—all need to learn to analyze different points of view. Academic service-learning brings such teaching techniques into the classroom.

Linked service project and textbook. At this point in my class, we moved our desks into a horseshoe-shaped half-circle facing the screen where I showed a slide presentation from *Camp Sharigan*. At the close of class, I said, "your textbook lists seven behaviors that are important for motivation. For our next class session, I want you to read the chapter and come to class ready to discuss and plan how we can create an intrinsically motivating learning environment for these children emphasizing these seven behaviors. I do not want your opinions. I want what it says in the textbook. I want to know how the textbook says we can bring out these seven motivational behaviors with the children. The text does not discuss rewards, ice cream parties, or other extrinsic bribes. We're talking about real motivation. Come to class prepared to outline what we need to do."

Linking service and learning. I used the service-learning project to help teach the textbook theories about motivation that my students needed to learn. Service-learning challenged students to start thinking about motivation on the first day of class. As this example shows, academic service-learning integrated theory into the class discussion.

Creating an intrinsically motivating environment in the university classroom. One of the ways that I chose to create a motivational environment was to teach students how to create a motivational learning environment for the children at *Camp Sharigan*.

Emphasizing academic service-learning. The service project was introduced on the first day of class. The opening group discussion stressed the difference between community service and service-learning. Then, I demonstrated that difference through the methods that I used to teach the class. The students received assignments that directly pulled the information from the textbook into the work that they needed to do for the service-learning project. Service and learning were linked.

Summary

Active learning ties directly into the theoretical concept of academic service-learning. When we combine active learning and service together to form academic service-learning, we pull together the best of both concepts. Academic service-learning increases cognitive development, empathy, thinking skills, intellectual growth, interpersonal relationships, cultural awareness, and commitment to social justice. When coupled with active learning to build higher test scores and a better understanding of the theories and knowledge being taught, academic service-learning creates a strong foundation for student engagement and learning in the classroom.

Building a Service-Learning Pedagogy

Questions to Help in Course Planning

1. What are your course goals? Review the goals that you set in Chapter 1.
2. How will you employ active learning in your class? Which active learning instructional techniques will you use in class? How will you relate these teaching techniques to the information that you want students to learn?
3. How will you measure student engagement? Will you incorporate reflection activities, especially as related to the service-learning project? Will students keep a journal?
4. What will you do to create an intrinsically motivating environment?
5. How will you measure learning and knowledge gained throughout the course? This is more than just the usual exams. What else will you do to measure how much students are learning?

Troubleshooting Checklist

1. Is your class truly interactive or do you fall back into lecturing?
2. Will you use problem solution strategies? If so, what problems will you use?
3. What accommodations will you make for diversity among the students in your class? How will you help students who are having difficulty?
4. How will you discourage competition between students during class discussions? How will you encourage cooperation?
5. How do you encourage acceptance and kindness to others during your class discussions?

Planning Guide Sheet

1. Keep class goals in mind as you plan teaching strategies.
2. Outline active learning teaching strategies that you would like to use.
3. List at least 5 things that you can do to help create an intrinsically motivating learning environment in your classroom.
4. List 5 active learning teaching strategies that you plan to use in your classroom.
5. List 5 ways that you can encourage student engagement in your course.
6. List 5 ways that you can include critical thinking in your classroom discussions.

Case Example

While we all say that we want our students to be kind, polite, and not teasing or bullying other students, it is sometimes difficult to make that happen. If you deliver a lecture where you do all the talking, then teasing and bullying take place outside the classroom. When you open the class to group discussion, you need to be prepared and aware of the fact that you might encounter rude comments made by one student to another student. How will you handle such behavior?

> Unfortunately, one day a student said, "that's the dumbest idea I've ever heard."
>
> I immediately replied, "we are a team and personal attacks are not allowed. Apologize please. Then, let's evaluate the idea, not the person."

Every university classroom should be a place of acceptance, a place where everyone's ideas are included. No, that does not mean that they are not evaluated, but the evaluation is not a personal attack. Set criteria, and evaluate to the criteria, not the person. Evaluate the ideas, not the students who present them.

My classroom becomes a learning laboratory, and an example for how personal problems and conflicts can be handled later during the service project with the children and also in life. I inform my students on the first day that we are a team, not a competitive team, but a team that strives to work together to build the very best reading camp for children in need. It is each student's responsibility to help their neighbor. The class helps students to build moral responsibility that I hope will translate into moral development throughout their lives.

References

Angelo, T. J. (1995). Classroom assessment for critical thinking. *Teaching of Psychology, 22*, 6-7.

Astin, A. W. (1992). *What matters in college? Four critical years*. San Francisco: Jossey-Bass.

Barnett, M., Silver, P. T., & Grund, T. S. (2009). Implementing service-learning pedagogy: A case example. *Journal of Higher Education Outreach and Engagement, 13,* 117-134.

Bleske-Rechek, A. L. (2001). Obedience, conformity, and social roles: Active learning in a large introductory psychology class. *Teaching of Psychology 28*, 260-262.

Bringle, R. G., & Hatcher, J. A. (2017). Innovative practices in service-learning and curricular engagement. *New Directions for Higher Education, 147*, 37-46. https://doi.org/10.1002/he.356

Clanton Harpine, E. (2024). *Camp Sharigan: A ready-to-use group-centered intervention for grades 1-3* (3rd ed.). Corpus Christi, TX: Group-Centered Learning.

Cooper, J. L. (1995). Cooperative learning and critical thinking. *Teaching of Psychology, 22*, 7-9.

Deslauriers, L., & Wieman, C. (2011). Learning and retention of quantum concepts with different teaching methods. *Physical Review Special Topics – Physics Education Research, 7,* 010101-1-010101-6. https://doi.org/10.1103/PhysRevSTPER.7.010101

Deslauriers, L., McCarty, L. S., Miller, K., Callaghan, K., & Kestin, G. (2019). Measuring actual learning versus feeling of learning in response to being actively engaged in the classroom. *Proceedings of the National Academy of Sciences, 116*, 19251-19257. https://doi.org/10.1073/pnas.1821936116

Dewey, J. (1933). *How we think: A restatement of the relation of reflective thinking to the educative process*. Lexington, MA: D. C. Heath and Company.

Eddy, S. L., & Hogan, K. A. (2014). Getting under the hood: How and for whom does increasing course structure work? *CBE Life Science Education, 13*, 453-468. https://doi.org/10.1187/cbe.14-03-0050

Eyler, J., Giles, D. E. Jr., Stenson, T., & Gray, C. (2001). *At a glance: Summary and annotated bibliography of recent service-learning research in higher education* (3rd ed.). San Diego: Learn & Serve America National Service-Learning Clearinghouse.

Forsberg, E. , Bäcklund, B. , Telhede, E. & Karlsson, S. (2019). Virtual patient cases for active student participation in nursing education —students' learning experiences. *Creative Education, 10*, 1475-1491. https://doi.org/10.4236/ce.2019.107108

Freeman, S., Eddy, S. L., McDonough, M., Smith, M. K., Okoroafor, N., Jordt, H., & Wenderoth, M. P. (2014). Active learning increases student performance in science, engineering, and mathematics. *Proceedings of the National Academy of Sciences, 111*, 8410–8415. https://doi.org/10.1073/pnas.1319030111

Haak, D. C., HilleRisLambers, J., Pitre, E., & Freeman, S. (2011). Increased structure and active learning reduce the achievement gap in introductory biology. *Science Magazine, 332*, 1213-1216.

Hake, R. R. (1998). Interactive-engagement vs. traditional methods: A six-thousand-student survey of mechanics test data for introductory physics courses. *American Journal of Physics, 66*, 64–74. https://doi.org/10.1119/1.18809

Hartlep, K. L. & Forsyth G. A. (2000). The effect of self-reference on learning and retention. *Teaching of Psychology, 2*, 269-271.

Harton, H. C., Richardson, D. S., Barreras, R. E., Rockloff, M. J., & Latane, B. (2002). Focused interactive learning: A tool for active class discussion. *Teaching of Psychology, 29*, 10-15. https://doi.org/10.1207/S15328023TOP2901_03

Holtz, R. (2004). Group cohesion, attitude projection, and opinion certainty: Beyond interaction. *Group Dynamics: Theory, Research, and Practice, 8*, 112–125. https://doi.org/10.1037/1089-2699.8.2.112

Kothiyal, A., Murthy, S., & Iyer, S. (2014). Think-pair-share in a large CS1 class. *Proceedings of the 2014 Conference on Innovation & Technology in Computer Science Education-ITiCSE '14*, 137–144. https://doi.org/10.1145/2591708.2591739

Krsmanovic, M. (2022). Fostering service-learning and leadership development through first-year seminar courses. *Journal of Service-Learning in Higher Education, 15*, 54-70.

Latane, B. (2002). Focused interactive learning: A tool for active class discussion. *Teaching of Psychology, 2*, 10-16.

McKeachie, W. J. (1988). Teaching thinking. *Update. 2*, 1.

McKeachie, W. J. (1987). Teaching, teaching, and research on teaching. *Teaching of Psychology, 14*, 135-139.

Shields, C. & Gredler, M. (2003). A problem-solving approach to teaching operant conditioning. *Teaching of Psychology, 30*, 114-116.

Stains, M., Harshman, J., Barkers, M. K., Chasteen, S. V., Coles, R., Dechenne-Peters, S. E., … Young, A. M. (2018). Anatomy of STEM teaching in North American Universities. *Science, 359*, 1468-1470. https://doi.org/10.1126/science.aap8892

Steffens, M. C., von Stülpnagel, R., & Schult, J. C. (2015). Memory recall after "learning by doing" and "learning by viewing": Boundary conditions of an enactment benefit. *Frontiers in Psychology, 6*, 1-10. https://doi.org/10.3389/fpsyg.2015.01907

Strage, A. A. (2000). Service-learning: Enhancing student learning outcomes in a college-level lecture course. *Michigan Journal of Community Service Learning, 7*, 5-13.

Sukacke, V., Pereira de Carvalho Guerra, A. O., Ellinger, D., Carlos, V., Petroniene, S., Gaiziuniene, L., Blanch, S., Marba-Tallada, A., & Brose, A. (2022). Towards active evidence-based learning in engineering education: A systematic literature review of PBL, P JBL, and CBL. *Sustainability, 14*, 1-31. https://doi.org/10.3390/su142113955

Theobald, E. J., Hill, M. J., Tran, E., Agrawal, S., Nicole Arroyo, E., & Behling, S. (2020). Active learning narrows achievement gaps for underrepresented students in undergraduate science, technology, engineering, and math. *Proceedings of the National Academy of Sciences, 117*, 6476-6483. https://doi.org/10.1073/pnas.1916903117

Uttl, B., White, C. A., & Gonzalez, D. W. (2017). Meta-analysis of faculty's teaching effectiveness: Student evaluation of teaching ratings and student learning are not related. *Studies in Educational Evaluation, 57*, 22–42. https://doi.org/10.1016/J.STUEDUC.2016.08.007

Wang, Y., & Rodgers, R. (2006). Impact of service-learning and social justice education on college students' cognitive development. *NASPA Journal, 43*, 316-337.

Warren, J. L., & Sellnow, T. L. (2010). Learning through service: The contributions of service learning to the Communication discipline. In D. L. Fassett & J. T. Warren (Eds.), *Handbook of communication and instruction* (pp. 129-145). Thousand Oaks, CA: Sage Publications.

Williams, K. C., & Williams, C.C. (2011). Five key ingredients for improving student motivation. *Research in Higher Education Journal*, 12, 104-122.

Chapter 3
Why Is It Important to Select the Right Service-Learning Project?

Camp Sharigan is a hands-on, make-believe, wonder-filled reading camp that meets for two hours a day for one week. Treasure hunt maps and colorful banners direct the children to ten exciting workstations that change each day. Mount Reading helps children work their way through "tricky" spelling words as they climb to the summit to find a good book to read. Children practice letter sounds at the Friendship Tree. Children hook on to new adventures at Lake Read with a fishing pole and magnet while they practice puppet plays. There's also a tent full of buzzing mosquitoes, a grapevine, a campfire, a snake pit with a friendly snake named Sharigan, and a make-believe poison ivy patch that helps the children capture new words. At the camp library, children become the author, write a story, and make a book. At the camp cabins, children make a pop-up book cover for their story. The compass at the Read and Hike Trail points the way to stories hidden under inflatable rocks, while the Road to Nowhere but Reading is lined with funny stories. At the Camp Stop Sign, everyone stops to play a word game, while learning something from a nonfiction book. The pace is lively as each workstation works on remedial reading skills. This will be our service project. Our goal is to make learning fun. The result is to instill a love for reading and make reading a life-long habit. To do so, we must teach children how to read.

This is the written description that I give to my students on the first day of class.

A well-planned description gets my students excited on the first day, but selecting a service project that sounds exciting is not enough. Do not just pick any project that comes along. Selecting the wrong project can lead to disaster, even to having students learn the opposite of what was intended. A poorly selected service project might reinforce stereotypes, prejudices, and misinformation.

E. Clanton Harpine, *Service Learning in Higher Education*,
https://doi.org/10.1007/978-3-031-51378-7_3

Guidelines for Selecting an Academic Service-Learning Project

Choosing a service-learning project is more than simply finding a community worksite. Just because a community agency is eager to recruit volunteers does not necessarily make them a good fit with your course objectives. Academic service-learning courses integrate the service project into the course content. It is this linking of service and learning that makes academic service-learning so successful. As discussed in Chapter 2, the course you are teaching and the way you plan to use active learning to teach the course will determine the type of service project you wish to select. *For academic service-learning to be effective, you must select (1) a project that enhances student learning, (2) a project that is successful, and (3) a project that provides a positive impact for the community and your students.* Let's examine these three requirements more thoroughly.

Enhance student learning. Academic service learning is a teaching method, and the primary purpose for using academic service-learning is to enhance learning in the university classroom. Helping others is wonderful and is definitely one of the motives for using academic service-learning. First and foremost, however, the service project must enhance student learning. Academic service-learning produces higher student outcomes, better retention and graduation, stronger student engagement, commitment, persistence, and improved self-efficacy (Bringle and Hatcher 2017; Howard 1998; Krsmanovic 2022; Warren and Sellnow 2021). This happens if and only if service and learning are linked in the classroom and at the community worksite. Academic service-learning becomes the method for teaching the course. So, before selecting a service project ask, *how will this service project enhance student learning in the classroom*?

Service project must be successful. Success comes from how well you link the service project with your course content. A major question to consider is, *how can you be sure the service project fits the course*? Since each professors' course goals are different, a project must be selected that fits the course's specific requirements. This is crucial for academic service-learning's success. For example, *Camp Sharigan* stresses rebuilding self-efficacy and uses intrinsic motivation to teach children to read. These are theories that my psychology of motivation students are studying. If *Camp Sharigan* did not teach children how to read or improve their reading as well as link with course content in motivation, then it would be a failure as an academic service-learning project. The service project must successfully meet a community need (overcoming reading failure) and must also help teach the course content.

Positive impact for the community and the students. First, make sure that the service project fulfills a need in the community. Identify the need, causes of the problem, and how your students can help. The service project should also build a positive relationship between the community and the university. So, select a service project that will benefit both the students and the community.

What Kind of Service Project Will You Select?

Throughout this chapter, we will strive to answer questions that will help you plan an effective service-learning project. Before you begin to talk with community leaders about a worksite, work through the following four pre-planning questions. Examples from *Camp Sharigan* will illustrate the planning strategies discussed.

The first question to ask is, will faculty choose the service project or will the students? Since the primary purpose of academic service-learning is to enhance student learning, it is better for the faculty member(s) to choose the service project. Furthermore, if you allow students the option of which service project to choose, valuable class time becomes wasted haggling over which project would be better.

Academic service-learning requires instructors to link the service project with the course content. Therefore, you need to find a community worksite that fits with the goals and objectives of your course. This must be done before the first day of class.

A second question is, should I do one project or have multiple projects? Multiple service projects simply do not work with academic service-learning. You do not want to have students doing different types of service projects because it is impossible to link 30 or 40 different projects to one set of course goals and objectives. For example, it would never work to have one student working at Habitat for Humanity, a student working with a homeless shelter, another student working at the food bank, one student working over at the school, still another student working at a nursing home, someone else building a playground, and the list could go on and on. Obviously, these could all be wonderful service projects, but it would be next to impossible to coordinate that many different projects with the goals, objectives, and curriculum for a single course. Since academic service-learning requires that the service project and course curriculum be linked together, it is better to select one class project. Indeed, several classes could even work on the same project. Let's look at an example.

> At *Camp Sharigan*, there are 10 workstations. Each workstation may be directed by one or more than one student. For example, *Mount Reading* is a spelling workstation. If I have several students, I stress teamwork. One student reads the spelling words, another helps the children use the *4 steps* to learn the spelling words. A third student assists while the children write the words correctly. Still another waits on the mountain, to help children find a book to read or to read to the children. So, the workstation can function with only one volunteer, or the volunteers can work as a team and further enhance the children's learning.

Therefore, it is possible to use a single service project with a large university class or multiple classes, with everyone working on the same project. Just make sure all students are fully involved with the hands-on fulfillment of the project.

A third question in pre-planning is, will the service project be required? Many faculty struggle with this question. My answer is yes. If you're integrating the service project into your class sessions, you cannot have some students participating in the service project while others go to the library and complete a research paper. As one wise professor stated, you do not give your students a choice as to whether they do or do not read the textbook. Nor do you ask a student's permission before assigning supplementary reading material. Therefore, simply explain on day one that you are teaching an academic service-learning course. Participation is required. I'll talk more in Chapter 8 about required participation and how to accommodate student schedules.

A fourth question is, must my academic service-learning project be a group project? Not necessarily. If you prefer, you may use individual projects, just make sure that everyone is working on the same type of project.

> If I want my college students to work individually, I integrate one-on-one tutoring. My tutoring program (Clanton Harpine 2022) uses the same *vowel clustering* method as *Camp Sharigan*. Students may be at a local school, community center, or after-school program, but they are all using the same tutoring packet. I can send an entire class out to tutor, or I can just make the tutoring packet available to students whose work or family schedule does not permit them to participate in *Camp Sharigan*. Since everyone is doing the same kind of work, it is easy to include a student's individual service project in the classroom discussions and problem-solving exercises. The packet has also been tested with college students to prove that they can individually use the packet effectively with both children and teens which provides flexibility. For example, a 5th grader reading at the third-grade level with low comprehension tested at the 6th grade reading level with high comprehension after only 21 weeks of one-hour, once-a-week tutoring using this packet.

The key to linking individual projects with the course curriculum is to use identical projects, so that all students are doing the same service, just at different locations.

Planning an Academic Service-Learning Project

There are many kinds of projects that can work with academic service-learning. Before you go out looking for a community worksite, stop and ask yourself, what kind of project will work best with your course curriculum? Remember, as research cited in Chapter 2 proved, a service project tacked on to a lecture is not academic service-learning, nor will it reap the benefits of academic service-learning (Deslauriers et al. 2019). With academic service-learning, the service-learning project becomes part of the pedagogy or way that you teach the course. It is also essential to choose or design a project that will succeed with students and the community. Both students and the community must experience a positive, productive service outcome. A failed service project neither teaches students nor helps others. There are three basic types of service projects to choose from: (1) your students may join an ongoing project in the community, (2) you may choose to use a research-based service-learning project (like *Camp Sharigan*), or (3) decide to design your own service project. Let's look at each of these options. I have included examples and planning questions at the end of each section to help you decide which option is best for your students and the course you are teaching.

Joining an ongoing community project. Some professors choose to join an ongoing service project (such as Habitat for Humanity), or nursing students might work at a free community health clinic to apply what they are learning in class. The professor can then focus on interweaving the project into the course.

- *Planning questions to think about:* How will the ongoing project fit with your course goals from Chapter 1? Will the ongoing community project be effective and safe for university students? What will your students learn from the ongoing community project?

It is essential for the ongoing community project to fit with the course you are teaching.

Choosing a research-based service program. Other faculty may choose to use a research-based service project that has been tested and proven to be successful in the community, as I did with *Camp Sharigan*. If you are selecting a research-based service program to use with your course (1) make sure it has been tested with college students and (2) make sure the program itself has been tested and proven to be effective with the community population you are going to be working with.

- *Planning questions to think about:* How will the research-based ready-to-use program chosen relate to your course goals from Chapter 1? How does the research-based program fit with the needs of the community and the university students in the course that you are teaching?

Camp Sharigan has been tested with middle school, high school, and college student volunteers in both large and small communities. Research has also shown that *Camp Sharigan* is effective. In 2009, children participating in *Camp Sharigan* outscored one-on-one tutored children. One year later, the *Camp Sharigan* children were still ahead (Clanton Harpine and Reid 2009). In 2019, children participating in *Camp Sharigan* exhibited significant improvements in reading, spelling, and sight word recognition, while children in the control group "...showed no improvement in any category" (Clanton Harpine and Pazda 2019).

If you select a research-based ready-to-use service project, make sure that it fits with the requirements of an academic service-learning taught course.

A self-designed project. Still other faculty may choose to design their own academic service-learning project. Designing your own project can help you fine-tune the service project to the course that you are teaching. If you are designing your own project, you should pre-test it before using it with your students. Just because a project sounds wonderful and creative does not mean that it will be what you need. Since our goal is to increase student engagement, improve academic success, and boost student retention, the service-learning project must be effective in teaching the course.

- *Planning questions to think about:* Why would designing your own service-learning project sometimes be the best option for students with the course you are teaching? Why would it not?

Service and learning must be linked, not just added on. We will talk more about how to achieve this intertwining of service and learning in Chapter 6.

Never hesitate to seek help. Before you start, check to see if your university offers workshops or assistance in planning an academic service-learning project.

Many universities have staff who will help you design a service-learning project. Do not be afraid to seek help. Make sure that you tell them that you're working on an academic service-learning project. Insist that service and learning link together.

Step-by-Step Guidelines for Designing an Academic Service-Learning Project

Did you find an ongoing community project that works for your course? Did you decide on a ready-to-use program? Or have you decided to design your own service-learning project? Either way, make sure that you are developing an academic service-learning project. Some projects are better suited to community service rather than academic service-learning. The link between service and learning is essential.

Getting started. All academic service-learning projects should achieve the three goals that we stated at the beginning of this chapter: to enhance student learning, to be a successful project, and to provide a positive impact for the community and the students. The service-learning project must also fit the needs of the course that you are teaching. If you are seeking a more comprehensive how-to guide on program design, I have published two books with step-by-step details: *Group-Centered Prevention Programs for At-Risk Students* (Clanton Harpine 2011) and *After-School Prevention Programs for At-Risk Students* (Clanton Harpine 2013).

Testing is the key to success. It is wise to test your program before using it, especially if you are creating your own design. It took years to develop, test, and refine my design for *Camp Sharigan*. Testing is important because you want students to have a positive and effective service experience.

Design questions. Regardless of whether you are joining an ongoing project, using a ready-to-use program, or designing your own project, working through the following step-by-step list of questions will help you develop a successful academic service-learning project. Examples from *Camp Sharigan* show how I answered each question.

Step 1: What type of academic service-learning project do you wish to develop? Give the project a name. Identify the community need or problem that you are working to correct. How will your service project correct this community need or problem? Why does this project fit well with your course? How will your students work with the service project? What will your students learn? Will your students work in the community for one week, a month, or longer?

> *Camp Sharigan* fulfills a community need and fits well with my class because it emphasizes intrinsic motivation. According to the Nation's Report Card, more than 60% of students in the fourth, eighth, and twelfth grade cannot read at grade level (National Center for Educational Statistics 2019). *Camp Sharigan* has been proven through research to help struggling students learn to read (Clanton Harpine and Reid 2009; Clanton Harpine and Pazda 2019). Both undergraduate and graduate students can work together as a team on this project.

Step 2: List five goals and objectives that you want students to achieve with this service project. How will you make sure that students achieve these goals and objectives? How many students will be working at the worksite? Will the students come from one class or multiple classes? What skills do your students need to learn to be successful with this project? How will you teach these skills to your students? Will students work in small groups, as teams, or one-on-one? How will you make sure that the service-learning project is beneficial for the students and for the community?

> My goals for the students are leadership, organizational skills, problem-solving, rebuilding self-efficacy, and using intrinsic motivation effectively. Students will achieve these goals through interactive class sessions and hands-on work at the worksite. Multiple classes will work together. I want students to experience the success of helping a child overcome reading failure. Everything the students need to organize the reading camp is contained in a ready-to-use program packet that includes step-by-step directions for the students to follow. The program packet can also be used in class for planning, decision-making, problem-solving, teamwork, skill-building, and leadership development. The students practice working in teams and with *vowel clustering* in class, so students are prepared. I also work all week at *Camp Sharigan,* so I'm always there if a problem arises.

Step 3: List five goals and objectives that you want students to achieve in the course that you are teaching. Briefly tell what you want students to learn from the course and the service project. How will you relate the service project to the course that you are teaching? Review the goals that you wrote in Chapter 1.

My learning goals from Chapter 1 were:

To challenge students to discover the complexities of motivation for self and for others.

To change student opinions about motivation.

To increase positive student engagement in the course.

To rebuild and/or improve each student's self-efficacy about their ability to learn and succeed at the university.

To create an intrinsically motivational learning environment in my classroom and teach my students how to apply intrinsic motivation in a real-world setting.

To demonstrate the benefits of working in a cohesive group atmosphere in our classroom and at *Camp Sharigan*.

> *Camp Sharigan* is easily intertwined into the course curriculum because learning to read is essential. Scientists, mathematicians, and even business majors training to be CEOs had to learn to read. As one computer science professor said, "we cannot teach coding to people who cannot read." Therefore, university students easily identify with helping struggling children learn to read. Motivation is also a component in every class; therefore, it applies very easily. *Camp Sharigan* enhances student learning and fulfills a definite community need.

Step 4: What type of reflection will be included for students? Reflection is very important with academic service-learning because it gives students a chance to explain what they have learned. Will students write reflection papers? How many? How will the reflection assignments be related to the course and textbook?

At *Camp Sharigan,* my students work individually, as teams, and as a total group. Both undergraduate and graduate students also keep a journal. I assign real-life observation exercises throughout the semester. They describe and then evaluate these observed behaviors in keeping with what we are learning in class. The observation exercises provide training and teach the skills that the students will need at *Camp Sharigan*. The students complete both observation and reflection assignments based on their work at *Camp Sharigan.* For example, I always emphasize that reflective exercises relate to textbook theories and information from class. A mere description of what happened is not enough. Students also tell what they learned and explain whether they think the service project helped them learn more from the textbook than they would have been able to do without participating in service. Reflection connects the service project with classroom instruction and provides another component of the learning process.

Step 5: Write an outline or description of what you want students to do during the service project. Be specific. What do you want your students to achieve from this project? How will they help the community? Will they bring about change? How will you make sure that the change is positive for the community? How do you expect students to grow and change in civic and cultural understanding, academically, and personally? How will students apply the course's content to the service project?

Camp Sharigan has 10 workstations. The university students assist in setting up, organizing materials, and helping the children read and follow directions at the workstations. Children travel around the room going to each workstation. There is a different task at each station for all five days. The reading camp utilizes intrinsic motivation, a *vowel clustering* teaching method, and rebuilding self-efficacy. Everything is built into the program. All the university students must do is read and help the children follow the directions. Research has shown that children do improve in reading after attending *Camp Sharigan*. *Camp Sharigan* builds an intrinsically motivational learning environment to make sure that the learning experience is positive for both children and university students. We measure change and improvement through pretests and posttests with the children. My university students grow intellectually in their understanding of cultural differences by the communities that we work in, academically by the content taught in class and interwoven into the service project, and personally from the experience of knowing they helped a child learn to read better.

Organizing an Academic Service-Learning Project

If you're using a research-based program (like *Camp Sharigan*) the program packet will probably explain how to set up and run the program (Clanton Harpine 2024). If you join an existing project, then you will need to coordinate with the project leader. Together you and the project leader will need to decide how to link the service project with your course goals. For example, if you want your students to work at Habitat for Humanity, you contact Habitat and sit down to work out exactly how your students can help at Habitat while fulfilling your course goals. If you are designing your own project, you will outline the organization needed as part of your design. Regardless of whether you are using a research-based ready-to-use program, joining an ongoing service project in progress, or designing your own service project, it is still your responsibility to integrate the service project into your daily class sessions. The link between service and learning is essential for academic service-learning to be successful.

Where do I go to find a community worksite? Obviously, that depends on the kind of project that you want to do. It may also depend on the course you are teaching. I usually start by contacting social services or other community offices that offer assistance. Social services can tell you about local needs, identify ongoing group projects that might accept student help, and are usually very supportive. Local churches often know about the community's needs. Your university may also have an outreach department that works directly with the community. First, decide on the age group or type of project that will fit best with your course goals and objectives.

Children and teens. If you plan to work with children or teens, good contacts can be Brothers and Sisters, Boys and Girls Club, the YMCA or YWCA, community health clinics, or even the schools. Some schools have restrictions, while others are open to university students coming in and working. Check with your local school.

Senior citizens. If you want to work with seniors, assisted living facilities, nursing homes, or community health clinics are often pleased to have groups come. There may even be a community center where seniors gather.

Construction jobs. If you're looking for a more physical construction-type project, I always suggest Habitat for Humanity. They are usually easy to work with. You may also find local religious groups that are building ramps for handicapped residents, repairing roofs, painting homes for those in need, or remodeling older homes. Keep student abilities in mind, making sure the construction project is safe for all students.

Music or art. If you teach music, you might have students go to nursing homes or homeless shelters to play music. Art students may also teach seniors to paint.

Fulfilling community needs. You may work at or start a community garden to have students raise vegetables for needy families. Check with the city.

Campus. If you teach seniors or a graduate class, you might have your students tutor freshmen on campus. Beginning students often need writing tutors. You might also have your students design and create a quiet outdoor study garden on campus. The possibilities are endless.

Did you establish a solid link between service and learning? Did you find a worksite that fits with the goals of your course? You are not just going out into the community to do community service. Your service-learning project must help those in need as well as teach the principles and theories from the course. Remember, *the important aspect of academic service-learning that makes it so effective is that service and learning are linked together in the university classroom.* Without the link between service and learning, students will not receive the full benefit of academic service-learning.

Will the service project require supplies? If so, what do you need? Cost? Will you apply for grants or donations? There are often groups willing to support student projects. Check with the university before requesting funds. Secure all funding and permissions prior to introducing the project to the students. Having a proposed project rejected by the university or service organization is not a good learning experience.

Other questions that may arise. You may not have the answers to all of these questions right now, but think about student concerns and university rules as you plan. Does your university have a policy about students working off campus? How many students will work at the project? Will you use teams? Will you be working alongside the students at the worksite? What duties will students be assigned to do at the community worksite? The answer to some of these questions will depend on the type of service-learning project and the course you are teaching.

Transportation. What about transportation to the worksite? Select a site that is close to campus and encourage carpooling from campus. Again, check university rules and regulations. Does your college have rules about students carpooling?

Accommodations. How will you handle bad weather or when students are sick? How will you accommodate student work schedules? See Chapter 8.

How many service hours will you require? I require two hours but most of my students volunteer for the week for ten hours. The number of hours you require does not make your service project better or provide a stronger link between service and learning. A positive impact is derived from what you do in the classroom as well as at the worksite. The way you intertwine service and learning together is the key to success with academic service-learning. We will discuss service hours in Chapter 8.

Permission. Do you need permission to have students work on a service project? Obtaining official permission beforehand is part of the planning process.

How to Evaluate the Quality of an Academic Service-Learning Project

Whether you chose to join an ongoing project in the community, use a research-based program, or design your own service project, all service projects must be evaluated as to their effectiveness. For a project to be classified as academic service-learning, the service-learning project must fulfill seven essential requirements.

Requirement #1: Academic service-learning must be linked to the course being taught. The service project you have selected must include in-class preparation and training, learning about the community need(s), and linking the service project to the subject being taught in the classroom. This can be hard. For example, unless faculty can link donating to a food bank with the course being taught, donating food, although an excellent community service project, does not fulfill the requirements of academic service-learning. However, the project could be transformed by having students build shelves and restock the food bank. Meet and learn more about the recipients by helping distribute food. In class, students could learn about the social needs that cause people to rely on food banks. If you are teaching economics or sociology, you might examine the financial benefits of foodbanks for those in need and for society. Students might even develop publicity to enable the food bank to reach more people. So, yes, donating food could be converted into an academic service-learning project, but there must be a meaningful link between service and the course. Service cannot just be tacked on. Yet, there are numerous ways to link service and learning.

Questions to consider when evaluating the service project.

- Does your selected community service-learning project fulfill the course goals set in Chapter 1? Give five examples.
- What will your students learn from this service project?
- What significance does the service project have for the course?

Requirement #2: Academic service-learning must include active learning. Students must be involved in the service-learning project from the first day of class to the last day of class. Sitting and passively listening is not student involvement, and the service project cannot simply be tacked on at the end of the course. Mechanical engineering students might design and build a playground in an underprivileged community. It's a wonderful project, but it must be incorporated into the curriculum throughout the entire course. The service project must become part of the course. Students might study playground design, safe construction materials, needs of the children, or even how communities can finance such projects. Academic service-learning teaches students how to apply the course's content to real-life problems and encourages students to problem-solve to find solutions to those problems.

Questions to consider when evaluating the service project.

- Does your selected community service-learning project teach or reenforce knowledge from the course?
- Who will plan and organize the service project? Will students work with community leaders? Or will all planning be on campus by your class?

Requirement #3: Academic service-learning must provide meaningful service that successfully fulfills the needs of the community and the university students. University students must have a positive, successful service experience. The goals of the service project should also be attainable during the semester. For example, professors might have their students work at a Habitat for Humanity building site--a wonderful and meaningful community project. Even though a house cannot be built in one semester, there are several aspects of building a house. Accounting classes could work with the family to establish budgets; architect and engineering students may work on the actual building process; interior design or art students may help the family plan the interior; political science and sociology students may study the effects Habitat has in the community and volunteer to help. Social work and education students might work directly with the family to help children adjust to a new neighborhood. The list could go on. An ongoing project (such as building a house) can work with academic service-learning, but you must connect the service project with the needs and interests of the university students as well as what you are teaching in the course.

Questions to consider when evaluating the service project.

- How will you make sure that the service project is a successful experience for university students?
- How will you make sure that the service project is successful for the community?

Requirement #4: Academic service-learning must teach problem solving skills. Academic service-learning should promote evaluation and problem-solving. Academic service-learning also teaches group decision-making, organization, helps students explore communication, and critically analyze misinformation and opinions. For example, a university class might feed the homeless. It's a wonderful community service project, but the class may be totally unaffected by the project because it was just a one-time instance of going out to provide food for the homeless. Yet, the service project takes on new meaning when the needs of the homeless are interwoven into the course structure and connected with the curriculum. No, the students will not solve the problem of homelessness, but they may be able to find a way to have an ongoing effect with the homeless in their community. Becoming more concerned for the needs of others should be part of the university experience. Students may also set service-learning goals or problem-solution criteria. Then, evaluate whether they are meeting those goals and criteria. Academic service-learning stresses student learning.

Questions to consider when evaluating the service project.

- Does your selected academic service-learning project teach skills? What skills should university students learn from the service project?
- What problems or difficulties do you foresee students encountering with the service project?

Requirement #5: Academic service-learning must teach critical thinking. Faculty are responsible for providing active learning opportunities in the classroom that help students critically analyze and evaluate what they are doing and why. Visiting seniors at an assisted-living facility can be a wonderful project, but if it is not tied to the course curriculum, it is not an example of academic service-learning. Remember, enhancing student learning is one of our main objectives. Let's look at how three related academic service-learning projects were used in a single entry-level course.

> I taught a freshman-sophomore course on lifespan development. It covered development from birth to death. Students came from many departments, and most did not have training in psychology. My course design would give the students three service-learning opportunities: early childcare, elementary school (the *Camp Sharigan* project), and assisted living with seniors. I wanted the students to critically analyze the differences and the similarities between these three age groups. The students kept a semester-long journal. I gave an assignment at the end of class for them to go into the community and locate a particular behavior that we were studying in class. They wrote their observations in their journals. For the next class session, we would compare and contrast their observations with the information from the textbook for that developmental age group. In small groups, we would then analyze and apply the observational and textbook material to one of the three groups that they would be working with. For example, they were to observe childlike behavior (tantrums, crying, or such) in different age groups. They were to list examples in their journal. The students were always shocked at how similar behavior could be between the children and the college students. We then applied their observations to the three groups they would be working with. *Camp Sharigan* incorporates hands-on crafts as teaching tools. The students then

selected crafts from *Camp Sharigan* that they thought would be appropriate for the other two groups. I organized a 30-minute craft session with preschool early childhood children, and a one-hour craft session with seniors at a local assisted living facility. The students could not believe how similar the seniors at the assisted living facility were to the early childhood and elementary students. Observations and hands-on service-learning helped students see these developmental stages with deeper understanding than any amount of classroom discussion could have facilitated.

Academic service-learning increases critical thinking and understanding of the text; therefore, you must incorporate critical thinking and evaluation into your service project design. Use the service project to teach the theories from the text. Academic service-learning does not just provide community service; it demonstrates and teaches.

Questions to consider when evaluating the service project.

- Does your selected community service-learning project encourage critical thinking? How? Give five examples.
- How would the service project help students learn textbook theory? Give five examples.

Requirement #6: Academic service-learning must offer leadership training. Do not send students off to a community worksite unprepared. One such disaster occurred when a professor sent students to work at a local hospice without training. First, most of the students had no idea what hospice was. Second, the students had no idea how to help and work in such an environment. Needless to say, it was a disaster. Weave adequate training into classroom instructional sessions before the service project begins. Active learning sessions in the classroom should help students be ready to work and feel confident in their ability to help when they arrive at the community site.

One semester, a criminal justice professor who mostly taught students planning to go into law enforcement requested permission for his students to participate in my reading clinic. I knew the professor was not using academic service-learning. Therefore, I would need to provide training. When the training session started, I looked out at a very bored group of uniformed law enforcement students. The service project did not interest them at all. I needed to relate this project to law enforcement while teaching them what they needed to know to succeed at *Camp Sharigan*. So, I began the training program by explaining that 70% of American prison inmates cannot read above the fourth-grade level (National Center for Adult Literacy 2007). I went on to explain that inmates who learn to read in prison show only a 16% probability of returning to prison, while inmates who do not learn to read while in prison show a 70% likelihood of being reincarcerated (The National Center for Education Statistics 2016). Heads began to lift; the law enforcement students were suddenly interested in what I was talking about. I went on to explain that 85% of adolescents and youth who find themselves in the court system are classified as "functionally illiterate" and unable to read (National Center for Adult Literacy 2007). When I cited the Department of Justice's statement that "… crime was welded to reading failure" (Brunner 1993), the law enforcement officers were ready to go to work at *Camp Sharigan*.

Questions to consider when evaluating the service project.

- What type of training would be needed for students to work successfully with the service project?
- Who would provide the training?
- When will the training be conducted?
- How will you know that your training has been effective?

Requirement #7: Academic service-learning must include opportunities for reflection. These can be both written and oral reflections. Reflection is much more than just describing what happened. Reflection must include critical evaluation, observations, and relating experiences back to textbook knowledge and information. Reflection should link the service project with the course objectives. Reflection should show how the service project enhances the course being taught. Reflection should occur throughout the course and not just at the end of the semester. Reflection goes beyond mere description; reflection requires the student to evaluate their real-life service experience in relation to what they have learned in the class.

One semester I was teaching educational psychology to junior level education majors who were preparing to become public school teachers. In another class, they were required to make six observations in a public school classroom—just observations, no teaching. In my class, they worked to organize and direct *Camp Sharigan* as well as completing a two-hour observation on teaching methods at *Camp Sharigan*. They had to identify the teaching method, and then tell whether the teaching method was effective or not. Then, we compared and contrasted teaching methods from their visits to the schools with those employed at *Camp Sharigan*.

Questions to consider before choosing a service project.

- Does your service-learning project include student reflection?
- What type of reflection assignments?

Finalizing Plans for an Academic Service-Learning Project

Why is academic service-learning the best way to teach your course? Yes, I understand that you may be embarking upon organizing an academic service-learning project because of a university requirement, but still, why will academic service-learning be the best possible way to teach the course? Return to Chapters 1 and 2 where we talk about benefits and student outcomes. Return to the course goals that you set in Chapter 1. What community needs will your students be fulfilling? Make sure that you are planning a service project that supports what you want your students to learn. Then, select or design a service project that supports these course goals.

Summary

Regardless of whether you are designing your own program, choosing a program, or joining a service project in the community, the first thing to remember is that, to reap the academic benefits we seek, you must fulfill all the requirements of academic service-learning. There are no shortcuts, and you cannot leave requirements out. Academic service-learning projects become the course's teaching pedagogy.

Building a Service-Learning Pedagogy

Questions to Help in Course Planning

1. Will your service project bring about a change in the community?
2. What are the advantages of the service-learning project you've selected?
3. What will the university students learn from the service project?
4. Will the service project fit into the semester-long requirements of your course?
5. Will this service project be safe and ethical for college students to participate in?

Troubleshooting Checklist

1. Are there language barriers or cultural differences for students to adjust to?
2. How will you adapt for diversity among the members of the community?
3. Does the community in which you are working have special needs?

Planning Guide Sheet

1. Is there a community need? Will this project fill that need?
2. Will the community welcome and be eager to work with you on your project?
3. Will the project provide a balance between community and student needs?
4. Will your students need special training?
5. Does your service project incorporate adjustments for diversity? How will the service project be adapted for handicapped or international students?
6. Does the service project adjust for work schedules and student class schedules?
7. How will transportation be handled?
8. How will you ensure that your project succeeds?

Case Example

As I mentioned earlier, testing the service project with university students and the community is essential. I spent 10 years developing *Camp Sharigan* and traveling to over six states to test its effectiveness, resulting in two published studies. Over those 10 years, I made many changes and revisions to fine-tune the effectiveness of *Camp*

Sharigan with the children and to ensure that university students would be able to work with the program effectively. It is critical to the success of academic service-learning that you include testing and that your service project produces a positive service experience for both college students and the community.

References

Bringle, R. G., & Hatcher, J. A. (2017). Innovative practices in service-learning and curricular engagement. *New Directions for Higher Education, 147*, 37-46. https://doi.org/10.1002/he.356

Brunner, M. (1993). *Retarding America: The imprisonment of potential.* Portland, Oregon: Halcyon House.

Clanton Harpine, E. (2011). *Group-centered prevention programs for at-risk students.* New York: Springer.

Clanton Harpine, E. (2013). *After-school prevention programs for at-risk students: Promoting engagement and academic success.* New York: Springer.

Clanton Harpine, E. (2022). *Why can't we teach children to read: Oh, but wait, we can: A step-by-step plan for teaching your child to read.* Corpus Christi, TX: Group-Centered Learning.

Clanton Harpine, E. (2024). *Camp Sharigan: A ready-to-use group-centered intervention for grades 1-3* (3rd ed.). Corpus Christi, TX: Group-Centered Learning.

Clanton Harpine, E. & Pazda, A. (2019). Is group centered better than classroom instruction for teaching reading? The need for a group centered approach. Testing two group methods. In E. Clanton Harpine (Ed.), *Afterschool programming and intrinsic motivation: Teaching at-risk students to read.* (pp. 29-47). Cham, Switzerland: Springer Nature.

Clanton Harpine, E., & Reid, T. (2009). Enhancing academic achievement in a Hispanic immigrant community: The role of reading in academic failure and mental health. *School Mental Health,* 1, 159-170. https://doi.org/10.1007/s12310-009-9011-z

Deslauriers, L., McCarty, L. S., Miller, K., Callaghan, K., & Kestin, G. (2019). Measuring actual learning versus feeling of learning in response to being actively engaged in the classroom. *Proceedings of the National Academy of Sciences, 116*, 19251-19257. https://doi.org/10.1073/pnas.1821936116

Howard, J. P. F. (1998). Academic service learning: A counternormative pedagogy. *New Directions for Teaching and Learning, 73,* 21-29.

Krsmanovic, M. (2022). Fostering service-learning and leadership development through first-year seminar courses. *Journal of Service-Learning in Higher Education, 15,* 54-70.

National Center for Adult Literacy (NCAL). (2007). The condition of education 2007 (NCES 2007–064). National Center for Education Statistics, National Institute of Literacy. Washington, D C: U.S. Department of Education.

National Center for Education Statistics (NCES). (2016). The condition of education 2016 (NCES 2016-144). Washington DC: Institute of Education Sciences, US Department of Education.

National Center for Education Statistics (NCES). (2019). The nation's report card: Reading 2019 (NCES 2019-457). Washington DC: Institute of Education Sciences, US Department of Education.

Warren, J. L., & Sellnow, D. D. (2021). Increasing learning while serving the community: Student engagement as the key to learning in a basic public speaking course. *Journal of Higher Education Outreach and Engagement, 25*, 25-35.

Chapter 4
How Does Academic Service-Learning Help Students Learn in the Classroom and from the Textbook?

It happens every semester. A student will ask, "how did you get into reading? I thought you were a psychologist." I respond that I'm a motivational psychologist, and I specialize in working with children who are struggling or failing in reading. I design group-centered prevention programs that teach children how to rebuild their self-efficacy as they learn to read. The basis for my focus on reading is that reading failure is one of the underlying reasons for dropping out of school before graduation, youth aggression and crime, and even teenage depression and suicide. The key to overcoming reading failure is to use teaching methods that work with the brain rather than teaching methods that work against the brain. We've even had children move up four grade levels in reading in one year during our year-long after-school program.

We have a similar problem in university classrooms. We often use teaching methods that work against how the brain processes information instead of methods that work with the brain. In Chapter 2, we reviewed the research showing that academic service-learning produces higher student outcomes (GPA, test scores, and knowledge learned), better retention and graduation, stronger student engagement, commitment, persistence, and improved self-efficacy (Bringle and Hatcher 2017; Krsmanovic 2022; Warren and Sellnow 2010). Have you ever wondered how academic service-learning produces better student outcomes? Or why academic service-learning works better than other teaching methods? The answer lies in how we learn. Academic service-learning creates a positive and stimulating learning environment that increases a student's ability to learn. Academic service-learning teaches students how to work with textbook theories, analyze, and evaluate the importance of information being learned, instead of just memorizing facts. Academic service-learning also uses hands-on learning experiences to help shape the brain and stimulate the learning and retention of knowledge. Academic service-learning works with the brain and how the brain processes information. Therefore, students learn and retain what they learn. Before building our academic service-learning pedagogy, let's pause to get a better understanding of how academic service-learning works with the brain.

E. Clanton Harpine, *Service Learning in Higher Education*,
https://doi.org/10.1007/978-3-031-51378-7_4

What Is the One Teaching Strategy That Helps University Students Learn Best?

Students learn best when they are fully engaged or involved in the learning process (Bringle and Hatcher 2017). Student engagement is measured by how many different ways a student is evaluating and applying what they are learning. Professors therefore need to engage their students on a multisensory level, a critical thinking and analytical level, and on an individual or emotional level (Banich et al. 2009). The more fully a student is engaged in the learning process, the more a student will learn (Bringle and Hatcher 2017). Academic service-learning provides the pedagogy (teaching method) that enables university professors to engage their students through multisensory teaching, hands-on instruction, critical thinking, analysis, evaluation, problem-solving, and reflection, in a personal real-world community experience.

Students must do more than simply listen. Student engagement requires more than mere listening; it requires interaction (Anderson 2003). Sitting and listening to someone talk only activates one of the learning senses (hearing). Even adding question-answer sessions still only uses hearing. The student(s) who ask a question are using investigative skills, but the remainder of the class is still just listening. As shown by the research discussed in Chapter 2, students from even the most outstanding lectures scored lower than students participating in active learning classes in the same subject (Deslauriers et al. 2019; Freeman et al. 2014). Why? Because passive listening is not how the brain learns and stores long-term knowledge for later recall, such as for a test (Horvath 2019). It is possible for a student to sit listening for an entire hour and learn nothing. Learning requires that what the student hears from a lecture, question answer session, or discussion be transferred into actual knowledge. Such transference requires critical analysis, evaluation, and application (Halpern and Dunn 2022).

Listening is not interactive. Students must constructively interact with new information to learn new information (Horvath 2019). Passively listening lacks the same impact (Brown et al. 2014). In a traditional college classroom, most of the instruction time involves the instructor lecturing while the students take notes. Yet, note-taking has not proven to always be helpful. Note-taking does not guarantee that a student will critically analyze and evaluate what they have written in their notes. So, how do we move our students from listening to learning? By the way we teach.

How Does the Brain Learn?

For students to learn, their brains must change. Most of us do not think about the brain changing as we learn, but the brain is constantly changing (Brown et al. 2014). Before you start saying that this sounds scary or resembles your favorite science-fiction movie, stop and realize that, if the brain does not change, students will not learn. Every time students learn something, their brain changes. Not in a bad way, but in a good, constructive way. *Learning doesn't actually take place until permanent changes or neural connections are created in the brain* (Horvath 2019). Let's explore some of these changes.

How does the brain change when students learn? When a student hears new information, the new idea, theory, or concept is transmitted through neural pathways to the student's temporary short-term or working memory. Short-term memory is where students perform the work of thinking and comprehending (Halpern and Dunn 2022). They evaluate, analyze, and try to make sense of what they have heard. In a lecture, there isn't time to stop and evaluate, and note-taking is often not accurate enough to allow for later analysis. Therefore, the student either accepts the new information or rejects it as unimportant. This is one of the ways that academic service-learning works with the brain to help students learn. Classroom discussions, critical analysis, and problem-solving in class help students decide whether new information is important and should be accepted or simply rejected as unimportant. Rejected information (perceived to be unimportant) is never remembered for next week's test.

Students accept new information that they perceive as being important. The accepted new information is carried by neural pathways in the brain to the student's existing long-term storage (Shahbaba et al. 2022). These neural pathways construct the foundation upon which learning is based (Brown et al. 2014). For successful learning to take place, the new information must move from short-term to long-term memory.

Long-term memory is where learning occurs. Students learn by connecting the information being taught in class with prior knowledge or experiences stored in their long-term memory (Desautels 2023; Stiles and Jernigan 2010). When new and old information connect, they form a bond. This bond provides easier recall and more comprehensive learning (Shahbaba et al. 2022). When students add a new bit of knowledge to an existing memory, the new connection becomes stronger, more permanent, and easier to retrieve later when needed (Banich et al. 2009). As teachers, we want to help students build neural pathways between the information that we are teaching in class and the knowledge stored in the student's long-term memory.

How can professors help students learn? Interactive teaching methods can increase the formation of this bond. When students interact with the course content, instructors strengthen the student's ability to learn and remember what they learned (Brown et al. 2014). As one of my students said on the end of class evaluation: "I liked the way the information was presented in the class." Students like academic service-learning because it helps them learn. Academic service-learning uses visual, hearing, hands-on, critical analysis, problem-solving, reflection, class discussion, and real-world application to build interaction into the classroom, keep students focused on the learning process, and create a deeper level of learning.

Students need to be personally involved. When we add personal experience to the learning process, it enhances instruction (McTighe and Willis 2019). When the brain is required to remember an actual experience, especially an emotional experience, the student is more likely to learn, and the information learned is easier to recall. As academic service-learning prepares students to go out to help others, students are learning how to apply the theories and information being taught in the classroom to a real-world community—a community they are personally working in.

Does the Brain Filter the Information it Receives or Accept Everything?

The brain is programmed to look for new, unique information (Lieberwirth et al. 2016). As new information is received, either from class or while reading the text, the brain immediately starts making comparisons between the new information and the existing information stored in the student's long-term memory. If the brain already has this new information, the brain simply rejects the new information as being redundant. If the new information is not contained in the student's long-term memory or does not contradict information that the student has retained, then this new information becomes a new memory for later recall (Lieberwirth et al. 2016; Shahbaba et al. 2022). In essence, the brain changes as new connections are made between old and new information.

> For example, in my psychology of motivation class, if students already believe that intrinsic motivation is better than extrinsic, then their brains most likely filtered out much of the research data stating that intrinsic is better than extrinsic as mere duplicated information. While students who have never heard of intrinsic motivation, found the information about intrinsic as totally new and most likely stored it as a new memory. Nevertheless, if students believe that extrinsic motivation is either just as good as intrinsic or even better, then the new information presented in class contradicts what they believe.

What Happens When New Information Contradicts What Students Believe?

Regardless of research data, the textbook, facts, truth, or actual knowledge, some students will hold firmly to their opinions, even when no real evidence supports their ideas. Every teacher has encountered this problem. History, political science, and science professors must often reteach factual information that has become distorted. Math, chemistry, and computer science professors often reteach methods as well. When students receive contradictory new information, the brain temporarily stores these new ideas in short-term memory (Merzenich 2013). Then, the student's brain goes to work immediately to explain the discrepancy (Mansvelder et al. 2019). If the course content presented is well supported and seems logical, the student's brain makes the new information part of its long-term memory (Brown et al. 2014).

What happens when the student disagrees? Sometimes, instead, the student does not believe the new information. Maybe it is not supported with facts from a trusted source. Or, if the student does not feel that the new information presented is useful, then the student's brain most likely will delete the new information and continue with the thoughts it already possesses (Ambrose et al. 2010; McTighe and Willis 2019). This can lead to inaccurate knowledge being stored. When knowledge is recorded inaccurately or as a misconception, it may be very difficult for a professor to refute or change a student's opinion (Ambrose et al. 2010). Even the slightest change or correction may be difficult (Galakhova et al. 2022). Refusal to accept new ideas is often grounded in fear and uncertainty (Salvi et al. 2023).

Academic service-learning helps students overcome rigid perceptions, misinformation, and to analyze their thought processes. Academic service-learning uses multisensory instructional methods, analytical reasoning, problem-solving, critical thinking, comprehension, and interactive classroom activities. This instructional approach encourages students to test, disprove, and overcome their reluctance to changing incorrect theories or beliefs (Brown et al. 2014). When students use critical thinking to justify their reasoning or use problem solution strategies to show how a certain idea just cannot work, it is one of the best pedagogical teaching methods for helping students undo misconceptions or wrong information (Ambrose et al. 2010; Salvi et al. 2023).

How to change inaccurate information. Sometimes, information may be incomplete, or just not retained correctly. Students are not refusing to believe; they are just confused. To correct confusion, students need to actively interact with the course content being taught. Academic service-learning helps students to analyze, evaluate, and in some cases, problem-solve. Hands-on involvement often gives new insight. This enables students to correct their misconceptions and to learn the new material correctly.

Academic service-learning can help students correct contradictions. If you are teaching course content that contradicts student beliefs, you must help students change their opinions. Simply telling students they are incorrect will not work.

As stated in Chapter 2, I needed to change my students' opinions about intrinsic and extrinsic motivation. Simply telling my students in my psychology of motivation class that intrinsic motivation is better than extrinsic wasn't going to convince them. The more engaged my students were with the learning process, the more likely they were to change their opinions. Therefore, I used academic service-learning and classroom interaction with the course content and the textbook to bring about a new way of thinking about intrinsic and extrinsic motivation. Let's look at an example of how this can be accomplished.

Academic service-learning increases student engagement through group interaction in class. I had students work in small groups. Each group defined intrinsic motivation and told why it was important. Students used multisensory learning by discussing, analyzing, and applying textbook information.

Academic service-learning provides support for textbook knowledge. I used slides from *Camp Sharigan* to demonstrate how real-world research validated textbook and course content. Pre and post-test reading scores from the children displayed their improvement. Group discussion and analysis reinforced that intrinsic motivation created this change with the children.

Academic service-learning uses real world significance. I took it one step further and showed graphs from multiple research studies conducted at *Camp Sharigan*. This showed how the very service project that the students would be working with helped the children.

By linking the service project with the text, I built another layer of understanding and strengthened the student's long-term memory connections with textbook content.

Academic service-learning applies classroom learning to the real world. Then, I took my students to *Camp Sharigan* and allowed them to work with intrinsic motivation. This provided a real-world learning experience, working hands-on with the children. Learning about intrinsic motivation became a personal event to strengthen the long-term memory bond even further. Academic service-learning strengthens student learning by attaching textbook information to the real world and by getting students personally involved in that real world.

Academic service-learning reinforces textbook learning. I reinforced the textbook by having students write a research paper about intrinsic motivation. Students gave presentations and conducted discussions about their research.

Academic service-learning calls for reflection. I sent students out to observe intrinsic motivation on campus, and they wrote in their journals about seeing intrinsic motivation in real life. Then, students wrote a reflection on how intrinsic motivation had affected their learning in our university classroom.

When we link the new information that students are learning in the classroom with their own personal experiences, it becomes much easier for students to remember and even recall the new information being taught. The more personally involved my students were with intrinsic motivation, both in the classroom and at *Camp Sharigan*, the more likely intrinsic motivation would become a lasting, permanent memory. Hands-on techniques created a stronger connection for understanding intrinsic motivation.

Do Students Learn More from Classroom Instruction or the Textbook?

Students must interact with course content in the classroom and with content from the textbook (Halpern and Dunn 2022). Unfortunately, students do not always learn when reading the textbook. Yes, it is possible for a student to read the assigned text but not learn from what they read because the student's brain is not interacting with the textbook material. How can we increase interaction with course content?

Taking notes does not always strengthen learning or neural connections. Students write notes either in class as they listen or as they read the textbook, but notes are not interactive. Inaccurate or incomplete notes may even lead to confusion and reduced learning (Eskritt and Ma 2014). Course content and the textbook are more easily understood when students are interactively engaged with the information they are learning, rather than simply taking notes (McTighe and Willis 2019).

Students need to do more than merely highlight the text. While many believe that highlighting the text improves comprehension and test scores, research does not support this theory. Research found that self-referencing (becoming personally involved) was more effective than lecturing, reading the text, or underlining the text (Hartlep and Forsyth 2000). Research showed that group problem-solving techniques improved the understanding of difficult textbook material, and, when students were required to apply theories from the text to real-life situations, self-referencing strengthened the retention of the textbook material. By relating textbook material to everyday life, the students were able to produce a higher score on a test one week and even two weeks after the class material was presented (Hartlep and Forsyth 2000). Academic service-learning helps students understand the textbook because it helps students analyze, evaluate, and apply the textbook to real world problems. Being able to discuss the textbook and the new information being introduced in class helps students interact with the course content and develop a deeper understanding.

Do Students Learn Through Repetition?

Many believe that students learn through repetition; unfortunately, research shows that is not the case (Brown et al. 2014). Unless you are teaching students a skill (like playing the violin), repetition can actually be harmful. While some forms of learning do need repetition, most forms of classroom learning are not strengthened by repetition. However, as most musicians will tell you, for repetitive practice to be effective and increase learning, the student must repeatedly practice correctly. Practicing mistakes or incorrect information causes more harm than good. Mere repetition of information does not build stronger neural pathways that lead to stronger retention. Merely hearing a new idea over and over does not necessarily help students learn a new idea (McTighe and Willis 2019). Rereading the text multiple times will not automatically enable a student to remember. Writing a word down five times to teach the spelling (rote memorization) or practicing memorizing over and over only produces unconnected neural networks and feeble memories (McTighe and Willis 2019).

Repetition is not enough. The more a student encounters information through multiple teaching methods, the better the student will be able to learn the new information. Repetition is only one type of instruction, even with multiple exposure. Students need more. Just reading the text is not enough (Brown et al. 2014). Students need to critically analyze, apply, and evaluate the information being learned from the classroom and from the textbook (Banich et al. 2009). If a teacher wants students to learn something new, the students must interact with that information in as many ways as possible (Ambrose et al. 2010). Students also need to see relevance.

Teach relevance. New information that the brain does not feel is important will eventually be rejected (Grill-Spector et al. 2006). Therefore, simply repeating that intrinsic motivation is better, over and over, will not convince my students. They must experience the difference. They must work where intrinsic motivation is being applied.

Academic service-learning provides multiple encounters with new information. With academic service-learning, students are given the opportunity to evaluate, analyze, explore, and apply what they have learned in the classroom to the real world.

This is much better than mere repetition. As you build your academic service-learning pedagogy, help students incorporate what they are learning in the classroom into the service project. Service and learning must be tied together.

How Does Academic Service-Learning Work with the Brain to Help Students Learn?

When students have the chance to discuss, evaluate, and analyze, they can better understand and accept new information (Horvath 2019). To really learn, however, students must apply what they are studying in class. This is where academic service-learning excels in bringing the classroom to life.

Academic service-learning directs a student's attention toward learning. Students have the power to self-direct their thoughts; therefore, professors must find teaching methods that redirect a student's attention. If students are not involved with the information being taught, students can literally sit for a full hour without learning (Ambrose et al. 2010; Horvath 2019). How can teachers prevent this from happening?

Academic service-learning encourages student engagement. Getting a student's attention is not enough (Brown et al. 2014; Horvath 2019). When most students enter a university classroom, they sit down, take out their notebooks or laptops, and get ready to take notes. In an academic service-learning course, students start interacting the minute they enter the classroom and continue until they leave. This interaction provides focus and a way for students to become fully engaged in the learning process. Student engagement grows out of interaction (Anderson 2003). Student engagement strengthens neural connections in the brain and the process for how students learn.

Academic service-learning creates an active classroom. The classroom learning environment determines whether or not students learn (Ambrose et al. 2010; Horvath 2019; McTighe and Willis 2019). How accepted students feel even affects the learning process. We'll say more about learning environment in Chapter 5. For now, we will just highlight that classroom environment is necessary for students to learn.

For learning to occur, students must apply new information to the real world. If students lack the opportunity to apply what they have learned to a real-world setting, then the new information being taught is unlikely to attach to other information stored in the brain. When students participate in academic service-learning courses, students show improved problem-solving skills, critical thinking, application of knowledge, and higher levels of cognitive development (including remembering and decision making) (Barnett et al. 2009). Students learn because they are engaged in the learning process instead of sitting in the audience as passive listeners.

Summary

The brain is constantly changing. The brain changes each and every day. Every time a student learns something new, the brain physically changes. That is why it is so important to teach in the same way that the brain learns. Neurons transmit information along neural pathways, but students cannot learn new information, theories, or concepts unless such new knowledge is stored, in one form or another, in the student's memory. Although there are various levels of memory, memories do not occur unless there is a physical change in the brain. Actual learning only takes place when the brain changes. When we work with the brain, not against the brain, we are teaching students in the way the brain learns best. When academic service-learning, active learning instructional techniques, and an intrinsically motivational learning environment combine to create the teaching pedagogy, students are more likely to succeed.

Building a Service-Learning Pedagogy

Questions to Help in Course Planning

1. Review the goals that you set in Chapter 1.
2. Did you add any new goals? Are there goals that you would like to add after reading this chapter?
3. How will you change your teaching strategies to work with the brain? List five examples.

Troubleshooting Checklist

1. How will you include everyone?
2. How will you challenge your students?

Planning Guide Sheet

1. List five academic service-learning instructional techniques that you plan to use.
2. How will your teaching strategies increase stronger neural connections in the brain? List five examples.
3. How will you encourage critical thinking?
4. What steps are you taking to make sure that your academic service-learning pedagogy is designed to work with the brain instead of against the brain?

Case Example

Let's return to the example presented in Chapter 1 to see how I applied the principles for how the brain learns. Emphasizing interaction, academic service-learning is textbook-based and allows students to analyze and develop a deeper understanding of the course content being presented both in class and in the text.

Start with a challenge. On the first day of psychology of motivation, I teach two specific principles that contradict what students have learned from prior experience.

First contradiction. I teach that it is not possible to motivate another person (Clanton Harpine 2015; Reeve et al. 2007). My students know the word *motivation*, but they commonly associate motivation with rewards or being rewarded for doing something they are told to do. If I am to teach students about intrinsic motivation, I must contradict this commonly held idea. I must challenge and change my students' established beliefs. I do this by referencing the textbook. Therefore, I encourage students to work in small groups, read the statement from the textbook that says you cannot motivate another person, and then critically analyze and justify the reasons for either agreeing or disagreeing with this statement. As stated earlier, to connect new information to old ideas, teachers must call up the old established ideas stored in the brain before such incorrect ideas can be changed. Often, when students see the validity of new ideas, it is easier for them to change their opinions (Ambrose et al. 2010). It's called plasticity, meaning how nerve cells change through new experiences.

Second contradiction. I also teach that intrinsic motivation is better than extrinsic rewards. I explain that information is not stored on a single neuron (McTighe and Willis 2019). The memories held in long-term storage for recall are only "tiny memory pieces" connected to other neurons in their network (McTighe and Willis 2019). I'm challenging my students on this second principle of intrinsic motivation to improve how solidly the new information on intrinsic is connected in long-term storage.

Relate to past personal experiences. My students have come up since elementary school being showered with extrinsic rewards. It is not enough to merely tell my students that you cannot motivate another person or that intrinsic motivation is better than extrinsic rewards (Deci et al. 1999; Murayama & Elliot 2011). Therefore, I must provide new experiences with intrinsic motivation.

Building new connections in the brain. One method for changing established ideas and connections in the brain is to show the longevity of research that has established that extrinsic rewards do not last and that extrinsic rewards undermine intrinsic desire (Deci et al. 1999). However, it is not until students experience intrinsic motivation firsthand at *Camp Sharigan* that they truly begin to believe the research. No matter what the research shows, students must personally experience the benefits of intrinsic motivation before they ever change their established opinions.

Case examples help students become personally involved in the learning process. I want my students to become personally committed, even on the first day, to helping the children at *Camp Sharigan*. Therefore, I tell the students about a case study that explains why it is important to teach with how the brain processes and learns new information.

> The child was a third grader, very bright, but could not read. The school tried and the parents had even hired a one-on-one tutor, but still the child could not read. He was referred to my year-long reading clinic, where I work with children having severe reading problems. Some children need more than the one week that *Camp Sharigan* provides. The after-school program uses the same ten teaching methods, hands-on learning techniques, intrinsic motivation, and a step-by-step procedure to rebuild self-efficacy. The longer year-long curriculum simply provides a lengthier program. An intrinsically motivating learning environment can be very powerful. For this little boy, it was a struggle, but he was reading beginning chapter books by the end of the year. Why? Because we were teaching with methods that directly related to how the brain learns.

When we teach with the brain instead of against it, almost any student, of any age, and in any classroom can learn. Failure is often not a student's fault. Yes, students can and do sometimes contribute to their failure, but so does the way we teach. The teaching method can be the determining factor in whether a student learns or fails to learn.

*Academic service-learning is a powerful teaching too*l. Even when I use neuro-imaging slides that visually reveal how intrinsic motivation creates more meaningful changes in the brain than extrinsic (Murayama & Elliot 2011), it is personal experience and reflection on that experience that causes students to change their beliefs and ideas. Personal hands-on experience in a real-world setting makes the difference.

References

Ambrose, S. A., Bridges, M. W., DiPietro, M., Lovett, M. C., & Norman, M. K. (2010). *How learning works: Seven research-based principles for smart teaching*. San Francisco, CA: Jossey-Bass

Anderson, T. (2003). Modes of interaction in distance education: Recent developments and research questions. In M. G. Moore & W. G. Anderson (Eds.), *Handbook of distance education* (pp. 129–144). Mahwah, NJ: Lawrence Erlbaum Associates Inc.

Banich, M. T., Mackiewicz, K. L., Depue, B. E., Whitmer, A. J., Miller, G. A., & Heller, W. (2009). Cognitive control mechanisms, emotion and memory: A neural perspective with implications for psychopathology. *Neuroscience and Biobehavioral Reviews, 33*, 613–630. https://doi.org/10.1016/j.neubiorev.2008.09.010

Barnett, M., Silver, P. T., & Grund, T. S. (2009). Implementing service-learning pedagogy: A case example. *Journal of Higher Education Outreach and Engagement, 13*, 117–134.

Bringle, R. G., & Hatcher, J. A. (2017). Innovative practices in service-learning and curricular engagement. *New Directions for Higher Education, 147*, 37–46. https://doi.org/10.1002/he.356

Brown, P.C., Roediger, H.L. & McDaniel, M.A. (2014). *Make it stick: The science of successful learning*. Cambridge, MA: Harvard University Press.

Clanton Harpine, E. (2015). *Group-centered prevention in mental health: Theory, training, and practice*. New York: Springer.

Deci, E. L., Koestner, R., & Ryan, R. M. (1999). A meta-analytic review of experiments examining the effects of extrinsic rewards on intrinsic motivation. *Psychological Bulletin, 125*, 627–668.

Desautels, L. L. (2023). *Intentional neural plasticity: Moving our nervous system toward post-traumatic growth.* Deadwood, OR: Wyatt-MacKenzie Publishing.

Deslauriers, L., McCarty, L. S., Miller, K., Callaghan, K., & Kestin, G. (2019). Measuring actual learning versus feeling of learning in response to being actively engaged in the classroom. *Proceedings of the National Academy of Sciences, 116*, 19251–19257. https://doi.org/10.1073/pnas.1821936116

Eskritt, M., & Ma, S. (2014). Intentional forgetting: Note-taking as a naturalistic example. *Memory and Cognition, 42*, 237–246. https://doi.org/10.3758/s13421-013-0362-1

Freeman, S., Eddy, S. L., McDonough, M., Smith, Nnadozie Okoroafor, M. K., Jordt, H., & Wenderoth, M. P. (2014). Active learning increases student performance in science, engineering, and mathematics. *Proceedings of the National Academy of Sciences (PNAS), 111*, 8410–8415. https://doi.org/10.1073/pnas.1319030111

Galakhova, A. A., Hunt, S., Wilbers, R., Heyer, D. B., de Kock, C. P. J., Mansvelder, H. D., & Goriounova, N. A. (2022). Evolution of cortical neurons supporting human cognition. *Trends in Cognitive Science, 26*, 909–922. https://doi.org/10.1016/j.tics.2022.08.012

Grill-Spector, K., Henson, R., & Martin, A. (2006). Repetition and the brain: Neural models of stimulus-specific effects. *Trends in cognitive sciences, 10*, 14–23. https://doi.org/10.1016/j.tics.2005.11.006

Halpern, D. F., & Dunn, D. S. (2022). Thought and knowledge: An introduction to critical thinking (Vol 2) 6th ed. NY: Routledge.

Hartlep, K. L. & Forsyth G. A. (2000). The effect of self-reference on learning and retention. *Teaching of Psychology, 2*, 269–271. https://doi.org/10.1207/S15328023TOP2704_05

Horvath, J. C. (2019). *Stop talking, start influencing: 12 insights from brain science to make your message stick. Chatswood, Australia: Exisle Publishing.*

Krsmanovic, M. (2022). Fostering service-learning and leadership development through first-year seminar courses. *Journal of Service-Learning in Higher Education, 15*, 54–70.

Lieberwirth, C., Pan, Y., Liu, Y., Zhang, Z., & Wang, Z. (2016). Hippocampal adult neurogenesis: Its regulation and potential role in spatial learning and memory. *Brain research, 1644*, 127–140. https://doi.org/10.1016/j.brainres.2016.05.015

Mansvelder, H. D., Verhoog M. B., & Goriounova N. A. (2019). Synaptic plasticity in human cortical circuits: Cellular mechanisms of learning and memory in the human brain? *Current Opinion in Neurobiology,* 54, 186–193. https://doi.org/10.1016/j.conb.2018.06.013

McTighe, J., & Willis, J. (2019). *Upgrade your teaching: Understanding by design meets neuroscience.* Alexandria, VA: ASCD.

Merzenich, M. (2013). Soft-wired: How the new science of brain plasticity can change your life (2nd edition). San Francisco, CA: Parnassus Publishing.

Murayama, K., & Elliot, A. J. (2011). Achievement motivation and memory: Achievement goals differentially influence immediate and delayed remember–know recognition memory. *Personality and Social Psychology Bulletin, 37*, 1339–1348. https://doi.org/10.1177/0146167211410575

Reeve, J., Ryan, R. M., Deci, E. L., & Jang, H. (2007). Understanding and promoting autonomous self-regulation: A self-determination theory perspective. In D. Schunk and B. Zimmerman (Eds.). Motivation and self-regulated learning: Theory, research, practice (pp. 223–244). Mahwah, NJ: Lawrence Erlbaum.

Salvi, C., Iannello, P., Cancer, A., Cooper, S. E., McClay, M., Dunsmoor, J. E., & Antonietti, A. (2023). Does social rigidity predict cognitive rigidity? Profiles of socio-cognitive polarization. *Psychological Research.* https://doi.org/10.1007/s00426-023-01832-w

Shahbaba, B., Li, L., Agostinelli, F., Saraf, M., Cooper, K. W., Haghverdian, D., Elias, G. A., Baddi, P., & Fortin, N. J. (2022). Hippocampal ensembles represent sequential relationships among an extended sequence of nonspatial events. *Nature Communications 13*, 1–17. https://doi.org/10.1038/s41467-022-28057-6

Stiles, J., & Jernigan, T. L. (2010). The basics of brain development. *Neuropsychology Review*, 20, 327–348. https://doi.org/10.1007/s11065-010-9148-4

Warren, J. L., & Sellnow, T. L. (2010). Learning through service: The contributions of service learning to the Communication discipline. In D. L. Fassett & J. T. Warren (Eds.), *Handbook of communication and instruction* (pp. 129–145). Thousand Oaks, CA: Sage Publications.

Chapter 5
Creating an Intrinsically Motivating Learning Environment: Promoting Student Engagement and Intrinsic Motivation

A student commented on the first day of the Camp Sharigan service project: "How did you find this place? We're around the corner from campus, but it's another world back here. You said we were working at a free community clinic, but I never...." The university student's opinions changed while walking into the gymnasium where Camp Sharigan was being held. "Hey, look at this. The kids are going to love those balloons, the bridge, the rainbow, that mountain, and they are going to go wild over those fuzzy little snakes in the snake pit." Yet, the most interesting comment of all came when the same student said at the end of the first day: "Wow, the kids at my station worked. They were reading better after just one day, but every kid I talked to said he hated reading. I don't think they figured out they just spent two hours reading."

Every teacher's goal is to create a learning experience that will make students want to learn. When students are engaged in the learning process, they become interested in mastering new challenges. They remember information and demonstrate more commitment for studying (Bringle and Hatcher 2017). Students need intrinsic motivation to successfully engage in learning, and student engagement is indeed essential for acquiring new ideas and information (Halpern and Dunn 2022).

What Is Intrinsic Motivation?

Richard Ryan and Edward Deci (two leaders in intrinsic motivation) define intrinsic motivation as the desire "...to seek out novelty and challenges, to extend and exercise one's capacity, to explore, and to learn...." (Ryan and Deci 2000 p. 70).

Persistence and commitment arise from intrinsic motivation. Research has demonstrated that student desire, willingness, and persistence are essential for student engagement (Miller et al. 2011). Academic service-learning combines active

E. Clanton Harpine, *Service Learning in Higher Education*,
https://doi.org/10.1007/978-3-031-51378-7_5

learning and intrinsic motivation to form a strong, high-quality intrinsically motivating learning environment that encourages student engagement and learning.

What Is an Intrinsically Motivating Learning Environment?

An intrinsically motivating learning environment for a university is the setting or conditions that encourage a student to learn for their own personal satisfaction and sense of accomplishment. With intrinsic motivation, there is no external reward or competition. Instead, motivation stems from a student's genuine interest and desire to learn. A student's motivation arises from their perceptions (beliefs and opinions) of self and others. The student's previous life experiences (especially in school) work to shape the student's intrinsic desire to learn (Deci 1975). As teachers, it is our job to reshape these perceptions, thus creating new positive learning experiences. Since we are using academic service-learning, the learning environment will include both the classroom and the service worksite. We want to create teaching strategies and service-learning projects that stress intrinsic motivation. How does intrinsic work in the classroom?

An intrinsically motivating learning environment is inclusive. An intrinsic environment ties into the student's need to belong, be accepted, feel competent, and have a sense of positive relatedness (Baumeister and Leary 1995). The concept of an intrinsic learning environment is based on the theory that students have an inherent desire to learn and strive to reach their full potential in life (Ryan and Deci 2000).

In college, students often feel overwhelmed, pressured, fearful, controlled, and even angry. The American College Health Association (2018) has estimated that 63% of college students are suffering from "overwhelming anxiety." An intrinsically motivating learning environment allows students to relax, feel accepted, and focus on learning.

An intrinsically motivating learning environment helps encourage cohesion. Cohesion means the unity and solidarity of the class. Cohesion helps students become more accepting and supportive of one another. As students grow in their ability to use textbook knowledge, the class will start learning to work together more cooperatively. As students learn new skills and apply these skills to the service project, they become a more cohesive group. Cohesive classroom interaction is central to creating an intrinsic environment that will reinforce academic service-learning and student engagement.

An intrinsically motivating learning environment supports better student outcomes. Research shows that intrinsic motivation leads to better test scores, better retention of textbook material, and better overall learning outcomes (Ryan and Deci 2017). It is intrinsic rather than extrinsic motivation that generates persistence (the will to keep trying) (Cerasoli et al. 2014). Students have even reported an increase in the desire to learn textbook material because of academic service-learning (Hart and King 2007). Academic service-learning, intrinsic motivation, and active learning combine to create a strong and effective teaching pedagogy.

Why Is the Learning Environment Important?

Learning in college improves when students participate in a high-quality learning environment (Ahn and Class 2011; Freeman et al. 2014). A high-quality learning environment helps students to become intrinsically engaged with the curriculum. It makes classroom sessions relevant and applicable to real life, and creates a cohesive, accepting group structure (Blumberg 2008; Weimer 2013). This is why the way you interweave the service project into class sessions is so important. The service project gives the class relevant, real-life application. Incorporating active learning along with hands-on experience at the service worksite can help show students the significance of what you are teaching. When you stress intrinsic motivation, academic service-learning creates a high-quality learning environment.

Does classroom structure make a difference? The classroom structure is crucial. Structure means more than just the arrangement of desks, or lecture hall vs. tables. Classroom structure describes how a professor teaches, works with students, and how student progress is measured across the semester (Bergsmann et al. 2013). The class atmosphere can be either positive or negative. Obviously, we want to strive for a positive classroom structure and an intrinsic environment. Students in college need to feel safe and intrinsically motivated in order to explore new ideas and learn new skills (Deslauriers et al. 2019). An intrinsically engaging learning environment offers students a sense of accomplishment, fulfillment, and acceptance (Ryan and Deci 2000).

A positive environment enhances learning. Every learning environment has both positive and negative aspects. As faculty members, we want to strive for a positive learning environment. Positive aspects encourage learning. Students should display a high level of interest or intrinsic desire to learn: the will to try and keep trying. Intrinsic motivation creates a perfect atmosphere for encouraging learning. Students also learn more when goals and learning objectives seem achievable. Students need to believe that they can learn the material being taught (self-efficacy). The way a class is taught is crucial to whether students do or do not learn. Students want the support of their peers, strong student engagement, and an interesting or engaging teaching approach (Palmer 2016). Academic service-learning makes it easier for students to learn because of its intrinsically motivating learning environment.

A negative environment hinders learning. There are also aspects to every college classroom that can discourage learning. For example, if students believe the course is too hard, they develop low self-efficacy (lack of belief in their ability) and have no hope.

Furthermore, if students do not see value in the course or otherwise lack interest, there is no intrinsic desire to learn. In contrast, students who are intrinsically motivated have a desire to learn and get involved in the course. As one of my students said, "I liked everything. This was actually the one class that I enjoyed coming to this semester. And actually, only one of a few that I have enjoyed throughout college." Obviously, this student liked academic service-learning. If students are seeking a more interactive teaching style, they may be bored in a traditional lecture class. This can result in a negative learning experience. Other aspects of a classroom that can discourage learning are lack of sleep, hunger, exhaustion, or overall fatigue. Even an unmotivated peer group can be discouraging (Palmer 2016). In contrast, academic service-learning creates a positive learning environment that helps students become engaged in the learning process and makes students want to learn. An intrinsic environment encourages students. A negative environment encourages no one.

Do students have a preference? Students are requesting interaction. When researchers surveyed 230 students to get a better understanding of student preferences, students stated that they wanted "a more active pedagogy." They wanted more student participation, more collaboration, different group sizes (both small and large), and flexible learning options (Valtonen et al. 2021). An academic service-learning pedagogy encased within an intrinsically motivating classroom environment provides each of these requests. Academic service-learning teaches the textbook through interactive discussions. Students stay focused and increase their engagement.

Advantages of Incorporating Intrinsic Motivation into Academic Service-Learning

When the teaching pedagogy (the way the curriculum or course content is taught) makes use of a strong intrinsically motivating learning environment, the likelihood of success for students in a university classroom greatly increases. With academic service-learning, intrinsic motivation is required.

Why must the learning environment include intrinsic motivation? Numerous research studies have shown that intrinsically motivated university students display less anxiety over assignments and tests, while producing higher levels of achievement, critical thinking, and test scores (Brady et al. 2016; Di Domenico and Ryan 2017). One study of 418 undergraduates found that the way a course was taught directly affected student outcomes, engagement, and student self-efficacy (Shin and Bolkan 2020). Intrinsically motivated students attach more meaning to what they are studying, better retain textbook material, have higher perceptions of competence, and better overall learning outcomes (Azila-Gbettor et al. 2021; Bandura 1997; Ryan and Deci 2017; Shin et al. 2018). Therefore, college professors should include intrinsic motivation in their classes.

Intrinsic motivation encourages higher-order thinking With intrinsic motivation, students show more determination to learn (Deci and Ryan 2012). Students also demonstrate greater originality and depth of thinking (Reeve et al. 2018). For example, when 110 college students participating in a semester long service-learning project were tested, intrinsic motivation was the determining factor that made the difference in their success or failure (Shin et al. 2018). When university students are intrinsically motivated in a class using academic service-learning, they often participate in classroom discussions and engage in service-learning activities for the sense of accomplishment that such learning brings. This type of learning is totally different from a student who works only for a grade and memorizes for the test, while having no intention of using any of the information from class once the course has ended.

Intrinsic motivation encourages teamwork. Intrinsic motivation heightens students' internal desire to explore and to help others, as well as encouraging persistence (Cerasoli et al. 2014; Reeve et al. 2007). During classroom discussions, an intrinsically motivating learning environment encourages more in-depth thought processes, critical thinking, and higher-level decision-making (Deci 1975; Reeve et al. 2018; Ryan et al. 2019).

> One semester, my students worked in groups to analyze the best way to get the children at *Camp Sharigan* excited about reading. Each group had good ideas but refused to compromise. It happens. One student spoke up and said, "Wait, we're supposed to be a team, a cooperative team, a team that works together. How are we going to teach a bunch of kids if we can't even agree?" It was a simple statement, but it brought forth the importance of the intrinsically motivating learning environment. The student reminded everyone that the goal was to work together, not insist that their idea was the best.

You need teamwork if you are going to succeed at a service worksite. Academic service-learning teaches teamwork. Intrinsic motivation helps to build the partnership.

Academic service-learning uses intrinsic motivation to help students learn. Intrinsic motivation increases students' willingness to put forth more effort. In an intrinsically motivating environment, students are more inclined to display rational decision-making, better control and regulation of emotions and behavior, less pessimistic thinking, and reduced negativity and hopelessness, while showing a stronger desire to study (Cerasoli et al. 2014). Intrinsic motivation enables students to take control over their lives, to stop avoiding the problems they face in school, and to learn to confront hard tasks and difficult situations (Ryan and Deci 2020; Yampolsky and Amiot 2013).

How Can an Intrinsically Motivating Learning Environment Be Added to a Course?

Creating such a learning environment is not as easy as placing a bowl of candy on a desk. Nor can intrinsic motivation be generated by simply smiling and saying kind words. Even though an intrinsic environment takes work, it is well worth the effort. When a professor creates a course that stresses intrinsic motivation, students strive harder to participate, cooperate with others, and be their best. These are skills that we want in a college classroom.

First, remember, you cannot motivate a student. Yet, it is possible to create a learning environment in which students can motivate themselves (Clanton Harpine 2015; Deci and Ryan 1985). Students are motivated when they perceive that the task they have been asked to do or learn has value and is purposeful, as well as when they believe (self-efficacy) that they have the ability to understand and complete the task (Bandura 1997). When combined with active learning, academic service-learning provides the perfect foundation for building this intrinsic learning environment.

There are five steps for building an intrinsically motivating learning environment. The steps are: (1) generate excitement, (2) teach acceptance, (3) teach teambuilding, (4) remove negative distractors, and (5) use intrinsic motivation to encourage student engagement. Let's look at each step individually.

Step #1: Generate excitement. As John Dewey explained, a curious student is alert and exploring (Dewey 1933). You want your students to be curious and alert; you want them to explore new information. Introduce the service-learning project on the first day. Explain the real-world benefits. Make it sound interesting, not boring. If available and applicable, use pictures or videos from the community service worksite.

A curious student will learn more. Curiosity often includes a bit of mystery and surprise. Don't be afraid to challenge your students. Show how the service-learning project is applicable for all students, no matter what their major is.

Use the service-learning project to create excitement and teach at the same time. Let the service-learning project help you teach the content and theory from the textbook. For example, if your course benefits from teamwork (most do), then talk about how the class can work together as a cooperative team. Students often find it rewarding to engage in a positive, worthwhile task (Forgas et al. 2005).

> With my psychology of motivation students, I started building my learning environment on the first day of class. As illustrated in the case example in Chapter 2, I presented my students with an exciting service-learning project—*Camp Sharigan*. A colorful slide presentation from *Camp Sharigan* helped to get the students excited, but pure excitement is not enough. By helping a failing child learn to read, students knew they could change a child's life forever. In class, I reinforced the concept of helping the children by having students review research telling the number of children helped in the past at *Camp Sharigan*. The college students became eager to go to work to help a new group of children.

The service-learning project helped to create a positive intrinsic learning atmosphere to initiate the semester's learning experiences. Acceptance and teamwork were already becoming important elements in the university classroom. These are skills that employers often seek and that can be applied to any course at a university or college.

Excitement is not enough. Research has demonstrated that learning-by-doing or the intentional hands-on use of the information from the textbook increases the university student's ability to remember and recall knowledge learned (Ekwueme et al. 2015; Freeman et al. 2014; Kibga et al. 2022). Hands-on learning, project-based activities, and especially real-world academic service-learning increase a college student's motivation and engagement. Student engagement plays a major role in determining how much a student learns and retains for recall later. Hands-on learning can take place in the classroom or at the community worksite.

> *Camp Sharigan* uses hands-on learning techniques to build an intrinsically motivating learning environment for the children, such as a pop-up book (made by each child) that

> encourages children to write their own story, practice spelling words, and work on their comprehension skills as they follow step-by-step directions. Making a paper pop-up book is exciting and motivating. The children are willing to challenge themselves and complete hard tasks so they can complete their book. Having the group work on a project together builds acceptance. Being accepted and included is a key concept at *Camp Sharigan* and for all university students. Working together to teach hands-on reading skills brings the university students closer together as a cohesive, cooperative team.

Why is a paper pop-up book motivating? It is motivating because it ties into self-efficacy (belief that you can accomplish a task). Struggling students read and follow directions to complete an interesting task. Positive self-efficacy is motivating.

> The pop-up book is a strong motivator for both the children at *Camp Sharigan* and for the university students. Although the book is easy to make, it looks complicated. When the college students first look at the project, they think that making a book pop up is too hard. It's not. Showing the children how easy a pop-up is to make generates motivation for the students as well as the children.

Accomplishing a task that looked hard or impossible builds self-efficacy (belief that a person can learn a particular skill). Self-efficacy builds motivation. It is the challenge of completing a task that one might have thought to be impossible that makes it so motivating. Hands-on teaching techniques both in the college classroom and at the worksite increase excitement and intrinsic motivation, and thereby increase learning.

Step #2: Teach acceptance. Positive thoughts are good, but just giving students positive feedback or making positive comments during class is not enough. An intrinsically motivating learning environment begins with acceptance. Teachers as well as students must accept every student in the classroom, even the students who are not the most cooperative. Acceptance doesn't always mean agreement. Yet, acceptance does mean being willing to work with someone who may have different ideas than your own. Acceptance is a life skill that all students need to develop.

Acceptance grows out of a cohesive group structure. Each class includes an array of students. Students have different backgrounds, life experiences, feelings about school, family lives, positive or negative opinions, biases, and, in some cases, even negative or bigoted judgments (Yampolsky and Amiot 2013). Students bring each of these ideas and feelings (positive and negative alike) into the university classroom and to the service worksite. An intrinsically motivating learning environment helps students learn to work together, even when they do not share the same feelings and beliefs. Working together in small groups in class will help your students learn to work together better when they are at the community worksite or on the job in their later careers.

Every student learns differently. No two students, not even identical twins, learn in the same way. When building a supportive, intrinsically motivating learning environment, consider the learning needs of each student. Build a cohesive, accepting, and supportive group atmosphere that accommodates learning differences, physical differences, and different life experiences. The classroom learning environment and the overall group structure of the class are two of the main determining factors for student success in the classroom (Ryan and Deci 2000). The instructor must provide emotional support and acceptance to all students. Faculty must create hope, generate involvement, and provide support for students when they struggle.

Step #3: Remove negative barriers. Motivation is the guiding energy that explains why students perform and behave as they do; however, motivation can be either positive or negative. As you create an intrinsic environment, be careful to make sure that your teaching strategies are truly intrinsic. It is harder for students to learn in a negative environment. So, build intrinsic motivation into every class session.

When building a learning environment, do not add extrinsic rewards. Grades, fear of failing, and parental pressure are all extrinsic. Even the desire to go to college to get a better job is extrinsic. That is why some students start out enthusiastic, then just seem to fizzle. Extrinsic rewards may temporarily induce a student to perform a certain action, but extrinsic motivation is short-lived. Temporary compliance is not true motivation (Clanton Harpine 2015; Reeve et al. 2007). Even the fear of failure pushes a student only so far; it does not last (Bandura 2012; Deci and Ryan 2012).

Sometimes extrinsic rewards seem to work at first. Yes, rewards can appear to work at first, but extrinsic rewards eventually become a detriment to learning (Ryan and Deci 2020). If students expect extrinsic rewards, they will not perform the desired learning task unless given the promised reward (Ryan et al. 1983). Extrinsic rewards do not produce the learning environment needed for academic service-learning.

Extra credit. Some professors may be saying, "but my students respond so well to extra credit." Unfortunately, research shows that students actually become less motivated as they progress through the course when the class relies on extrinsic rewards (Deci et al. 2001; Reeve et al. 2003; Ryan and Deci 2020). Extrinsic rewards, such as extra credit, do not create high-quality learning or engagement in learning.

> One semester, another professor and I were teaching the same lifespan development course, using the same textbook. This was a beginning freshman course required by several different departments at the university. Most of the students had no desire to take the course. I taught using academic service-learning. The other professor taught using traditional lecturing but had students work at *Camp Sharigan*. My students spent the semester preparing for *Camp Sharigan* as they learned about the stages of development. I offered a training program and slide presentation for the other class, but, otherwise, they were not involved until *Camp Sharigan* began. Students in both classes were required to spend two hours working at *Camp Sharigan*. Almost all of my students requested permission to volunteer for extra hours (without receiving any kind of bonus or extra points—these were not psychology majors or my motivation students; these were general study students). The other professor's students only agreed to work when the professor offered extra credit.

An integrated academic service-learning project had a stronger motivating influence than a project simply tacked-on to a lecture. The academic service-learning students were intrinsically involved and committed; they wanted to do their best for the children.

Never ignore rudeness. Ignoring rudeness destroys cohesion and gives it permission to grow and fester. Always keep discussion, analysis, and evaluations positive and never personal. Make it clear from the very beginning that acceptance is required. Always develop criteria for evaluating solutions to problems and to evaluate group decisions. Establish criteria before group discussions begin.

> Early in the semester a student said, "that's the dumbest idea I've ever heard; you're an idiot; that won't work." I responded by saying, "go back to the criteria that we set at the beginning for evaluating our ideas. We never attack each other or make rude comments to another person. We are here to generate ideas and to learn, after all how would you feel if someone made such a response after something you said. Think before you speak, do not just say the first thing that comes to mind. Analyze your words before you talk. We are a team, and we work together cooperatively, please apologize."

As a teacher, it was my responsibility to step in immediately and resolve this controversy; such a comment could destroy interaction in the classroom from that day forward. If students are worried about being criticized, they will not speak up in class discussions. When you open the classroom to discussion, you must be prepared to handle negative comments or personal problems that arise between students.

Never allow competition. Never permit competition, bullying, rude comments, or negativity to be a part of the classroom atmosphere. We all have an internal desire or need to belong (Baumeister and Leary 1995). Negative comments, competition, personal conflicts, or pressure to perform can destroy the intrinsic learning environment that you're trying to create (Grant and Dweck 2003). An intrinsically motivating classroom environment is totally non-judgmental. Create a classroom structure that offers trust, cooperative teamwork, but not competition.

Negative classroom behavior destroys cohesive acceptance. Make it clear that students are responsible for their words and actions in the classroom and at the service-learning worksite. Learning how to handle rude comments is important for the students because, more than likely, they will encounter rude comments at some point at the worksite. People tend to speak before they think. This is an important lesson for every college classroom. It is also important in life because such events not only happen at the university, but indeed throughout the world. In the age of social media, the problem is even more obvious. Teach students how to be kind, considerate, and accepting of others.

Generate a cohesive working environment at the service worksite. Acceptance must carry over to the community site. Students must be accepting of the people they are working with in the community. Students also need to be accepting of each other while working in the community. Even though you cannot motivate a student, you can teach acceptance. Kindness and consideration for others must be taught.

Step #4: Teach teambuilding. College students, like everyone else, need to experience success. Working in a group to complete a service-learning project generates pride and the belief that they can accomplish something worthwhile. Academic service-learning teaches leadership skills, and how to help people in the real world.

The first step is to teach nonjudgmental communication. Teach cooperation; teach students how to work together. Teach respect by demonstrating how to be respectful.

Teambuilding begins the first day of class and continues till the end of the semester. Teambuilding takes practice. Students read, learn about, and then have the opportunity through class discussions and the service-learning project to apply teambuilding skills.

> One semester, I was teaching developmental psychology to a class of nursing students. They honestly did not see why they needed to take a class in developmental psychology; after all, they were getting a degree in nursing. When I began to talk about *Camp Sharigan*, they were certain that they were in the wrong course. As the semester progressed, I introduced the effects of stress, frustration, and anger on physical health. As I explained, reading failure is not only an educational problem. It is also a mental health problem, and mental health problems often cause physiological health problems. By helping the students make the connections between reading failure, mental health, and physical health, the students began to see why the class and service project were important for them. They became a strong team that worked very well at *Camp Sharigan*. On the end of the year evaluations, many of the nursing students expressed how much they learned about life from working with the children. One student even said that she now planned to train to become a pediatric nurse.

Develop an intrinsically motivating learning environment to help teach the information, concepts, and theories. Help students apply textbook information to the service worksite. Building an intrinsically motivating learning environment can work in every university classroom with every subject taught at any university.

Step #5: Encourage student engagement. Student engagement needs cohesion and acceptance. Cohesion is the harmony and supportive nature of your class. Group cohesion begins with acceptance. Cohesion is only possible in the classroom if students feel safe expressing their ideas and suggestions. Work to build a cohesive classroom atmosphere that works together cooperatively. Working together is the key to an intrinsically motivating environment, but students do not simply walk in the classroom door, sit down, and begin working together cohesively. Remember, cohesion means being accepting and understanding of others. Instructors must model and teach the class how to work together cohesively. Students need to feel that they belong and that there is a bond that pulls all students together. Truth and honesty are important, but the group must always keep student feelings and acceptance at the forefront. Cohesion is only possible when you have open and honest interaction between all class members. Such free communication does not include rude or offensive comments.

How can intrinsic motivation be built into the course pedagogy? Let's look at an example from my psychology of motivation course. This example shows how I worked to build an intrinsically motivating learning environment. The students had previously discussed the difference between intrinsic and extrinsic motivation.

Building a classroom structure conducive to intrinsic motivation. Before class, I arranged the desk into four groups so that, as the students arrived, they would have to select a group to join. Yes, it helps to have movable desks, but the same teaching technique can be used in a lecture hall. It works. Just be a bit more creative.

Rationale for rearranging desks. Why did I rearrange the desks? My intention in rearranging the desks was not to prevent friends from working together in the same group. That doesn't bother me. The purpose was to have equally sized groups.

Sometimes, if you tell students to put their chairs in a group, you will have 15 in one group and five in the other. As I tell my students, "You are welcome to work with your best buddy, but if you have 500 buddies in the class, you and your best friends will need to split up into different groups. The desks stay as arranged." Sometimes a little humor helps. Another reason is that small groups are more cohesive than large groups. Small groups also achieve acceptance faster than large groups. I wanted cohesion. To achieve cohesion, I needed to start with acceptance and the desire to work together.

Build onto previous knowledge taught. At the previous class session, my motivation students had been instructed to read the text and come to class ready to discuss seven behaviors listed in the textbook as being important for motivation. When they arrived, they worked in small groups to work with the seven behaviors from the textbook.

Small group discussion helps to reinforce and teach the text. Their first task was to set a group criterion for evaluation. Then, they decided on one group technique they would use at *Camp Sharigan* to encourage intrinsic motivation. Starting with the service-learning project always generates excitement. This is a teambuilding exercise, one of the methods used to generate intrinsic motivation in class.

Teach teambuilding. Leadership and team building need cooperation. Small groups also provide an opportunity for teambuilding. Teambuilding is important at *Camp Sharigan* and in the classroom alike. It is also a skill that employers often seek.

Group discussion and critical thinking helps students apply textbook theories to real life. The next step was for us to come back together as a total class. We established our group criteria for evaluation. Then, sitting in one large circle, each group explained their suggestions for the first day of camp. We analyzed each suggestion in accordance with the established criteria. The main question was, will the idea help to create intrinsic motivation with the children at *Camp Sharigan?* Then, we discussed how would the children respond to each suggestion. When you enable college students to analyze information that they have learned from the textbook, it strengthens learning.

"Think before you speak" became our class motto. Students learned that, when we analyze ideas, we are analyzing information, not the people or group who presented the idea. Helping students remember to focus on information rather than the person giving that information is one of the first steps toward building an intrinsically motivating learning environment in a classroom. It is essential to get past negative comments, such as having people say, "that's a dumb idea" or "that won't work." Analyze instead.

Use the service-learning project as a teaching tool. Students were reminded that children at the camp will occasionally be negative toward one another. So, I asked, how are you going to handle negative comments from the children? What will you say to the children? Reducing negativity at the service-learning worksite is just as important as reducing negativity in the university classroom. Learning to be kind is essential. Consideration for others must be taught. It doesn't happen naturally.

Real-world experience. Camp Sharigan has intrinsic motivation built into the program design. This makes it a perfect project for teaching students about intrinsic motivation as well as for integrating intrinsic motivation into the course pedagogy.

Does Academic Service-Learning Need Intrinsic Motivation to Be Successful?

The foundation upon which academic service-learning is built is active learning, but, just as a house cannot be built on bumpy ground, active learning instructional techniques must be employed within an intrinsically motivating environment. It's like building a house. The ground must be prepared before the foundation upon which to build the house can be laid. So, yes, we need intrinsic motivation.

Academic service-learning and intrinsic motivation work together to encourage higher-order thinking. When 1671 faculty members from 19 different universities in the United States were surveyed, those who supported and employed intrinsic motivation were more likely to use teaching strategies that called for higher-order thinking, reflection, or integrative and collaborative learning (Stupnisky et al. 2018). Academic service-learning provides this high-quality learning environment.

Academic service-learning focuses on teaching course content. Academic service-learning strives for a level of student engagement that helps students learn new textbook information, build meaning from that information, and understand how such information can be used in real-life situations. Service and learning are linked together in the active learning instructional techniques entwined within the course's content.

> One day at *Camp Sharigan,* a little boy asked one of the university students if he would be receiving a prize for finishing his puppet. (We use puppets as teaching tools at *Camp Sharigan,* but we do not give prizes or rewards. The puppet was covered with words that the child was learning to read and spell that day.) The university student replied, "no, we're doing something better. We're going to have a puppet play. Would you like to be a reader (which in actuality meant more work for the child)?" The child was so excited that he actually begged his mother to let him stay when she arrived early to take him home. The child said, "I have to stay. I'm a reader." That is intrinsic motivation in action. The university student had been a very strong supporter of extrinsic rewards when he started the semester. After studying intrinsic motivation in class and from seeing intrinsic motivation in action at *Camp Sharigan*, the university student became a strong supporter of intrinsic motivation over extrinsic rewards.

A real-world experience at the service worksite brought the textbook to life. Academic service-learning teaches the textbook and teaches how to apply the text to real life.

Summary

For academic service-learning to succeed, it must be built upon the foundation of a positive, intrinsically motivating learning environment. Creative ideas or exciting activities alone are not enough. Intrinsic motivation is the key. Even though it is not possible for a professor to motivate students, it *is* possible to create a classroom environment that helps students find the desire to become motivated. Intrinsic motivation is an internal desire to explore or learn for the pleasure and enjoyment that it brings to the student. Intrinsic motivation determines how much effort students are willing to invest in learning and the persistence that students display in learning a new concept or theory. Intrinsic motivational strategies lead to better test scores, better retention of textbook material, and better overall learning outcomes. These are skills that we want in the college classroom. The first step is to develop an intrinsically motivating learning environment. There are five steps for building an intrinsic learning environment: generate excitement, teach acceptance, teach teambuilding, remove negative distractors, and use intrinsic motivation to encourage student engagement. Intrinsic motivation is essential for academic service-learning to be successful.

Building a Service-Learning Pedagogy

Questions to Help in Course Planning

1. Review the goals that you set in Chapter 1.
2. Are there any new goals you would like to add?
3. How will you build an intrinsically motivating learning environment in your classroom? At the service worksite?

Troubleshooting Checklist

1. How will you handle negativity when it occurs in the classroom?
2. How will you discourage rude comments and judgmental statements toward other students?
1. How will you include everyone in your class discussions?
2. How will you challenge your students?
3. How will you make sure that you're using only intrinsic motivation rather than extrinsic rewards in the classroom?

Planning Guide Sheet

1. List five intrinsic motivational techniques that you plan to use in creating an intrinsically motivating learning environment.
2. List five teambuilding strategies that you plan to use in your course.
3. List five ways that you will teach acceptance and respect in your classroom.
4. List five ways to generate excitement through the service-learning project.

Case Example

This example comes from a class session in developmental psychology when I was teaching nursing students about how the brain learns. The nursing students had some background knowledge, but I wasn't sure how much. At this point in the semester, they were still apprehensive about the idea of a service-learning project; therefore, I was trying to build cohesion and acceptance.

Start with excitement. "At *Camp Sharigan*, we often tell the children 'let's train our brain.' They love it. You'll often hear one of the children walking around the room saying, 'I'm training my brain.' We do this to introduce the concept of change. We are using *vowel clustering*. This technique has proven to be very successful. Children have even moved up four grade levels in reading in one year. We want the children to realize that they will be learning a new method; therefore, we turn it into a game called *Match the Sound* where they train their brains to listen for sounds."

Generate interest in the service project. I *s*how slides from *Camp Sharigan* and the *Match the Sound* game to generate interest in the service-learning project with my college students. *Camp Sharigan* is colorful; therefore, when students see the pictures, it always generates excitement. At this point, I'm trying to build interest.

Hands-on activities generate motivation and make learning personal. I pass out *Match the Sound* gameboards, and we work on playing the game. I explain that one of the tasks that they will be doing at *Camp Sharigan* is helping children play this game. Hands-on activities intrinsically motivate university students to interact with the learning process and with other students in the class. When hands-on activities are tied to real-world service, their significance doubles.

Teach acceptance. The game is fun but sometimes even challenging for college students because they are not accustomed to thinking about words as sounds. This provides an excellent opportunity to work on cohesion and acceptance in class.

University students also often have low self-efficacy. Learning a new skill boosts the self-efficacy of the university students, especially when the game is tied to the service project. A positive self-efficacy is intrinsically motivating. Students who were at first reluctant in the course began to show stronger persistence and willingness to learn textbook information to help failing children at *Camp Sharigan.*

Teach teambuilding. One of the best ways to unite a group and build a team is to help someone in need. I emphasize that the children we will be working with are failing in reading at school. Student commitment increases.

Build group cohesion, understanding, and acceptance. I try to encourage my students to think back to when they were in school. "Think for just a moment when we played the game how difficult it was for you to change how you think about words. Most of you learned in school using phonics or whole language. The same is true for the children we will be working with. Unfortunately, phonics and whole language have both failed with these children. They need a new approach. Think about how you would feel if you were in their place. How do you think they feel in elementary school knowing that they have failed to learn to read?"

Use the service-learning project to teach the textbook. Give a question to work on:

> "Let's look at our textbook reading for today to see why these children might be doing so much better with *vowel clustering* than with phonics or whole language."

Small group work. Small groups generate cohesion and encourage teambuilding better than a large group. Send students into small groups with their textbooks to answer the question: How does the brain work?

Large group. Come back together as a total group to discuss small group answers. I always want to make sure that all students correctly understand the concepts from the textbook, so we return to a large group after small group work.

Provide background knowledge, summarize, and provide clarification. I always make sure that I give a summary statement to make sure that students understand the information being taught correctly. I explain, "As stated in the text, the brain is composed of about 86 billion neurons. Most of these neurons existed at birth and are wired and rewired throughout life forming approximately 150 trillion connections or synapses in the adult brain. Although a baby is born with the same number of neurons as an adult and has almost all of the neurons the person will have throughout life, a baby is born with only around 50 trillion connections between these neurons. By age 3, the child's brain has developed approximately 1000 trillion synaptic connections—almost double."

Make learning personal. I do not want the students to sit and listen passively, even though I have lots of information to cover; therefore, I ask a question:

> "Does the brain stop growing after age 3? What did the textbook say?"

After discussion, again summarize and clarify. "That is correct, the brain continues growing and developing until around age 25, but the brain continues to change and learn throughout a person's life. The rewiring and changing of connections between neurons continues even into old age; the brain never stops changing or loses the ability to learn. Even people my age can still learn."

Group process, evaluation, and critical thinking enhance learning. Therefore I use group discussion questions to help students process information: "So, if the brain is still growing, why are these children having so much trouble learning to read?"

Open group discussion. Orient the textbook directly to the nursing students. "Some of you mentioned that you cannot answer the question because you're not teachers. Let's think about nurses. Do nurses do any teaching?" [Most say no.]

Make the example more specific to nursing. "What if you have a patient who is diabetic and having trouble stabilizing their blood sugar? Does understanding how the brain works and knowing how to teach and work with others help you as a nurse help your patient?" [Allow student answers.]

Extend the connection between teaching and nursing. "What about if you're working with a cardiac patient who must relearn how to eat, exercise, and adjust to a new lifestyle? Are you teaching? Does knowing that the brain can continuously change help you help that patient? "After discussion, I move back to the textbook. I always want to tie the group discussions back to the text.

Application to the text. "The textbook talked about neuroplasticity. What is neuroplasticity?" Allow discussion.

Summarize and clarify. "Yes, it is the ability to reorganize and rewire synaptic connections, especially in response to learning new information and skills."

Group assignment to apply textbook information to service-learning project. "Neuroplasticity is the process that allows the children at *Camp Sharigan* to learn new information, especially using a new teaching method. With all of this new knowledge about the brain, I want you to work in groups to look over the workstation packets for the first day. See if you can identify when and how we will be working to help the children apply the principles of neuroplasticity and learn new words and vowel sounds. Make a list. Then, we will come back together and discuss your findings. Do you think that the learning process will be different for children of different ages? What does the text say?"

With that lesson, I was building group cohesion by switching from small group to large group discussions. Students could build intrinsic interest and acceptance within the class and toward the children. Academic service-learning allowed me to incorporate the information from the text into critical analysis during discussion to build a more intrinsically cohesive team.

References

Ahn, R., & Class, M. (2011). Student-centered pedagogy: Co-construction of knowledge through student-generated midterm exams. *International Journal of Teaching and Learning in Higher Education, 23,* 269–281.

American College Health Association. (2018). *American College Health Association-National College Health Assessment II: Undergraduate Student Reference Group Data Report Fall 2018.* Silver Spring, MD: American College Health Association.

Azila-Gbettor, E. M., Mensah, C., Abiemo, M. K., & Bokor, M. (2021). Predicting student engagement from self-efficacy and autonomous motivation: A cross-sectional study, *Cogent Education, 8*,1–14. https://doi.org/10.1080/2331186X.2021.1942638

Bandura A. 1997. *Self-efficacy: The exercise of control.* New York: Freeman.

Bandura, A. (2012). On the functional properties of perceived self-efficacy revisited. *Journal of Management, 38*, 9-44. https://doi.org/10.1177/0149206311410606

Baumeister, R. F., & Leary, M. R. (1995). The need to belong: Desire for interpersonal attachments as a fundamental human motivation. *Psychological Bulletin, 117*, 497–529. https://doi.org/10.1037/0033-2909.117.3.497

Bergsmann, E. M., Lüftenegger, M., Jöstl, G., Schober, B., & Spiel, C. (2013). The role of classroom structure in fostering students' school functioning: A comprehensive and application-oriented approach. *Learning and Individual Differences, 26,* 131–138. https://doi.org/10.1016/j.lindif.2013.05.005

Blumberg, P. (2008). *Developing learner-centered teaching: A practical guide for faculty.* San Francisco, CA: Jossey-Bass.

Brady, S. T., Reeves, S. L., Garcia, J., Purdie-Vaughns, V., & Cook, J. E. (2016). The psychology of the affirmed learner: Spontaneous self-affirmation in the face of stress. *Journal of Educational Psychology, 108*, 353–373. https://doi.org/10.1037/edu0000091

Bringle, R. G., & Hatcher, J. A. (2017). Innovative practices in service-learning and curricular engagement. *New Directions for Higher Education,147*, 37–46. https://doi.org/10.1002/he.356

Cerasoli, C.P., Nicklin, J.M. and Ford, M.T. (2014). Intrinsic motivation and extrinsic incentives jointly predict performance: A 40-year meta-analysis. *Psychological Bulletin, 140*, 980–1008. https://doi.org/10.1037/a0035661

Clanton Harpine, E. (2015). *Group-centered prevention in mental health: Theory, training, and practice*. New York: Springer.

Deci, E. L. (1975). *Intrinsic motivation*. New York: Plenum Press.

Deci, E. L., Koestner, R., & Ryan, R. M. (2001). Extrinsic rewards and intrinsic motivation in education: Reconsidered once again. *Review of Educational Research, 71*, 1–27. https://doi.org/10.3102/00346543071001001

Deci, E. L., & Ryan, R. M. (1985). *Intrinsic motivation and self-determination in human behavior*. New York, NY: Plenum Press.

Deci, E. L., & Ryan, R. M. (2012). Self-determination theory. In P. A. M. V. Lange, A. W. Kruglanski & E. T. Higgins (Eds.), *Handbook of theories of social psychology* (Vol. 1, pp. 416–437). Thousand Oaks, CA: Sage.

Deslauriers, L., McCarty, L. S., Miller, K., Callaghan, K., & Kestin, G. (2019). Measuring actual learning versus feeling of learning in response to being actively engaged in the classroom. *Proceedings of the National Academy of Sciences, 116*, 19251–19257. https://doi.org/10.1073/pnas.1821936116

Dewey, J. (1933). *How we think: A restatement of the relation of reflective thinking to the educative process*. Lexington, MA: D. C. Heath and Company.

Di Domenico, S. I., & Ryan, R. M. (2017). The emerging neuroscience of intrinsic motivation: A new frontier in self-determination research. *Frontiers in Human Neuroscience, 11*, Article 145. https://doi.org/10.3389/fnhum.2017.00145

Ekwueme, C. O., Ekon, E. E., & Ezenwa-Nebife, D. C. (2015). The impact of hands-on-approach on student academic performance in basic science and mathematics. *Higher Education Studies, 5*, 47–51. https://doi.org/10.5539/hes.v5n6p47

Forgas, J. P., Williams, K. D., & Laham, S. M. (2005). Social motivation: Introduction and overview. In J. P. Forgas, K. D., Williams & S. M. Laham (Eds.), *Social motivation: Conscious and unconscious processes*. (pp. 1–15). New York: Cambridge University Press.

Freeman, S., Eddy, S. L., McDonough, M., Smith, Nnadozie Okoroafor, M. K., Jordt, H., & Wenderoth, M. P. (2014). Active learning increases student performance in science, engineering, and mathematics. *Proceedings of the National Academy of Sciences (PNAS), 111*, 8410–8415. https://doi.org/10.1073/pnas.1319030111

Grant, H., & Dweck, C. S. (2003). Clarifying Achievement Goals and Their Impact. *Journal of Personality and Social Psychology, 85*, 541–553. https://doi.org/10.1037/0022-3514.85.3.541

Halpern, D. F., & Dunn, D. S. (2022). *Thought and knowledge: An introduction to critical thinking* (Vol 2) 6th ed. NY: Routledge.

Hart, S. M., & King, J. R. (2007). Service learning and literacy tutoring: Academic impact on pre-service teachers. *Teaching and Teacher Education, 23*, 323–328. https://doi.org/10.1016/j.tate.2006.12.004

Kibga, E. S., Sentongo, J., & Gakuba, E. (2022). Development of chemistry learners' problem-solving skills through hands-on instructional model. *International Journal of Evaluation and Research in Education (IJERE), 11*, 2029–2038. https://doi.org/10.11591/ijere.v11i4.22688

Miller, R. L., Ryceka, R. F., & Fritson, K. (2011). The effects of high impact learning experiences on student engagement. *Procedia-Social and Behavioral Sciences, 15*, 53–59.

Palmer, D. (2016). Motivation for learning: An implicit decision-making process. *Creative Education*, 7, 2380–2388. https://doi.org/10.4236/ce.2016.716229

Reeve, J., Nix, G., & Hamm, D. (2003). The experience of self-determination in intrinsic motivation and the conundrum of choice. *Journal of Educational Psychology, 95*, 347–392. https://doi.org/10.1037/0022-0663.95.2.375

Reeve, J., Ryan, R. M., & Deci, E. L. (2018). Sociocultural influences on student motivation as viewed through the lens of self-determination theory. In G. A. Liem & D. M. (Eds.) *Big theories revisited 2*, (pp. 31–60). Charlotte, NC: Information Age Press.
Reeve, J., Ryan, R. M., Deci, E. L., & Jang, H. (2007). Understanding and promoting autonomous self-regulation: A self-determination theory perspective. In D. Schunk and B. Zimmerman (Eds.). *Motivation and self-regulated learning: Theory, research, practice* (pp. 223–244). Mahwah, NJ: Lawrence Erlbaum Associates Publishing.
Ryan, R. M., & Deci, E. L. (2000). Self-determination theory and the facilitation of intrinsic motivation, social development, and well-being. *American Psychologist, 55,* 68–78.
Ryan, R. M. & Deci, E. L. (2017). *Self-determination theory: Basic psychological needs in motivation, development, and wellness*. New York, NY: Guilford Publishing.
Ryan, R. M., & Deci, E. L. (2020). Intrinsic and extrinsic motivation from a self-determination theory perspective: Definitions, theory, practices, and future directions. *Contemporary Educational Psychology, 61,* 1–11. https://doi.org/10.1016/j.cedpsych.2020.101860
Ryan, R. M., Mims, V., & Koestner, R. (1983). Relation of reward contingency and interpersonal contacts to intrinsic motivation: A review and test using cognitive evaluation. *Journal of Personality and Social Psychology, 45,* 736–750.
Ryan, R. M, Ryan, W. S., Di Domenico, S. I., & Deci, E. L. (2019). The nature and the conditions of human flourishing: Self-determination theory and basic psychological needs. In R. M. Ryan (Ed.), *The Oxford handbook of human motivation* (2nd ed.). New York, NY: Oxford University Press.
Shin, J., Kim, M., Hwang, H., & Lee, B. (2018). Effects of intrinsic motivation and informative feedback in service-learning on the development of college students' life purpose. *Journal of Moral Education,* 47, 159–174. https://doi.org/10.1080/03057240.2017.1419943
Shin, M., & Bolkan, S. (2020). Intellectually stimulating students' intrinsic motivation: The mediating influence of student engagement, self-efficacy, and student academic support. *Communication Education, 70,* 146–164. https://doi.org/10.1080/03634523.2020.1828959
Stupnisky, R. H., BrckaLorenz, A., Yuhas, B., & Guay, F. (2018). Faculty members' motivation for teaching and best practices: Testing a model based on self-determination theory across institution types. *Contemporary Educational Psychology, 53,* 15–26. https://doi.org/10.1016/j.cedpsych.2018.01.004
Valtonen, T., Leppänen, U., Hyypiä, M., Kokko, A., Manninen, J., Vartiaainen, H., Sointu, E., & Hirsto, L. (2021). Learning environments preferred by university students: A shift toward informal and flexible learning environments. *Learning Environments Research*, *24*, 371–388. https://doi.org/10.1007/s10984-020-09339-6
Weimer, M. (2013). *Learner-centered teaching* (2nd ed.). San Francisco, CA: Jossey-Bass.
Yampolsky, M. A., & Amiot, C. E. (2013). Priming self-determined and non-self-determined group identification: Effects on well-being and intergroup bias. *Group Dynamics: Theory Research and Practice, 17,* 137–149. https://doi.org/10.1037/a0032825

Chapter 6
Building an Academic Service-Learning Pedagogy: How Can a Course Incorporate Academic Service-Learning?

Two identical university classrooms sit directly across the hall from one another, same course, arrangement, desks, but in one room the professor stands before the class using the traditional lecture method in which the teacher talks, and the students sit listening and taking notes. In the academic service-learning classroom, the teacher engages students in discussion. The students work in small groups to solve problems, relate the textbook to the service-learning project being planned, and critically analyze theories and topics being discussed. With academic service-learning, out-of-class observations and the service-learning project give students the opportunity to relate the theory and principles being learned in class to real-life settings. Academic service-learning transforms the classroom from a passive listening environment to an active, fully engaged, discovery-oriented learning center. When general study students were asked if they liked the academic service-learning teaching approach, 71% said yes (Clanton Harpine 2003).

Academic service-learning is not a game or structured experience tossed in between lectures to generate interest. Nor is it a service project tacked on to fulfill a university requirement. Academic service-learning is a total restructuring of the classroom approach to college teaching. It is not enough for instructors to know and understand the subject that they are teaching. To teach a subject, professors must also know and understand the best way to convey that information to students.

The original version of the chapter has been revised. A correction to this chapter can be found at https://doi.org/10.1007/978-3-031-51378-7_11

E. Clanton Harpine, *Service Learning in Higher Education*,
https://doi.org/10.1007/978-3-031-51378-7_6

Do Universities and Colleges Need to Change?

In his book, *Creating Significant Learning Experiences: An Integrated Approach to Designing College Courses* (2013), L. Dee Fink, who has worked in higher education as an instructional consultant for over 30 years, said:

> "We can continue to follow traditional ways of teaching, repeating the same practices that we and others ... have used for years. Or we can dare to dream about doing something different.... Should we make the effort to change?" (1)

In this book, we are answering Fink's call for change through academic service-learning. Our goal is to build a pedagogy (teaching method) that works with the way students learn [reread Chapter 4 for review of how students learn best] so we can help students achieve their full potential. In this book, *pedagogy* means the way teaching and learning are facilitated in the classroom and at the service project worksite.

Why Should University and College Professors Change How They Teach?

Larry Spence, founding director of the Schreyer Institute for Innovation in Learning (2001) recounts a story of students he had taught as freshmen and then again as seniors. He said that he always assumed that when students didn't remember something they should have known that the subject had just been omitted from their instruction. Then, when he retaught the same group of students and he knew that they had been taught the information, he asked, what happened? Yes, he had taught the information to the students, and four years later when he tested them, they had completely forgotten everything he had taught. In his article *The Case Against Teaching* (2001), Spence calls for change and then goes on to explain that professors will never be able to meet the needs of students in higher education until they become "designers of learning experiences ... not teachers" (Spence 2001, p. 10). Spence and Fink are not alone in calling for a change in how university courses are taught. Today's campuses are inundated with many calls for change.

Are the businesses who hire college graduates calling for change? Many business leaders who are hiring college graduates are complaining that graduates cannot write well enough to satisfy the company's needs, cannot analyze (not even non-technical problems), and lack problem-solving skills. In their book *Academically Adrift: Limited Learning on College Campuses* (2011), Richard Arum and Josipa Roksa explain that 90% of employers rate written communication, critical thinking, and problem-solving as important skills for students to learn to work successfully in the business world. From their research with 2300 students from 24 different colleges and universities, Arum and Roksa found that 45% of students did not show improvement in critical thinking with a college education. Arum and Roksa also stated that only 26% of college graduates were well prepared in writing and only

22% in critical thinking, while 24% of college students could not even read a print or online version of a newspaper. So yes, the business community is calling for a change in how university courses are taught.

Are students calling for change? When 230 university students were surveyed, they requested more interactive teaching strategies and application to real life (Valtonen et al. 2021). Academic service-learning provides an interactive learning experience.

Math. A second group of researchers studied 124 introductory mathematics students and found that, when students regularly experienced an interactive classroom, 90% said that an interactive pedagogy "greatly helped" them learn the math concepts being studied. Unfortunately, when interactive group sessions were merely interspersed between lectures, only 39% found the interactive sessions helpful. The study concluded by calling for a more interactive pedagogy (Vroom et al. 2022).

Engineering. In still another study, when 261 engineering students were asked to identify the strongest influence on what they learned, they said 45% of technical skills and 62% of what they learned about professional skills came from service-learning (Carberry et al. 2013). The study recommended a stronger focus on service-learning.

Marketing. The call for change was supported by still another study. A professor in non-profit marketing used a variety of pedagogical approaches for teaching different sections of the same course (lectures, case studies, reading the text, guest speakers, exams, and service-learning). Students in the study identified service-learning as the most helpful of the pedagogical tools employed for increasing their knowledge and understanding as well as greatly contributing to their ability to learn and complete the course objectives (Mottner 2010). The study called for an increase in service-learning.

Why are the students in these studies calling for change? Because if a professor just teaches theory or a long list of facts that are not connected with the real world and real-world experiences, then theory and facts become meaningless (Knight and Wood 2005). Students memorize for the test, then forget. Therefore, students are calling for change.

Is there a call for change among faculty? Some researchers have been calling for an end to lecturing and multiple-choice testing for many years (Arum and Roksa 2011; Blaich and Wise 2011; Fink 2013; Freeman et al. 2014; Spence 2001; Sukacke et al. 2022). Many professors are finding that active learning and academic service-learning produce stronger student outcomes (grades), knowledge learned, and application to the real world (Freeman et al. 2014; Hart and King 2007; Krsmanovic 2022; Mottner 2010; Warren and Sellnow 2010). Let's look at some of the research findings.

No more lectures. One study tested a variety of courses taught by the same professor (some using active learning and others traditional lecturing). The researchers reached this conclusion: "Our results support calls to replace traditional lecturing with evidence-based, active-learning course designs" (Theobald et al. 2020, p. 6480). Faculty are still able to cover the same amount of material with active learning as with lecturing (Deslauriers et al. 2019), but research demonstrates that students understand course content better with active learning and academic service-learning (Freeman et al. 2014; Hart and King 2007; Kamuche 2006; Stains et al. 2018; Theobald et al. 2020).

Struggling students. Researchers also found that high-order learning experiences help poorly prepared students to be more successful in college (Theobald et al. 2020). A more interactive classroom that emphasized high-order cognitive skills helped "… close the gap between disadvantaged and nondisadvantaged students" (Haak et al. 2011).

Higher-order thinking. A deeper level of knowledge and understanding is possible when active learning and academic service-learning combine. Problem-solving and other high-order teaching strategies help students improve their class performance (Halpern and Dunn 2021). So, yes, there are professors calling for change.

Why Is Academic Service-Learning a Better Way to Teach?

Academic service-learning uses problem-solving, case studies, critical thinking (objective analysis and evaluation), and other group discussion methods. When used as the teaching method in a college course, research shows that academic service-learning has been very effective and has produced stronger student outcomes, higher grades and test scores, better retention and graduation rates, commitment, persistence, stronger student engagement, and improved self-efficacy (Bringle and Hatcher 2017; Hart and King 2007; Krsmanovic 2022; Warren and Sellnow 2010). Academic service-learning has also been shown to be effective even in large university classes (Salam et al. 2019).

Academic service-learning is better because it encourages student engagement and a deeper level of learning. Class discussions, group work, and problem-solving replace lectures. Students work either in groups or respond individually to demonstrate an understanding of the concepts being studied. Group discussions and problem-solving have been shown to have the greatest impact on critical thinking and performance on exams (Arum and Roksa 2011; Halpern and Dunn 2021). Critical thinking improves in the college classroom when faculty allow students to apply what is being learned to real-life situations. Academic service-learning includes learning in the classroom as well as at the community worksite. Academic service-learning becomes the method used to teach the course, but academic service learning can only be successful when service and learning are linked together.

Academic service-learning is better because it combines active learning with intrinsic motivation. An effective academic service-learning pedagogy must combine active learning instructional techniques with an intrinsically motivating learning environment. Intrinsic motivation is internal, real motivation, not based on rewards (Ryan and Deci 2000). An intrinsic learning environment improves learning, increases persistence, and helps students remember what they have learned longer. Chapter 5 discussed how to build an intrinsic environment. Now, we add active learning and discuss how we integrate both intrinsic motivation and active learning into a course.

What Is Active Learning?

There are many definitions of active learning. In this book, *active learning* means hands-on interactive instruction and analysis that applies to the real world. We mean interaction both in the classroom and at the service project worksite.

Active learning is a teaching method. In the classroom, we want to challenge students to think through problems, to analyze information from the textbook, and to apply knowledge to real-world situations. To accomplish this higher-level of learning, academic service-learning uses active learning instructional techniques that promote critical thinking, analytical reasoning, and problem-solving. Research has shown that a high-level of learning is essential before knowledge will transfer from the classroom to the real world, such as for a student's future job or profession (Richmond et al. 2015). Therefore, students need to be encouraged to analyze, not just memorize.

Active learning includes application. Academic service-learning uses active learning techniques that encourage college students to apply and improve on what they are learning (Paul and Elder 2006). This level of thinking and learning is not possible with lectures, question and answer sessions, or add-on activities and games (Hardiman 2003). To be effective, active learning must be tied to the real world.

> One semester I was teaching a graduate class of teachers working on their master's degree. They taught school by day and came to the university one night a week for a human growth and development seminar. When they discovered that I was a psychologist, they immediately assumed that I knew absolutely nothing about teaching, and they certainly did not have time for that service project I was discussing. They had papers to grade and lesson plans to write. Active learning began the moment that I called their attention to the *individual student project* listed on the syllabus. They were required to select a student from their public school classroom who they were having difficulty with. This could be a behavioral or learning problem. My class of teachers became immediately interested. From that point on, I oriented the textbook material through the *Camp Sharigan* project (Clanton Harpine 2024) and also through the problems they were having with their designated students. Active learning became the platform for change not only in the university classroom and at *Camp Sharigan*, but also at their individual schools with the designated students whose behavior or learning problems they had chosen to transform.

Academic service-learning produces a teaching pedagogy that enables professors to teach real problems and help students find real solutions to those problems.

Developing an Academic Service-Learning Pedagogy

Since research supports the benefits of using academic service-learning as a teaching method for the college classroom, let's concentrate on building an academic service-learning pedagogy and show how active learning can be incorporated into that pedagogy. To produce this high level of learning, an academic service-learning pedagogy must fulfill five requirements: teach course content, apply knowledge learned, encourage student engagement, use intrinsic motivation, and build upon prior knowledge or student's personal learning experiences. I offer 10 easy-to-follow steps to help you create a successful academic service-learning pedagogy. Each step includes (1) questions to assist with the development of the course pedagogy, (2) the rationale for including each principle in the pedagogy, and (3) an example showing application.

Step 1, build an academic service-learning pedagogy that teaches course content. First and foremost, academic service-learning stresses teaching content. Academic service-learning can only achieve higher test scores, better retention, and better understanding of the theories and knowledge being taught when active learning teaches content and when service and learning are combined. Academic service-learning also stresses executive function, which is a very important part of learning because organized thought patterns in the brain are easier to retrieve and recall (Ramos-Galarza et al. 2023). Executive function involves the mental processes that enable students to plan, focus, remember, organize, and implement self-control (Ambrose et al. 2010). Organization is a skill that every student needs to learn and practice.

Questions to aid in building an effective pedagogy. Start by looking at your course content. Review the goals that you set in Chapter 1. How can you best accomplish your course goals? *M*ake a "must teach" list of every topic that you want your students to learn. Then, cut the list in half.

When I first started teaching, my department chair said, "make a list of everything you want to teach. Then, cut it in half. The goal is not to see how much information you can cover. The objective is to see how much your students can learn."

It's true that sometimes we all try to cover too much information. Research does substantiate that you can cover the same amount of material with active learning as with lecturing (Deslauriers et al. 2019); therefore, you can still achieve all of your goals from Chapter 1. So, with the new list in hand, decide on an active learning instructional method for teaching each item on the altered list. Did you include group discussions, problem-solving, and critical thinking? How do you teach organization in your course? The service-learning project is an excellent opportunity for teaching organization, teambuilding, and leadership. How will you apply these skills to your subject area?

Rationale for using active learning to teach course content. Active learning goes by many labels. We've defined *active learning* as being analytical and investigative--not the same as merely adding on a game or fun class activity. Academic service-learning focuses on teaching course content through using problem-solving, critical thinking, application of knowledge, decision making, higher-order thinking, and application to real-world experiences (Barnett et al. 2009; Hart and King 2007).

In my motivation class, I used five different teaching techniques to clarify the meaning of the word intrinsic. I used small and large group discussions, application to the textbook definition, evaluation, and analysis with prior knowledge about motivation. Then I related intrinsic motivation to the service-learning project and the real world. I applied critical evaluation and hands-on learning to teach the meaning of intrinsic. I applied the new information about intrinsic motivation to what students already knew about motivation, and then

> I built onto and even challenged their prior knowledge of intrinsic and extrinsic motivation. [see Case Example in Chapter 2 for a more complete description].

I wanted my students to learn course content and how to apply what they had learned.

Step 2, an academic service-learning pedagogy must help students apply the knowledge learned. Do not assume that, just because students know a lot of facts, they know what to do with those facts. It's like learning about a skill but not knowing how to use it. Students need to practice integrating and applying knowledge. Academic service-learning teaches facts and information as well as how to relate that information to a service-learning real-world project. Academic service-learning provides students with an opportunity to practice applying new theories and information during interactive classroom sessions and at the service-learning worksite. Academic service-learning focuses on group discussions, critical analysis, case studies, problem-solving, and a hands-on service-learning experience interwoven into the course content. Let's create an example of how this teaching concept could be applied.

History students might put on a historical fair where they teach younger children about a particular period of history with costumes, wall hangings, hands-on historical crafts, and stories. Perhaps they could include stories that they write based on historical information that they learn from the text. Students must research and learn the historical information while they work in groups and teams to organize the event before they can present the fair to the children.

The service project teaches the course content. Showing students how to apply textbook material to a real-world situation helps students obtain a deeper understanding. They remember what they learned in class long after the test and the class have ended.

Questions to aid in building an effective pedagogy. Review your finalized "must teach" list from Step 1. Do you include interactive teaching methods? Circle any instance in which you might be prone to lecture. Are you falling back into the age-old tradition of lecturing or trying to squeeze just one or two lectures in? If so, think how you could switch the same content to an active learning teaching method. Academic service-learning does not include lectures. How can you teach the same material that you normally teach in a lecture by using interactive groups? How will you teach application of knowledge learned? Will you include group discussion or teamwork?

Rationale for using active learning to help students apply knowledge learned. In biology, chemistry, computer science, engineering, urban studies, geology, math, physics, nursing, education, and psychology, the research findings were the same—active learning produced higher student outcomes (Brail 2016; Deslauriers et al. 2019; Freeman et al. 2014; Hart and King 2007; Hartlep and Forsyth 2000; Knight and Wood 2005). Regardless of the subject being taught, active learning is better than lecturing.

Working in groups in the classroom provides a totally different learning approach than lecturing (Ahn and Class 2011). Group work produces better test scores and longer lasting knowledge learned. Remembering, understanding, and being able to apply new information learned in a course are critical for the future careers of college graduates. Professor Pai Obanya is quoted as saying in 2012 that students retain only 5% of what is said during a lecture but retain approximately 75% from active learning instruction (Ekwueme et al. 2015). Research clearly shows that classes using active learning instructional techniques outperform classes relying on lectures, even when compared to dynamic lecturing professors (Brail 2016; Deslauriers et al. 2019). The only problem is that faculty must be willing to switch from lecturing to academic service-learning (Sukacke et al. 2022). Academic service-learning using active learning teaching strategies provides real-world application, problem solving, as well as conceptual understanding of textbook theories and analytical skills for the classroom.

Step 3, an academic service-learning pedagogy must encourage student engagement. Engagement means involvement. Passively sitting and listening (even taking notes) does not engage students in the learning process. When teaching goals are intertwined with service and academic content, student engagement, learning, and persistence improve (Bringle and Hatcher 2017; Kuh et al. 2008). As one study reported, with academic service-learning, students reported an increased desire to learn textbook material and demonstrated stronger student engagement across the semester (Hart and King 2007). The more realistic a student's involvement with the subject, the more likely the student is to retain the information being taught (Pascarella and Terenzini 2005).

Academic service-learning provides a real-world experience and uses active learning instructional techniques that directly link with the textbook and what is being taught.

Questions to aid in building an effective pedagogy. Return to your "must teach" list from Step 1. How do you enhance student engagement to improve learning in your course? Investigative discussions help increase student engagement. Are you teaching problem-solving? Do you emphasize high-level critical thinking and analysis? If not, go back and add interactive class sessions that teach problem-solving, analysis, critical thinking, and in-depth evaluation of theories and topics from the textbook.

Rationale for stressing student engagement. When students are actively engaged in the learning process, their focus and attention are increased, higher-level critical thinking and analysis are involved, and consequently students learn more and remember what they learn longer (Biggs 2001). When you add a real-world experience (a service-learning project), the college classroom takes on a deeper level of instruction.

Step 4, an academic service-learning pedagogy must stress intrinsic motivation. Academic service-learning uses active learning techniques that cultivate a sense of belonging. Students who feel they belong (feel accepted as a member of the class) will display stronger student engagement and involvement with learning (Baumeister and Leary 1995). When active learning is used with intrinsic motivation, active learning encourages acceptance, inclusion, and positive self-identity.

> In my early career, I used a class exercise that involved children's building blocks. The set had to include a triangle. Students were told that each group was to build as tall a tower as possible by placing one piece on the uppermost surface of the other. Students would eagerly get down on the floor to carefully place each block, until someone would eventually place the triangle on top. Naturally, nothing can be placed on top of the pointed triangle. The game would end. Yes, some leadership skills would surface during the game, but the main concept that the students learned was that competition killed the intrinsic environment and the student who placed the triangle on the tower had ruined everything. I stopped using classroom games when I started teaching with academic service-learning. Instead, I now teach students how to make a pom-pom spider name tag for *Camp Sharigan*. The children and the university students love the silly little name tag, but more importantly, students also learn about leadership. Students learn in class how to follow the step-by-step directions and make the name tag so that they will be ready and able to help the children make a nametag when they arrive at *Camp Sharigan*. Leadership skills abound as one student helps another student. Then, university students discuss the best way to teach the children to make a name tag. Some classes chose to have the children sit in a circle and learn together at one time. Other classes laid out step-by-step directions at a workstation. Teaching a hands-on craft, such as a name tag, taught my students more about leadership than any game or lecture could ever have accomplished. Leadership and intrinsic cooperation were excellent lessons.

Leadership and organization are important skills for every college student to learn but learning to be an accepted member of a class is even more important. Academic service-learning teaches this sense of belonging through an intrinsic environment and active learning teaching methods that encourage acceptance and teamwork.

Questions to aid in building an effective pedagogy. An intrinsically motivational learning environment is not just something you build at the beginning of the course and then forget about. Intrinsic motivation must be nurtured throughout the course. Look at your teaching strategies. How are you including intrinsic motivation? What do you do to help students feel as if they belong, accepted? What role does intrinsic motivation have at the service-learning worksite? For help, reread Chapter 5. Do you have anything negative? Anything controversial? If you are discussing controversial topics (which can be good), how will you maintain cohesion and intrinsic motivation during those discussions? Controversial topics can be an excellent way to teach critical thinking. When discussing controversial topics, how will you ensure that all students are included and not made to feel inferior? It's excellent to discuss controversial issues and even negative topics, but make sure that acceptance, understanding of everyone's ideas, and intrinsic motivation prevail. Do you include competition or competitive games? Competition destroys intrinsic desire. Remove all competition.

Rationale for including intrinsic motivation. An intrinsically motivating learning environment provides a strong, supportive atmosphere for learning. Intrinsic motivation also increases a student's persistence or desire to keep working, even when the learning task is difficult. Research has shown that when students are intrinsically motivated, they learn better, remember what they learn longer, and are able to recall what they learned more easily (Murayama and Elliot 2011). Why? Intrinsic motivation works with the brain to make stronger neural connections that help students retain information (Merzenich 2013). High stress reduces a student's ability to concentrate and thereby learn. So, as you build your academic service-learning pedagogy, start with an intrinsically motivating environment, but remember that working with people in a real-world situation makes all the difference.

> Returning to our leadership example, competition with the building blocks destroyed any hope for teaching leadership. Yet, making a name tag (cooperation rather than competition) helped to teach the desired leadership skills. Why? Because playing a game or participating in an artificial leadership activity does not teach students how to be a leader when they are away from the game. By attaching leadership to the service project, leadership skills taught in class transferred to the real world. Students were practicing real leadership.

There are hundreds of leadership activities, but the skills do not transfer to the real world. Leadership games do not teach how to go out into the real world and apply leadership skills to a real problem, especially for careers and jobs.

Step 5, an academic service-learning pedagogy must build upon prior knowledge. It is not possible for a university student to sit in class and learn new knowledge, skills, or even to retain or recall new information unless the new information being taught is stored and connected with previous knowledge in the student's memory (Biggs 2001). Students must be able to link new information beyond the mere context (textbook) or setting (classroom) in which new information was presented or read. The more ways that a teacher finds to apply new ideas, the better the student will be able to learn, retain, and recall the information. An academic service-learning pedagogy must help students make connections with previous knowledge. Let's create an example of how a professor teaching poetry might use this approach.

> A college class could plan a poetry workshop for elementary or high school students. Almost all students learn about the different types of poetry. University students could work in small groups in class to find examples of each type of poetry. They could then interpret the poems. They can identify rhyme, meter, and imagery. The students might even try their hand at writing an example for each. Students could research the lives of the different poets to see how the poet's life influenced their poetry. As a class, they could read poems aloud, analyze, evaluate as to style, and even make a booklet of their poems. The university students could then teach children or youth about the types of poetry, help the children or youth write their own poems, and make a poetry booklet.

Look at how many different ways students are working with the information taught? Academic service-learning helps students learn the information taught in class as well as giving students the opportunity to fill a social need (Wang and Rodgers 2006).

Questions to aid in building an effective pedagogy. Review your "must teach" list from Step 1. How are you building onto prior knowledge and experiences? How will you determine what students do and do not know from previous courses? How many active learning techniques are you using to teach each theme, idea, or theory? Are you using high-order learning strategies? How are you linking your course content and service-learning project together? Are you using the service project to teach the textbook? Can you draw a stronger link between service and learning? What does the service project add to the course? Why is that important?

Rationale for building upon prior knowledge. It is important to develop a teaching pedagogy that boosts memory and recall. We need a pedagogy that helps students process information into their long-term memory and retain knowledge learned long after the class has ended (Shahbaba et al. 2022). Academic service-learning uses active learning to teach, then takes students into the community to apply that knowledge.

Step 6, an academic service-learning pedagogy incorporates group discussion. Group discussions are an excellent teaching technique because they encourage higher-order thinking skills and enable students to obtain a deeper level of understanding with course content. Small groups help you build cohesion faster and give more students a chance to practice leadership and analytical skills. Large groups give you, the instructor, a chance to summarize and make sure the textbook content is being presented correctly. [See the *Case Example* at the end of this chapter.] All group discussions must teach, be intrinsically motivating, and accepting—no negativity.

Questions to aid in building an effective pedagogy. Will you incorporate small and large group discussions as one of your teaching strategies? Which textbook topics will work best for in-class discussion? What will students learn during the class discussions? When will you use small group discussions? Which topics will you relegate to full class discussions? Why? How often will you use discussion to teach course content? How will group discussions be used to link textbook information with the service-learning project? Will you use discussions every day or only occasionally? How will you start the discussion? How will you incorporate the service project?

Rationale for using group discussions to teach course content. To build an effective pedagogy, promote useful group discussions, not just group talks but discussions that teach. While critical thinking, problem-solving, and case studies typically work best with small groups, there are times when you may want to bring your class together as a total large group. [See the Case Example at the end of this chapter.] Groups are a very effective teaching method and work well with active learning. When students work together in groups, multisensory networks are activated. Students are talking, listening, critically analyzing, experiencing emotions, problem-solving, and drawing connections between what is being discussed and what they have learned previously (Brown et al. 2014). Neither passive listening nor game-based class activities lead to this kind of multisensory learning. It is only through interactive teaching that students can learn and retain information, store this new information, and retrieve or recall this information later (Handelsman et al. 2006). Of course, this type of learning only occurs if you keep group discussions instructive and positive.

> If a problem arises, do not simply sit back and wait to see what will happen. If the disagreement is over information, refer the group to their textbook. If the problem is that one person is dominating the discussion, steer the group back on task. One approach that works is to say, "That's one idea. Now, let's see what the rest of the group has to say." You've neither declared the dominating speaker's idea good or bad; you have simply called for ideas from the rest of the group. Effective group interaction involves every group member.

A group decision is not a group decision unless every single member of the group has participated in making the decision. Don't allow competition, negativity, or rejection.

Step 7, an academic service-learning pedagogy uses teaching strategies that encourage critical thinking. Rote memorization for a multiple-choice test does not establish long-term memories that students can take with them into the workplace. Teaching critical thinking helps students develop a deeper level of learning.

Questions to aid in building an effective pedagogy. Look at your "must teach" list from Step 1. What is being learned from each of the class sessions that you've outlined? How are you incorporating critical thinking? Analysis?

Rationale for using critical thinking to teach course content. Critical analysis encourages students to justify their thinking. Having to justify and support one's thoughts with facts helps students to correct misinformation and misconceptions. It also encourages students to apply textbook information correctly. We want to use active learning strategies that teach students how to analyze information, use research, think rationally, and explain the purpose behind the information that they are learning (Paul and Elder 2006). In short, we want learning that lasts beyond the mid-term and the final exam. Let's create an example of how a professor might use this approach.

> Political science, sociology, mass media, communication, economic majors, or students in public administration could evaluate five different news or internet reports about an upcoming election. Each small group could work on a different report. They could evaluate the evidence, check the facts, analyze the accuracy of the reporting, and write (as accurately as possible) an unbiased description or report of the political event. Students and faculty alike will be amazed at how inaccurate media/internet reporting is. Students might then organize a town meeting. They could use their research to show the community how news can be distorted. Such a service project could help improve understanding of highly politicized reports and reduce misconceptions and distortions.

The key to teaching critical thinking is that you must be willing to use only provable facts, not opinions or political ideologies. Critical thinking can be used for any subject and can be linked directly to information being taught in class as well as a community-based service-learning project. This type of active learning strengthens knowledge.

Step 8, an academic service-learning pedagogy uses teaching strategies for problem-solving. Every university class can use a problem-solution teaching approach to generate discussion in class and teach course material. One example for using problem-solution techniques would be case studies. People often think that a case study can only be about an individual person. Case studies can be about a person, a group, or an event. A case study may also be about a company, organization, or a community. A case study involves in-depth analysis. Case studies look for patterns of behavior or causes. A case study may be related to the service-learning project, or it may be the entire project. A case study may also incorporate problem-solving.

> Problem-solving is how I start most of my class sessions. Students try to solve a problem in small groups. The class develops criteria for evaluation. Then, they evaluate the solutions they propose against theories from the textbook and the needs of people in a real community setting at the service-project worksite.

The service-learning project becomes a teaching tool that teaches course content.

Questions to aid in building an effective pedagogy. How can you use problem-solution group discussions to teach a particular theory or concept in your course? How could you link problem-solving with a case study(s) in your course? Does the case study support or explain the theory you are teaching? For problem-solution discussions, use a simple format: identify the problem, determine the cause of the problem, generate possible solutions, develop criteria for selecting the best possible solution, and implement the solution or test the solution for its effectiveness. Criteria are the guidelines you want to use for evaluating and finding the best solution. Evaluating in accordance with criteria avoids personal attacks or negative thinking.

Rationale for using problem-solving. This is one of the advantages of using an academic service-learning pedagogy. Pull problems from the service project, develop and evaluate solutions, and then, if appropriate, test proposed solutions. The professor must make sure all solutions are correct and appropriate. Absolutely never send students out to test an idea that could be harmful to the community or to the students. Never test an idea or solution just to see what will happen or to teach that the proposed solution will not work. Students should only implement approved workable ideas.

> One of my classes tackled the age-old problem of parking on campus. Students interviewed the administrators, students, and faculty to define the problem and gather suggestions for implementing a solution. They came back to class and worked in groups to analyze both the problem and the proposed solutions. They created criteria for evaluating each solution. They researched and prepared a formal proposal to present to the administration. From this project, students not only reinforced textbook knowledge on working in groups to solve problems but learned how to analyze and determine the effectiveness of proposed solutions. They also learned how to submit a proposal to an administrative body.

Academic service-learning taught the students to use the textbook and apply it to the real world—because the campus really did have a major parking problem.

Step 9, an academic service-learning pedagogy uses teaching strategies that stress higher-order thinking. Higher-order thinking pulls together analysis and evaluation to explain the information that students are learning.

Questions to aid in building an effective pedagogy. Make a list of higher-order thinking strategies for your course. Do your teaching strategies involve complex higher-order thinking, or have you simply listed games and add-on activities? Do you use small and large group discussions, problem-solving activities related to the service project, critical thinking, personal application of content learned, analysis of textbook information, or reflective analysis? Are you challenging your students to think?

Rationale for including higher-order thinking. Active learning teaching strategies that focus on higher-order thinking help students learn. When active learning was compared to traditional lecturing, the active learning students earned higher grades (Freeman et al. 2014). Therefore, an academic service-learning pedagogy needs to include critical thinking in the classroom and reflection activities that stimulate high-order thinking and analysis. At the worksite, implement hands-on application of the text as I did with my students in this example from my psychology of motivation class.

> From the very first day to the last-class session, *Camp Sharigan* is discussed every single day in class. *Camp Sharigan* is used to teach content from the textbook by applying the theory of intrinsic motivation to the needs of the children. Critical thinking, problem-solving, and evaluation are taught through class discussions. Leadership training and organizational skills (often sought by employers) are practiced in class and implemented at the service worksite.

Academic service-learning improves learning while engaging students in theoretical and textbook instruction. Students become more than passive listeners; they are actively working to uncover knowledge and apply it to the real world. The service-learning project becomes a teaching tool within the classroom. The key is to link service and learning together, a project that is merely tacked on will not reap the same benefits.

Step 10, an academic service-learning pedagogy employs reflection. Reflection is a crucial component that helps the students pull the learning from the classroom and the learning from the service worksite together, but reflection in isolation will not make academic service-learning successful. All reflective activities should incorporate critical thinking, analytical reasoning, and evaluation that takes a student back to the textbook and what has been taught in the course. When reflection and learning are connected, then reflection is a vital part of academic service-learning.

Rationale for using reflection to teach course content. Reflective activities can serve many purposes. One that I insist upon is that the reflection paper or journal entry must include evaluation—not just a description of what happened. Students must analyze why a particular event happened and then relate the entire reflection experience to the textbook and what they are studying in the course. With academic service-learning, all reflective writings must be a learning experience and tied to the course content and the service-learning project in the community.

> All of my classes keep an observation notebook. Students go out and observe behavior on campus or in the community in keeping with the subject of the course. They also reflect on their work at *Camp Sharigan*. Sometimes, students are requested to reflect on their own behavior. Students write learning goals and objectives each week. Students then reflect on how well they met those goals and objectives. What worked, what didn't, and why? Students are always encouraged to measure their own improvement. I remind students that other class members are not looking at their journal; this is their self-reflection.

Academic service learning includes reflection, but the learning process in the classroom is the key component that determines what the students will learn. Reflection alone does not teach critical thinking, problem-solving, or analytical reasoning.

Questions to aid in building an effective pedagogy. Look at your "must teach" list from Step 1. Do you include reflection? Do your reflection assignments challenge students to tell more than just a description of what happened? If students do not relate reflective assignments to the course content, reflection is incomplete. How will you use reflection in your course? How will you tie each reflective exercise or paper to your learning goals from Chapter 1? How many reflection assignments will you include? Will you use both oral and written reflection? What will you require students to include in their reflective assignments? For what purpose are you using reflection? What do you want your students to learn from the reflection assignment(s)?

Why Choose Active Learning Over Passive Learning?

As you have worked through the design steps for planning an academic service-learning pedagogy, each step has asked you to think of ways to use group discussion, problem-solving, critical thinking, analytical reasoning, and application to a real-world service-learning project. Hopefully, you are ready to embark upon this new approach to teaching. We have discussed this several times, and as many researchers have explained, getting faculty to switch from lectures to active learning is often the biggest hurdle that academic service-learning must overcome (Blumberg 2008; Sukacke et al. 2022; Weimer 2013). Even when research from 2000 classrooms, taught by 500 different professors, at 25 different United States universities clearly demonstrated that lecturing actually increased the likelihood of student failure, resistance remains (Stains et al. 2018). Why? Many researchers believe that some faculty and students resist the idea of changing from lecturing out of fear (Deslauriers et al. 2019; Freeman et al. 2014; Sukacke et al. 2022). Don't be afraid to change how you view education and learning (Sukacke et al. 2022). Adopt academic service-learning. It really is worth the change. As one of my students said: "Yes, you could see the process in action, then refer to sections in the book and think this is what they meant" (Clanton Harpine 2007).

Many professors are advocating for a change to academic service-learning. While some professors and students are reluctant to change to academic service-learning, other professors are enthusiastically advocating the switch to academic service-learning. As biology professors Jennifer Knight and William Wood, stated:

> "... easy accessibility of facts on the Internet is making long-term memorization ... less important. [students need to] ... apply conceptual knowledge to problem solving rather than simply to know many facts.... Therefore, teaching for conceptual understanding and analytical skills while encouraging collaborative activities makes increasing sense.... There is now a great deal of evidence that lecturing is a relatively ineffective pedagogical tool for promoting conceptual understanding." (Knight and Wood 2005, p. 298)

The research conducted by Knight and Wood tested and retested the difference between interactive teaching strategies and traditional lecturing. Each time, service-learning produced higher learning outcomes than traditional lecture. They also pointed out that leadership and working together as members of a team were important workplace skills that students needed to learn and practice (Knight and Wood 2005). An academic service-learning pedagogy infused with active learning and intrinsic motivation teaches teamwork and leadership.

Are you ready to embark on this new approach? How do you feel about academic service-learning, active learning, and creating an intrinsically motivating environment? If you are still reluctant, reread the benefits listed in Chapter 1.

Summary

A student's ability to learn grows stronger through multisensory exposure to different stimuli. Active learning that links with the real-world helps students to develop *cross-talk* between neurons and to store such information in long-term memory for later recall and use. It is these higher-order active learning instructional techniques such as group discussion on real topics, problem-solving with real-world activities, analysis of real information, or the application of textbook material to a real-world setting that create strong neural pathways and connections. The more neural pathways a teacher can link information with, the more likely the student is to learn the information being taught (Horvath 2019). When we apply active learning to academic service-learning, this is the kind of teaching that results. To be truly effective, however, active learning must be used in an intrinsically motivating classroom atmosphere.

Building a Service-Learning Pedagogy

Questions to Help in Course Planning

1. Review the goals that you set in Chapter 1.
2. Are there goals that you would like to add after reading this chapter?
3. What kind of active learning instructional techniques are you planning to use in your class? Give five examples.
4. Are you using only high-order thinking strategies? Give five examples.
5. How are you ensuring that an intrinsically motivating learning environment will be present in your classroom? Give five examples. Review Chapter 5 if needed.
6. How will your teaching strategies work with the brain to help students learn? Give five examples. Review Chapter 4 if needed.

Troubleshooting Checklist

1. How will you handle negativity when it occurs during class discussions?
2. How will you discourage rude comments and judgmental statements toward other students? How will you respond? What will you say?
3. How will you include everyone in your class discussions?
4. How will you handle a student who tries to dominate group discussions?
5. How will you challenge your students?
6. How will you make sure that you're using only intrinsic motivation rather than extrinsic rewards in the classroom?
7. Are you using lectures, simulations, role-plays, computer games, or contrived activities in class? Why? What will the cost to learning be for your students? How can you change to active learning? Give five examples.

Planning Guide Sheet

1. List five discussion topics that work with the course you are teaching.
2. List five problem-solution activities that you plan to use with your class.
3. How will you encourage critical thinking?
4. List five intrinsic motivational techniques that you plan to use in creating an intrinsically motivating learning environment. Does your learning environment include acceptance, teambuilding, cohesive interaction, and respect for others?

Case Example

This example comes from my junior-level motivation of psychology class. The students are still new to academic service-learning. For this case example, I emphasize critical thinking, group discussion, applying knowledge, executive function, problem-solving, neuroplasticity, and how to connect to prior knowledge. At the same time, students have a chance to see how to maintain and increase the intrinsic environment through enthusiasm, acceptance, cohesion, and teambuilding. This case example illustrates how to use active learning in an academic-service-learning pedagogy.

Topic for This Class Session: How to Rebuild Self-Efficacy

Establishing an intrinsic learning environment. It is the professor's responsibility to create the intrinsic learning environment in the classroom. This is an ongoing process (Clanton Harpine 2015). It will not happen all at once. Students must learn to trust before active learning can thrive. Start by building cohesion.

Creating group cohesion by having students work in small groups. I arranged the desks in small group clusters before the students arrived. Each group was given a case study. It is perfectly fine to have multiple groups doing the same case study.

Link with the textbook. The reading assignment was on self-efficacy, so the students have background knowledge. Having the students retrieve information from the textbook reading will stimulate their memory and reinforce previous knowledge.

Problem-solving in small groups. Each group was given 10 minutes to read and respond to a case study from *Camp Sharigan.* The students are to read and decide how they would help the child in the case study to rebuild self-efficacy. We start with small groups because, as explained in Chapter 5, small groups help to build cohesion and intrinsic motivation faster than large groups.

Analysis. Small groups regrouped into a full class circle to analyze and evaluate.

Critical thinking. "Let's establish our criterion and evaluate your group proposals." Before we could proceed, one group responded in a panic: "I don't think we did this right." I immediately responded, "That's okay. That's why we plan and organize. When you're sitting in the classroom, it's fine to have an idea that doesn't work. When we are at *Camp Sharigan*, we want to make sure we know what we're doing and why. We have 30 children depending on us. Confusing self-efficacy and self-esteem is very common." I am still building an intrinsic atmosphere; therefore, I reinforce students who are worried about completing the assignment incorrectly.

Link with the text and interactive engagement as a group. "Your textbook reading for today even talked about how these two terms are often confused. What did the textbook say is the difference between self-efficacy and self-esteem?" Since I'm emphasizing acceptance and teambuilding through my intrinsic environment, I do not want to critique the student responses. Yet, I definitely want to make sure that the correct answer is understood. Summarizing is a method that works without adding negativity. I frequently summarize from the text throughout the class session.

Summary refers back to the textbook. Again, after student responses, I summarize. "Self-esteem is how you feel about yourself; self-efficacy is what you feel you can accomplish. The problem is that self-esteem does not relate to learning. According to Roy Baumeister and Mark Leary (1995), who your text quotes, self-esteem does not increase one's ability to learn, improve test scores, or help the student remember and retain knowledge."

Using group discussion to teach. Who can think of an example of self-esteem and self-efficacy from the case study?

Summarize. If instructors critique student answers in a discussion, students become reluctant to respond. Yet, I always want to make sure that the correct answer is emphasized. I summarize and restate the correct answer, emphasizing the textbook.

Summary refers back to the textbook. "Albert Bandura (1997) (also quoted in your text) states that, unlike self-esteem, self-efficacy helps students apply the skills and knowledge that they are acquiring in the classroom while at the same time helping students generate persistence and willingness to learn difficult concepts and theories. There is even research to support that self-efficacy improves grades and test scores as well as helping students manage their behavior which fits in with our desire to improve executive function. So, how do we build self-efficacy into our learning environment at *Camp Sharigan*? Let's look at your proposals, and no, they do not need to be perfect. We are here to learn." Again, I reassure students as I continue to build an intrinsic environment, and students eagerly respond.

Link with the text and interactive engagement as a group. I ask, "What does Dr. Bandura say we need to do to rebuild self-efficacy?" This question asks for the textbook answer, not opinions. Students were eager to show that they read the assignment and responded with enthusiasm.

Summarizing textbook information. "Yes, Dr. Bandura clearly says that to rebuild self-efficacy, we must teach "mastery skills." Therefore, for our children at the reading clinic, we must teach them how to read. Their self-efficacy will not improve until they learn to read." I link theory from the text to the real-world service-learning project.

Application to the real world. I'm using the service project to apply textbook material to real life. This is important because many of my students also struggle with low self-efficacy, but if we discuss who does and does not believe they can learn the material being covered in this class, some of my students would feel inferior which would create a negative barrier. By applying the topic to the children at the reading clinic, students learn the same concepts while negativity is removed.

Creating new connections by engaging in multiple modes of interaction with the content being taught. "Let's slide our desks around to look at the screen. Since Dr. Bandura says that to rebuild self-efficacy we must teach skills, especially the skills that the child does not have, let's see how *Camp Sharigan* teaches skills." I show slides from *Camp Sharigan* showing how *vowel clustering* and vowel clustered stories teach children to read.

Return to small groups for critical thinking exercise and application to real world. All students now return to their original small groups. Never regroup, it wastes time. I passed out packets to each group for the first day at *Camp Sharigan.* At this point I keep the packets after class for later use, but for students who are interested, there is a complete copy of *Camp Sharigan* (Clanton Harpine 2024) available in the library.

Group assignment. The assignment is for small groups to make two lists each. For the first list, they are to write down every use of intrinsic motivation that they see for day one. The second list is to include every instance of rebuilding self-efficacy that they see for day one. I suggest that the best way to facilitate this task is to have one person in the group read the packet slowly while two group members silently write intrinsic motivation examples and two other members write self-efficacy examples.

Total class discussion closes out the day. Each group writes their lists on the board or computer screen if the room has the technology. Discussion reinforces the text.

Reflection assignment. For homework, after reminding students of their reading assignment, students have an observation notebook assignment. This gives students a chance to reflect on their own self-efficacy. I remind students that no one sees their notebook but me at the end of the semester; therefore, they are free to write their feelings without fear of criticism. They answer questions like these: How would you describe your self-efficacy? Is your belief in your ability to learn strong or is it weak? What were your goals and objectives when you started college as a freshman? Have your goals and objectives changed now that you are juniors in psychology?

Personal or emotional attachment. Obviously, my reason for the reflective assignment is to make self-efficacy personal for the students without embarrassing them. This helps the students see how this new information about self-efficacy makes a difference, not only for *Camp Sharigan,* but for their lives as well.

References

Ahn, R., & Class, M. (2011). Student-centered pedagogy: Co-construction of knowledge through student-generated midterm exams. *International Journal of Teaching and Learning in Higher Education, 23,* 269-281.

Arum, R., & Roksa, J. (2011). *Academically adrift: Limited learning on college campuses.* Chicago: University of Chicago press.

Ambrose, S. A., Bridges, M. W., DiPietro, M., Lovett, M. C., & Norman, M. K. (2010). *How learning works: Seven research-based principles for smart teaching.* San Francisco, CA: Jossey-Bass.

Bandura, A. (1997). *Self-efficacy: The exercise of control.* New York: Freeman.

Barnett, M., Silver, P. T., & Grund, T. S. (2009). Implementing service-learning pedagogy: A case example. *Journal of Higher Education Outreach and Engagement, 13,* 117-134.

Baumeister, R. F., & Leary, M. R. (1995). The need to belong: Desire for interpersonal attachments as a fundamental human motivation. *Psychological Bulletin, 117,* 497–529. https://doi.org/10.1037/0033-2909.117.3.497

Biggs, J. (2001) The reflective institution: Assuring and enhancing the quality of teaching and learning. *Higher Education, 41,* 221–238. https://doi.org/10.1016/0969-5931(94)00033-I

Blaich, C. F., & Wise, K. S. (2011). From gathering to using assessment results: Lessons from the Wabash National Study. (Occasional Paper No. 8). Urbana, IL: University of Illinois and Indiana University, National Institute for Learning Outcomes Assessment (NILOA).

Blumberg, P. (2008). *Developing learner-centered teaching: A practical guide for faculty.* San Francisco, CA: Jossey-Bass.

Brail, S. (2016). Quantifying the value of service-learning: A comparison of grade achievement between service-learning and non-service-learning students. *International Journal of Teaching and Learning in Higher Education, 28,* 148–157.

Bringle, R. G., & Hatcher, J. A. (2017). Innovative practices in service-learning and curricular engagement. *New Directions for Higher Education,147,* 37–46. https://doi.org/10.1002/he.356

Brown, P. C., Roediger, H. L., & McDaniel, M. A. (2014). *Make it stick: The science of successful learning.* Cambridge, MA: Harvard University Press.

Clanton Harpine, E. (2003, August). Interaction analysis versus classroom lecture. Poster presented at the annual convention of the American Psychological Association, Toronto, Canada.

Clanton Harpine, E. (2007). Applying motivation theory to real-world problems. *Teaching of Psychology, 34,* 111–113.

Clanton Harpine, E. (2015). *Group-centered prevention in mental health: Theory, training, and practice.* New York: Springer.

Clanton Harpine, E. (2024). *Camp Sharigan: A ready-to-use group-centered intervention for grades 1-3* (3rd ed.). Corpus Christi, TX: Group-Centered Learning.

Carberry, A. R., Lee, H. S., & Swan, C. W. (2013). Student perceptions of engineering services as a source of learning technical and professional skills. *International Journal for Service Learning in Engineering, Humanitarian Engineering, and Social Entrepreneurship, 8,* 1–7. https://doi.org/10.24908/ijsle.v8i1.4545

Deslauriers, L., McCarty, L. S., Miller, K., Callaghan, K., & Kestin, G. (2019). Measuring actual learning versus feeling of learning in response to being actively engaged in the classroom. *Proceedings of the National Academy of Sciences, 116,* 19251–19257. https://doi.org/10.1073/pnas.1821936116

Ekwueme, C. O., Ekon, E. E., & Ezenwa-Nebife, D. C. (2015). The impact of hands-on-approach on student academic performance in basic science and mathematics. *Higher Education Studies, 5,* 47–51. https://doi.org/10.5539/hes.v5n6p47

Fink, L. D. (2013). *Creating significant learning experiences: An integrated approach to designing college courses* (2nd ed.). San Francisco, CA: Jossey-Bass.

Freeman, S., Eddy, S. L., McDonough, M., Smith, M. K., Nnadozie Okoroafor, Jordt, H., & Wenderoth, M. P. (2014). Active learning increases student performance in science, engi-

neering, and mathematics. *Proceedings of the National Academy of Sciences (PNAS), 111*, 8410–8415. https://doi.org/10.1073/pnas.1319030111
Haak, D. C., HilleRisLambers, J., Pitre, E., & Freeman, S. (2011). Increased structure and active learning reduce the achievement gap in introductory biology. *Science Magazine, 332*, 1213–1216.
Halpern, D. F., & Dunn, D. S. (2021). Critical thinking: A model of intelligence for solving real-world problems. *Journal of Intelligence, 9*, 22. https://doi.org/10.3390/jintelligence9020022
Handelsman, J., Miller, S., & Pfund, C. (2006). *Scientific teaching: Diversity, assessment, active learning*. New York: W. H. Freeman & Co.
Hardiman, M. (2003). *Connecting brain research with effective teaching: The brain-targeted teaching model*. Lanham, Maryland: Rowman and Littlefield Education.
Hart, S. M., & King, J. R. (2007). Service learning and literacy tutoring: Academic impact on pre-service teachers. *Teaching and Teacher Education, 23*, 323–328. https://doi.org/10.1016/j.tate.2006.12.004
Hartlep, K. L., & Forsyth G. A. (2000). The effect of self-reference on learning and retention. *Teaching of Psychology, 2*, 269–271. https://doi.org/10.1207/S15328023TOP2704_05
Horvath, J. C. (2019). *Stop talking, start influencing. 12 insights from brain science to make your message stick*. Chatswood, Australia: Exisle Publishing.
Kamuche, F. U. (2006). Service learning and student performance. *Academic Exchange Quarterly, 10*, 187–192.
Knight, J. K., & Wood, W. B. (2005). Teaching more by lecturing less. *Cell Biology Education, 4*, 298–310. https://doi.org/10.1187/05-06-0082
Krsmanovic, M. (2022). Fostering service-learning and leadership development through first-year seminar courses. *Journal of Service-Learning in Higher Education, 15*, 54–70.
Kuh, G. D., Cruce, Ty M., Shoup, R., Kinzie, J. (2008). Unmasking the effects of student engagement on first-year college grades and persistence. *Journal of Higher Education, 79*, 540–563. https://doi.org/10.1353/jhe.0.0019
Merzenich, M. (2013). Soft-wired: How the new science of brain plasticity can change your life (2nd ed.). San Francisco, CA: Parnassus Publishing.
Mottner, S. (2010). Service-learning in a nonprofit marketing course: A comparative case of pedagogical tools. *Journal of Nonprofit & Public Sector Marketing*, 22, 231–245. https://doi.org/10.1080/10495142.2010.483274
Murayama, K., & Elliot, A. J. (2011). Achievement motivation and memory: Achievement goals differentially influence immediate and delayed remember–know recognition memory. *Personality and Social Psychology Bulletin, 37*, 1339–1348. https://doi.org/10.1177/0146167211410575
Pascarella, E. T., & Terenzini, P. T. (2005). *How college affects students: A third decade of research* (2). San Francisco, CA: Jossey-Bass.
Paul, R., & Elder, L. (2006). *Critical thinking: Learn the tools the best thinkers use*. Lanham, MD: Rowman and Littlefield.
Ramos-Galarza, C., Ramos, V., DelValle, M., Lepe- Martínez, N., Cruz-Cárdenas, J., Acosta-Rodas, P., & Bolaños-Pasquel, M. (2023). Executive functions scale for university students: UEF-1. *Frontiers in Psychology, 13*. https://doi.org/10.3389/fpsyg.2023.1192555
Richmond, A. S., Fleck, B., Heath, T., Broussard, K., & Skarda, B. (2015). Can inquiry-based instruction promote higher-level learning? *Scholarship of Teaching and Learning in Psychology, 1*, 208–218. https://doi.org/10.1037/st10000032
Ryan, R. M., & Deci, E. L. (2000). Self-determination theory and the facilitation of intrinsic motivation, social development, and well-being. *American Psychologist, 55*, 68–78.
Salam, M., Awang Iskandar, D.N., Ibrahim, D.H.A., & Farooq, M. S. (2019). Service learning in higher education: A systematic literature review. *Asia Pacific Education Review, 20*, 573–593. https://doi.org/10.1007/s12564-019-09580-6
Shahbaba, B., Li, L., Agostinelli, F., Saraf, M., Cooper, K. W., Haghverdian, D., Elias, G. A., Baddi, P., & Fortin, N. J. (2022). Hippocampal ensembles represent sequential relationships

among an extended sequence of nonspatial events. *Nature Communications 13*, 1–17. https://doi.org/10.1038/s41467-022-28057-6

Spence, L. (2001). The case against teaching. *Change: The Magazine of Higher Learning, 33*, 10–19. https://doi.org/10.1080/00091380109601822

Stains, M., Harshman, J., Barkers, M. K., Chasteen, S. V., Coles, R., Dechenne-Peters, S. E., . . . Young, A. M. (2018). Anatomy of STEM teaching in North American Universities. *Science, 359*, 1468–1470. https://doi.org/10.1126/science.aap8892

Sukacke, V., Pereira de Carvalho Guerra, A. O., Ellinger, D., Carlos, V., Petroniene, S., Gaiziuniene, L., Blanch, S., Marba-Tallada, A., & Brose, A. (2022). Towards active evidence-based learning in engineering education: A systematic literature review of PBL, P JBL, and CBL. *Sustainability, 14,* 1–31. https://doi.org/10.3390/su142113955

Theobald, E. J., Hill, M. J., Tran, E., Agrawal, S., Arroyo, E. N., Behling, S., Chambwe, N., Cintrón, D. L., Cooper, J. D., Dunster, G., Grummer, J. A., Hennessey, K., Hsiao, J., Iranon, N., Jones, L., 2nd, Jordt, H., Keller, M., Lacey, M. E., Littlefield, C. E., Lowe, A., … Freeman, S. (2020). Active learning narrows achievement gaps for underrepresented students in undergraduate science, technology, engineering, and math. *Proceedings of the National Academy of Sciences of the United States of America, 117*, 6476–6483. https://doi.org/10.1073/pnas.1916903117

Valtonen, T., Leppänen, U., Hyypiä, M., Kokko, A., Manninen, J., Vartiaainen, H., Sointu, E., & Hirsto, L. (2021). Learning environments preferred by university students: A shift toward informal and flexible learning environments. *Learning Environments Research*, *24,* 371–388. https://doi.org/10.1007/s10984-020-09339-6

Vroom, K., Gehrtz, J., Apkarian, N., Elizondo, T. A., Ellis, B., & Hagman, J. (2022). Characteristics of interactive classrooms that first year students find helpful. *International Journal of Stem Education, 9*, 1–17. https://doi.org/10.1186/s40594-022-00354-y

Wang, Y., & Rodgers, R. (2006). Impact of service-learning and social justice education on college students' cognitive development. *NASPA Journal, 43*, 316–337.

Warren, J. L., & Sellnow, T. L. (2010). Learning through service: The contributions of service learning to the communication discipline. In D. L. Fassett & J. T. Warren (Eds.), *Handbook of communication and instruction* (pp. 129–145). Thousand Oaks, CA: Sage Publications.

Weimer, M. (2013). *Learner-centered teaching* (2nd ed.). San Francisco, CA: Jossey-Bass.

Chapter 7
Designing An Academic Service-Learning Course: How Can Faculty Members Measure Learning and Student Reflection?

Students were asked to conduct an out-of-class observation. They picked the location. Their goal was to return to class with a list of ten sexually communicative explicit behaviors observed in public (shopping malls, grocery stores, campus) that they could share with the class and that would be classified as sexually explicit but acceptable public behavior. We then compiled a male and female list of sexually communicative explicit behaviors. Surprised to discover the differences, the students talked at great length about the behaviors listed as being sexually explicit. At the next class, we compiled a list of sexually harassing behaviors at the university and in the workplace. We combined the list of harassing behaviors with the list of sexually communicative behaviors typically tolerated in public and discussed the differences.

What did the students learn? How can such learning be measured? A traditional answer would be through tests and assignments, but as David A. Whetten (2007), Director of the Brigham Young University Faculty Center, a campus-support program that sponsors faculty development, stated:

> "…we are in the midst of an unfolding paradigm shift in higher education, from focusing on teaching to focusing on learning… the point of the teaching-learning distinction is that teaching does not automatically translate into learning." (340)

Are We Willing to Make the Change?

Whetten presents a challenge that requires faculty to change how they teach. Academic service-learning changes how professors teach as well as how students learn.

The original version of the chapter has been revised. A correction to this chapter can be found at https://doi.org/10.1007/978-3-031-51378-7_11

E. Clanton Harpine, *Service Learning in Higher Education*,
https://doi.org/10.1007/978-3-031-51378-7_7

How do we transform teaching into learning? With academic service-learning, we design the course to encourage interactive, in-depth learning. This design process calls for us to rethink how we teach and how we measure learning in the classroom. Academic service-learning provides the change that Whetten and others are calling for, by developing a course design that strives for a high-level of learning and engagement.

Academic service-learning uses active learning teaching techniques that stress critical thinking, problem-solving, group discussions, and analytical writing. Academic service-learning is most effective in an intrinsically motivating learning environment.

How can we make sure students are learning what we intend for them to learn? Whetten's answer is by making sure that our measurement of student outcomes is focused on learning, not testing (Whetten 2007). He goes on to say that one of the strongest influences over a student's mastery of knowledge is the way the instructor chooses to measure learning. Do you just give a quiz or a test? Or do you encourage additional learning (Whetten 2007)? Academic service-learning encourages additional learning. Measuring competency is important, and we'll take up the challenge of how to measure learning later in the chapter. But before we discuss different methods for measuring student proficiency, let's first focus on developing the *learning experience*.

What Is a Learning Experience?

A learning experience is a deliberate organized approach for teaching a course that involves focusing on learning goals and objectives as well as student engagement (Fink 2013; Krsmanovic 2021; Veletsianos 2020). The key is to focus course goals and objectives on learning rather than delivering content. Such a learning experience should be engaging, organized, interactive, effective, stimulating, and emphasize learning-by-doing (Fink 2013; Krsmanovic 2021; Nomme and Birol 2014). With academic service-learning, we also stress application to the real world. There is nothing passive about a learning experience. Students are totally engaged in the learning process. The true measure of an effective learning experience comes from how the course is taught and how it helps students learn (Spence 2001). I offer the following example to illustrate how learning and service can be blended together.

Case example. We will continue the example presented at the start of this chapter with general study students. The purpose of the course was to explore through an interactive classroom the principles and theories of psychological adjustment. This was an academic service-learning course that used active learning (problem-solving, critical thinking, case studies, observations, analytical writing, group discussion, and reflection) along with an intrinsically motivating learning environment. For the class sessions in this example, the textbook reading assignment was on sexually explicit behaviors (acceptable and not acceptable) and the course objective was to show how and why we adjust to the sexually acceptable norms of society. Let's look at the teaching strategies used in this learning experience.

Homework assignment to enable students to prepare for class. At the end of the previous class session, I requested that students make an out-of-class observation and list ten sexually communicative explicit but acceptable behaviors observed in public. The reading assignment defined sexually communicative explicit behaviors.

Non-graded reflection assignment. Students were also requested to write a brief reflection (150 words) describing the observation, their feelings about the behaviors they observed, and then tying it into the assigned textbook reading. The reflection paper was turned in for individual feedback but not graded. My purpose was to ensure that students understood the textbook reading and could apply the theory.

Gender specific small groups. In class, the students worked in gender-specific groups to focus on the difference between female and male perspectives as they compiled and discussed sexually explicit behaviors. Each group developed criteria for evaluating their observations and selecting which behaviors to submit to the class.

Total class discussion. Each group then placed their list on the board. Established an overall class criterion for evaluation. Discussed and analyzed the differences. Discussion was related back to the textbook and previous theories examined in class.

Homework assignment for second class session. Students were requested to make a list of sexually harassing behaviors at the university and in the workplace that would not be acceptable. The reading assignment discussed sexual harassment.

Analyzing differences. We built upon our previous work by working in mixed (male and female) groups to compile lists of sexually harassing behaviors. We combined the list of harassing behaviors with the list of sexually communicative behaviors and discussed the differences. Again, we related each item to the textbook.

Critical thinking. Open classroom discussion allowed students to engage in a deeper understanding of how members of the opposite sex interpret their verbal and nonverbal actions. Many students remarked afterwards that the class sessions helped them understand how others perceived their behavior.

Adjustment to the real world. We were able to analyze psychology in real life by using out-of-class observations. The goal was interpreting, and applying the principles being learned from the textbook to life today and to engage students in critical thinking.

Application to the service-learning project. The lesson was then applied to *Camp Sharigan.* Small groups used problem-solving to discuss: How would the children define appropriate but sexually explicit behavior? How will children interpret the way you dress or act? Students were reminded that we would be working in a gymnasium, sitting on the floor. I asked students to determine from the perspective of the children what would be appropriate to wear while working at *Camp Sharigan.* My purpose was to encourage perspective taking—a major goal of the course.

Measuring learning. In-class discussion enabled me to make sure students understood the theories and information from the text. An ungraded reflection paper gave students a chance to individually demonstrate their knowledge from the textbook. It also allowed me to give direct feedback to each student. This enabled students to know if their reflection paper was written correctly before being graded. Students could then rework the paper before placing it in their observation notebook for a grade. The take-home essay exam became more than just a graded exercise; it became a learning tool. The exam enabled students to pull their observational experiences, classroom information, and textbook knowledge together. An example is as follows,

> *The authors of our text contend that our perceptions of other people [both male and female] are influenced by physical appearance, including the clothes we wear. We send out a nonverbal message each and every day to others simply by the way we dress, wear our hair, walk, talk, and act. What aspects of our personality and self are we relying on to formulate these personal messages that we send to others? What is the role of the media, advertisements, and social expectations? What is the role of gender differences in encoding and interpreting these physical messages? When does gender difference (male or female) become sexual harassment—verbal or nonverbal?*

Why Is Course Design Important?

Designing a learning experience with academic service-learning entails the planning process for making sure that the course enhances student learning, higher-order thinking, student engagement, and real-world application. The way you design your course will determine whether students learn or do not learn (Fink 2013).

Academic service-learning focuses on what students are learning both in the classroom and at the service project worksite. Academic service learning does not reduce the amount of content that you teach; instead, academic service-learning increases what students learn over and above what is normally covered when lecturing (Jacoby 2015). The learning experience should stress the course goals, objectives, instructional material to be taught, real-world application, higher-order thinking, active learning, and then blend everything together to enhance student engagement.

An academic service-learning course should incorporate interaction, challenge, intrinsic motivation, and an active learning teaching approach. The course design may incorporate problem-solving discussions, analysis of textbook information and theory, evaluating case studies, and, of course, relating everything learned to a service-learning project. Converting to a learning focused style of teaching involves a change from a traditional course design, but if we are to increase student learning and engagement, we must embark upon this change. As Fink states,

> "... although faculty members want their students to achieve higher kinds of learning, they continue to use teaching practices that are not effective at promoting such learning" (Fink 2013, p. 3).

Academic service-learning promotes high-quality learning throughout the course.

What Should an Academic Service-Learning Course Include?

Now, it is your turn. From the beginning chapter, we have been creating an academic service-learning pedagogy. Each chapter has concluded with questions to help in designing this teaching pedagogy. Now, we are pulling all of the pieces together: how students learn best (Chapter 4), why the classroom environment is so important for learning (Chapter 5), and how to use high-order active learning strategies (Chapter 6). So, gather your answers to the pedagogical design questions at the end of each chapter, add the active learning teaching strategies from the 10 design steps in Chapter 6, and the goals for your course from Chapter 1. By the end of this chapter, we want to have created an academic service-learning pedagogy that transforms teaching into learning. Focus on what you want students to learn, not what you want to teach.

Are there active learning techniques that should be avoided? After Chapter 6, you should have your course outlined. Now, we want to review your teaching plans to make sure that your pedagogy fulfills the needs of an academic service-learning course. Remember, our goal is to help students learn. Some teaching methods used in college classrooms work against how the brain acquires and processes information [see Chapter 4]. There are also teaching techniques that are labeled *active learning* that do not provide higher-order thinking, analysis, or application to the real world. They are simply games or add-on activities. As you finalize your pedagogy, let's go back to your "must teach" list and the active learning strategies that you outlined from the 10 steps in Chapter 6. Undertake a final in-depth review. There are three areas that can undermine and destroy the effectiveness of academic-service learning that we want to avoid.

Do you want your students to learn high order thinking and analytical skills? If so, avoid using games or add-on style activities. Remember, active learning has many definitions. Not every idea labeled active learning is instructional. The Internet gives several lists for college faculty that range from scavenger hunts on campus, trivia games, ice breakers, to even charades in the classroom. The problem with games and other add-on style activities is that they do not encourage higher-order thinking (Bohyun 2015). Games are also not connected to the real world. Games introduce competition into the classroom. Competition destroys intrinsic motivation and group cohesion (Bandura 1997; Clanton Harpine 2015; Deci and Ryan 1985; Reeve et al. 2018). Students play the game, have fun, but nothing is learned. For example, students do not automatically draw the connection between leadership games and how to function in a leadership role. Academic service-learning requires more than mere classroom games or activities. Yes, games can be fun, but they do not always tie into the course content, and they do not teach in a manner that leads to knowledge being recalled years later (Richmond et al. 2015). Fictional activities, games, or even clickers (classroom response systems) do not help prepare students for the workplace. So, unless you are only interested in students memorizing facts for the next test, games and clickers are entertaining but not a form of high order instruction. Review your "must teach" list. Replace games, add-on class activities, or simulations with higher-order thinking skills.

Use the service-learning project in place of games, activities, or simulations.

Do you want your students to learn knowledge and skills that will transfer to the real world? If so, avoid relying on computer games or video simulations. Computer games and simulations are also being used in some college classrooms, but so far research is still weak on the value of computer games for student performance. Computer games do not encourage student engagement, analytical reasoning, or knowledge acquisition (especially from the textbook) (Vlachopoulos and Makri 2017). Games waste time and do not encourage real-world application (Kim 2015). When 230 university students were surveyed, they requested more participatory pedagogies and application to real life (Valtonen et al. 2021). Simulations are not real, and they do not teach students how to solve problems. Even simulations that attempt to re-create realistic problems are likely to fail. Simulations that try to generate strong emotions and reactions to a problem can actually be psychologically dangerous. As one history professor noted, make-believe simulations on slavery can actually be harmful; it is much better to reflect on modern day prejudices and injustice (Blight 2002). Students could learn more and have a deeper understanding of prejudice by working at a poverty-related service-learning program and connecting that project academically to classroom discussions.

Do you want your students to learn critical thinking and analysis skills? If so, avoid question and answer sessions. Questions and answers do not provide the same level of learning as in-depth class discussion, critical thinking, and evaluation (Deslauriers and Wieman 2011; Hart and King 2007). There are other approaches, such as "the minute paper," "flipped classroom," and "think-pair-share," but these do not provide analytical reasoning or a real-world experience. Some professors use role-playing to teach critical thinking, but role-plays do not teach critical thinking. Analytical reasoning and evaluation teach critical thinking. Role-plays can be entertaining, and students often enjoy role-plays, but role-playing rarely connects with textbook material, nor is there any evidence that role-playing improves test scores. It's entertainment, not a teaching strategy. Be careful, though, because role-playing can be embarrassing for some students. You do not want negative activities that detract from learning and an intrinsic environment. Review all teaching strategies and class plans. Yes, even "icebreakers" are often seen as embarrassing, by some students. Is there anything in your pedagogy that has the potential to embarrass students or create negative attitudes? Embarrassing students destroys intrinsic motivation and group cohesion.

Are there active learning techniques that should be included in every academic service-learning course? Now that we have checked your course design for teaching strategies that should be avoided, let's also check for active learning teaching strategies that should always be included in an academic service-learning course, regardless of the subject or course that you are teaching. Here are four steps for designing an effective learning experience: (1) select course goals, (2) write interactive course objectives, (3) intertwine service and learning, and (4) measure student learning. For each of these steps, I include questions to consider and examples for how I answered the questions with my own courses. We will save measuring student learning till Step 4.

Step 1: What are the goals for the course? Course goals outline the overall concepts and information students need to learn. Goals should answer two questions:

- What information do I want my students to know and understand?
- What skills should my students be able to perform?

If your department does not have established goals and you have not written goals, return to Chapter 1 and develop at least five learning goals for your course.

Questions to consider for Step 1:

What do you expect students to learn from taking your course?

Will students learn any new skills from taking your course?

What kind of sustained change are you striving to make in your students' lives by the end of the course? In five years? In 25 years?

How will academic service-learning help you achieve these goals?

Case example for Step 1.

For my psychology of motivation class, I wrote the following goals:

- **To challenge students to discover the complexities of motivation for self and for others.**
- **To change student opinions about motivation.**
- **To rebuild and/or improve each student's self-efficacy about their ability to learn and succeed at the university and in life.**
- **To increase positive student engagement in the course.**
- **To create an intrinsically motivational learning environment in my classroom and teach my students how to apply intrinsic motivation in a real-world setting.**
- **To demonstrate the benefits of working in a cohesive group atmosphere in our classroom and at *Camp Sharigan*.**

The goals are what you want students to learn by the end of the course. Goals should not include assessment. We will work on assessing how well students achieve these goals later, in Step 4. For now, just write goals—what you want students to learn.

Step 2: What are the course objectives? Course objectives are more specific than goals. Academic service-learning course objectives tell how you plan to use active learning to help students learn. Active learning requires that students interact and analyze rather than just sitting passively listening and taking notes (Freeman et al. 2014). As Fink (2013) explained, the course objectives should tell how students will encounter new information in the classroom, interact with this new information, and then apply the learned information. Course objectives should focus on designing an interactive classroom to enhance student learning (problem-solving discussions, critical thinking, both small and large group discussions, analyzing case studies, projects, analytical writing, and, of course, linking service and learning).

Focus on what you want students to learn, not what you plan to teach. Look at the topics and active learning strategies that you outlined from the 10 steps in

Chapter 6. Remember, each course objective leads to a form of measurement for the knowledge or skill that students have learned (not necessarily a test). As you write each objective, make sure the concept being learned can be measured, but do not get overly worried about assessment yet. We will discuss different ways to measure learning in Step 4.

Always check university requirements. Some university departments have very specific requirements for writing course objectives. If so, follow university guidelines.

Write specific learning objectives, not just general objectives. For academic service-learning, write at least one course objective for each class session. Don't worry about assessment. For now, work on writing course objectives. Stress interactive learning.

Questions to consider for Step 2:

1. First, when writing objectives, write what students are to learn from that particular class session. What should they know at the end of the class? Which active learning teaching techniques are you stressing with your course objectives to help students learn the information you are teaching?
2. Second, create a learning experience that will help students understand the information being taught. Remember, we are using only active learning (no lectures). Focus on how students will interact in class and learn the desired information. Academic service-learning needs objectives that tell students exactly what they are expected to learn, the actions or behavior students are expected to perform, and how the information they have learned will be applied to the service-learning project. Do your objectives include an intrinsically motivating environment?
3. Thirdly, when writing your objectives, intertwine the information being taught with the service-learning project. Use the service-learning project to help teach the information that you want students to learn. Academic service-learning is never just tacked on; it is woven throughout the teaching of the course content. How can you relate what you are teaching in class to the service-learning project? Does the service-learning project help apply textbook knowledge and theories to the real world? Which of the concepts and theories that you are teaching are best learned through service-learning? Why? Look at your course objectives, ask yourself, am I teaching with how the brain learns or against how the brain learns?

Case example for Step 2.

Again, I will turn to my psychology of motivation class and the objectives written for the case example presented in Chapter 2 so that you can see how I answered each of the questions listed above. Remember, the important concepts are how you bring active learning into the classroom and how you link learning and service together.

Answer for #1: Students will learn the difference between intrinsic and extrinsic motivation. Intrinsic and extrinsic motivation can be understood best by the students through their experiences at the service-learning project with *Camp Sharigan*. I can show real-world research data from *Camp Sharigan* showing how failing children improved at the reading clinic through the use of intrinsic motivation. Then, university students will be able to go to *Camp Sharigan* and see firsthand how intrinsic motivation works with the children.

Answer for #2: Students will use problem-solving group discussions and critical thinking, while analyzing information directly from the textbook to learn about motivation. As illustrated in the case example in Chapter 2, I needed to help students overcome incorrect concepts about motivation, particularly with intrinsic and extrinsic. Relating new concepts to prior knowledge and using critical thinking to evaluate incorrect perceptions on motivation would help students analyze the differences and then understand why intrinsic is better [see Chapter 2].

Answer for #3: Students will integrate the information being learned from the textbook and show how it can be applied in a real-world setting through the service-learning project. I use group discussion, problem-solving, case studies, and critical analysis to tie the textbook and service-learning project together. Students plan and organize details to get ready for *Camp Sharigan*. I maintain an intrinsically motivating environment in the classroom by focusing on acceptance, cohesion, and enthusiastic lively class sessions. I personalize the learning experience by having students reflect on the learning process. All reflection assignments link the textbook knowledge to the service-learning project.

Step 3: How will you link service and learning in the course? If academic service-learning is to be effective, service and learning must be intertwined from the beginning of the course until the end. The service-learning project is a teaching tool. We talked extensively in Chapter 3 about how to select a service project; therefore, in this section, we will focus only on evaluating how well the service project selected fits with the course being taught. The concentration is still on learning. We want to create a service-learning experience that helps to improve student learning.

Questions to consider for Step 3:

Which of your learning course objectives can best be accomplished through service learning? Why?

Why is the service project that you have selected appropriate for the course that you are teaching?

What type of knowledge and skills do your students need with this project?

Are there any campus departments or community agencies that will be helping you with your service-learning project?

Case example for Step 3.

I chose *Camp Sharigan* (Clanton Harpine 2024) for my service-learning project because it is a motivational reading clinic. It will provide my students with a hands-on experience working with children who struggle to read. *Camp Sharigan* demonstrates how effectively intrinsic motivation can be used to help children learn. Hands-on experience is the best way for my students to learn.

At this point, you should have your course developed and objectives written for each class session. You should have established what you want students to learn and which active learning instructional techniques you will use to bring about this learning experience. Academic service-learning brings a deeper level of learning to the university classroom. If you have not completed these steps, stop and finish developing the learning experience before going on to Step 4. Learning always comes first.

Step 4: How will student learning be measured? We are now ready to talk about assessment. There are typically two kinds of assessment at universities and colleges: departmental program assessment and individual student assessment. In this book, we are only talking about individual student assessment in a course.

Can learning be measured? Learning is a developmental process that brings about a change in how a student thinks, a change in the students' knowledge, and a change in how the student understands and replies to experiences (Lovett et al. 2023). Learning involves prior knowledge, motivation, the learning atmosphere, and the process of how a student learns [see Chapter 4 to review how the brain learns]. Learning is when students acquire knowledge, skills, or experiences. To truly measure learning, a professor must measure each aspect of the learning process (Whetten 2007).

What is individual student assessment? If assessment is measuring learning for the purpose of helping and improving how a student learns, then we must measure how the individual student is learning (Miller and Leskes 2005). Yes, you may want to do a pre-test to evaluate student knowledge upon entering the course. Then, follow with a post-test at the end of the course to evaluate improvement. For the most part, however, when we talk about individual student assessment, we are talking about tracking student improvement. What are the students' strengths and weaknesses? How can the student improve? How can we help students improve? Praise is wonderful; we all like kind comments, but students need "usable information" (Lovett et al. 2023). Does a bad grade give students usable information? Does a bad grade tell students how to improve? Individual student assessment means the process that the professor uses to lead students to change, to improve, to acquire new experiences and knowledge. Therefore, individual student assessment should focus on how the student learns and how the instructor can help the student learn (Whetten 2007; Deslauriers et al. 2019).

Does assessment mean testing? When most professors hear the word *assessment*, they think of exams, quizzes, or research papers. At universities, multiple-choice tests are the most common form of individual student assessment (Butler 2018). Yet nearly all universities and colleges assert that the purpose of student assessment is to improve student learning (Stassen et al. 2001). How does a test enhance student learning?

What do tests measure? Faculty typically rely on tests and grades to measure learning, but do tests measure learning? As research discovered, students may select the correct answer on a multiple-choice test while maintaining incorrect knowledge on the subject they were tested on (Couch et al. 2018). They simply guessed correctly. A similar situation occurred when multiple-choice tests were compared to constructed response tests, students could answer (guess) the multiple-choice questions but did not have enough knowledge on the subject to answer a constructed response test question (essay using analysis, critical thinking, and application) where they were to apply knowledge learned (McKenna 2019). Furthermore, having both correct and incorrect options on a multiple-choice test can lead to confusion or "false knowledge" (Roediger III and Marsh 2005). Time-limited in-class exams also put students with disabilities or language barriers at a disadvantage (Gernsbacher et al. 2020). The conclusion of most researchers was that traditional test procedures are not actually measuring learning. Academic service-learning needs a way to accurately measure what students learn.

Do traditional multiple-choice tests help students retain information? Research has shown that 50% of retention declines after approximately four weeks with traditional lecturing and testing (Kamuche 2006). Multiple-choice exams do not apply knowledge, engage critical thinking, or use analysis. Instead, multiple-choice tests encourage cosmetic learning that is easily forgotten, while test grades merely ascribe a number but do not tell students how to improve (Deslauriers and Wieman 2011; Stassen et al. 2001).

Are multiple-choice tests healthy for students? Research shows that 51% of college students report high anxiety over the traditional multiple-choice exam and 84% feel overwhelmed by testing (Nilson 2015). Research has also shown that tests do not inspire students to learn or enhance student learning (Fink 2013; Kamuche 2006).

How do multiple-choice tests fulfill employer requests? Employers are seeking graduates with written communication, critical thinking, and problem-solving skills (Arum and Roksa 2011). Do multiple-choice tests measure this form of learning? No, research demonstrates that tests and grades do not translate into success in the real world (Baird 1985; Tomlinson 2012). Just measuring whether students memorized a particular list of facts does not help prepare students for careers and jobs after college (Knight and Wood 2005). Students need a more useful form of measurement.

Do we need an alternative to testing? If our goal is to improve student learning, then, yes, we need an alternative to traditional multiple-choice testing. Changing to new teaching and assessment methods is not easy, but sometimes it is necessary, especially if we want to increase student engagement and a deeper level of learning.

Is there a form of assessment that would strengthen learning? Research has shown that students actually reach a deeper level of understanding when they are required to apply what they are learning (Fink 2013). Therefore, we need to measure learning in a way that would also help students apply knowledge.

What are the best ways to measure learning? With academic service-learning, we typically use reflection, journals, observations, research papers, problem-solving projects, self-evaluation, group discussions, critical thinking, analytical writing, and essay exams. Feedback needs to be continuous throughout the course and give the student usable information that tells how the student can improve. Individual student assessments need to stress analytical writing, critical thinking, and problem-solving with an emphasis on how the information being learned relates to the real world. I have given examples of many of these forms of measurement throughout the book; therefore, we will discuss only reflection in this chapter. Reflection is one of the most frequently used assessments with service-learning [for more examples, see Chapter 8].

What is reflection? Reflection strengthens learning by helping the student analyze what they are learning (Eyler 2002). Reflection assignments should give students an opportunity to discuss concepts being learned or situations experienced. Reflection is one suggestion that connects directly with what the business world says they are looking for from graduates: written and oral communication, critical thinking, and problem-solving skills (Arum and Roksa 2011). All reflection assignments should go beyond a simple summary of an event or opinions—mere descriptions achieve nothing.

Quality reflection includes analysis. For reflection to help students learn, reflection assignments must be quality assignments, not just opinions or descriptions. Unsupported opinions do not strengthen the learning process. Research supports that more challenging and rigorous reflection assignments produce better student outcomes and learning (Eyler and Giles Jr. 1999). Quality reflection assignments include analysis and critical thinking as well as reference to the text and theories being taught in class. Reflection strengthens the link between service and learning. Reflection assignments should explain what the student has learned (Ash and Clayton 2004). Professors should also provide guidelines to students for exactly what they classify as reflection [see guidelines presented in the case study below for an example].

Questions to consider for Step 4:

Do you offer guidelines on reflection for your students?

Will you use reflection multiple times or just at the end of the course?

How will your students demonstrate that they have learned the information?

Do your course goals go beyond mere memorization for a test?

How will your students show what they have learned from the service-learning project? Will you include reflection assignments? How many? When?

Are your assignments authentic, realistic, and related to the real world? How are your assignments linked with the service-learning project?

Case example for Step 4.

In my psychology of motivation class, my students keep an observation journal. They complete a reflection assignment for the journal at the end of each class session. Sometimes the daily reflections are graded but often not (the journal is collected and evaluated at the end of the course). These might be very simple observations and reflections, but each assignment relates back to the text and what is being taught in class. Some of the reflections are self-evaluations of what the student has learned. For example, I might ask at the end of class: "For your journal assignment, I want you to write what you learned from the class discussion today. Did you agree or disagree? Why?" Many of the journal assignments also connect directly to the service-learning project. Let's look at how I answered the questions from Step 4 in my case example.

Reflection guidelines. To improve the quality of my student's reflection assignments, I provide guidelines that can be used with all reflection assignments.

- Are you writing about a specific event or situation that occurred? Remember, we are not looking for general descriptions. Be specific.
- Did you critically analyze the situation using your textbook as a reference? Do theories or information in the text help explain why the event or situation

happened? Does the text explain how the situation could have been avoided or corrected? Be sure to cite your textbook correctly. Follow our 3-word rule. If you use more than three words written in the text or from another source, use quotation marks and APA citation correctly.

- Plagiarism is not permitted.
- Did you integrate theory and facts from the text in a meaningful way?
- Go back and review what you have written. Can you elaborate or explain the relevance of what you're trying to say? Does what you have written show that you understand the concepts being discussed? How?
- Do a final edit. Check for spelling, punctuation, and grammar. Did you give specific details? Simplify your writing and be more concrete in explaining your ideas? Remember, we never use names in our papers.
- Did you fulfill the assignment? Did you follow the word count requirements? Is your reflection paper typed and ready to turn in?

Students demonstrate what they have learned. I gave students the following case study to individually analyze, reflect on, and turn in to be graded. I encouraged students to use perspective taking (consider how someone else may feel) in their reflection. Then, the students analyzed and discussed the same case study in class. The textbook topic was "helplessness" and how to help rebuild self-efficacy (belief in self) and intrinsic motivation.

Case study: A college student is sent to the university counseling center. The note from the advisor reads: "This kid needs help: he's failing in four subjects, his apartment landlord still hasn't turned the heat on even though our daytime highs are only 45 degrees; consequently he's got a bad cold, his car stalled out on the highway in the construction zone three days ago; another car rear ended him; both cars had to be towed. The kid has a car repair bill over a thousand dollars, no insurance, and the kid's boss just fired him because he couldn't get to work; he works the late shift, long after the buses run. Can you help this guy?"

The students used their individual reflection assignments and paired up in class. The assignment called for concrete solutions based on the principles explained in the textbook. Unsupported opinions were not accepted. After ten minutes, each pair joined another pair to form a small group, and again they established criteria and reevaluated their proposal for helping this student; this time with the goal of presenting a unified plan to the entire class in ten minutes. Each group's proposal was presented and evaluated against the class criteria. As this example demonstrates, I use case studies in class, but the in-class case studies are never graded. I do not grade group discussions, but problem-solving allows students to use analytical skills, critical thinking, and information learned in class from the textbook. If I want a grade, I send case study assignments home for students to do individually. This allows students to work on their writing skills, which employers say is one of the most important requirements for graduates. I grade each student individually because it is really not possible to grade a group fairly.

Realistic assignments related to the real world. Academic service-learning uses realistic assignments that require application to the real world. The more realistic an assignment is, the more likely students are to apply the knowledge in class to their career goals or life in general. A more realistic assignment also reduces the anxiety and pressure that many students feel from traditional testing by allowing students to rehearse, practice, consult the textbook, and even rework their paper or project. One of my objectives with this assignment was for students to think about their own self-efficacy. Asking for personal reflection in class could have negatively impacted the classroom intrinsic environment. Also, you never want to embarrass a student. By using a case study, students would automatically think about their own life. I also wanted my students to think about how they could improve their self-efficacy. Commenting on their reflection papers allowed this option. The reflection assignment led into the class discussion.

Analysis of a case study allowed me to determine if the students were learning and understanding theories discussed in class as well as information from the text. By not allowing mere opinions, the class discussions became a teaching tool that required students to use knowledge learned from the text.

Beyond memorization for a test. Research has shown that multiple-choice tests are not conducive to learning and retaining information (Butler 2018). Essay exams, research papers, and observation journals that incorporate reflection encourage deeper thinking and work better for individual student assessment. Through the graded portion of the assignment, I was able to establish how well students were understanding the textbook information. Reflection is a very critical component of academic service-learning, and a part of how you combine service and learning. Reflection alone, however, is not enough. The primary learning structure of academic service-learning lies in how you integrate learning and service. I used group discussion, especially problem-solving. The active learning teaching strategies that you use in the classroom are just as important as the reflection assignments. Students learn more when you integrate service and learning from the beginning of the course until the end.

Relating to the service-learning project. The final step of the in-class discussion on the case study was to apply the same self-efficacy concept to the children at *Camp Sharigan.* Questions discussed: How can we help the children believe they can learn to read? How can we create an intrinsically motivating environment and help the children rebuild their self-efficacy and try again? I started with a case study about a college student because I knew it would help my students identify with the feeling of helplessness and low self-efficacy. They could empathize with a downtrodden student. Then, I had them take the same principles from the text and apply the theories to the children at *Camp Sharigan.* Children failing in reading often display a sense of helplessness and low self-efficacy.

When using reflection assignments as one of your teaching strategies, make sure that reflection is used throughout the semester, even before students go to the service -learning worksite. I frequently set a word count limit on written reflection assignments because brevity is wonderful when you're grading. It also helps students to strengthen their writing skills and understanding of the topic. Instead of rattling on endlessly, students learn to condense and focus on details.

Summary

A learning experience is about what you want your students to learn. A learning experience includes the course goals, objectives, and the content or instructional material to be taught, and it blends everything together with the teaching method or pedological approach. Course objectives describe exactly what you want students to learn. Case studies can be used to genuinely assess what students have learned while also enhancing student learning. Service-learning has been determined by students to be the most effective teaching strategy for helping students learn content and theory. Quality reflection assignments are a key component for creating a learning experience with academic service-learning. Reflection assignments must connect service and learning.

Building a Service-Learning Pedagogy

Questions to Help in Course Planning

1. Review the goals that you have set for your course.
2. Did you add any new goals? Are there goals that you would like to add?
3. What are your course objectives? You need at least one course objective for each class session that you teach throughout the semester.
4. Are you using only higher-order thinking strategies? Give examples. How do these strategies relate to your course goals and course objectives?
5. How are you working active learning, an intrinsically motivating learning environment, and the service-learning project into your course design?
6. How are you measuring learning? Did you go back and outline how you would measure learning for each course objective?

Troubleshooting Checklist

1. Do all of your course goals and objectives link with your service-learning project? How are you measuring learning at the service project?
2. Are your assignments clear and easily understood by the students?
3. What do you think will be the most difficult concept for your students to learn? How will you help students learn this concept? How will the service-learning project help? How will your individual student assessments help students learn?

Planning Guide Sheet

1. What steps are you taking to make sure that your academic service-learning course goals and course objectives are designed to work with how students learn best? Refer back to Chapter 4 for help.
2. Do you need to have your class goals approved by the department chair?
3. Do you have a course objective written for each class session? How will you implement these objectives? Refer back to the planning guide questions for Chapter 6. What teaching strategies will you employ?

4. How will you measure learning with each course objective? Do you include analytical writing, critical thinking, reflection, and problem-solving?
5. How did you link service and learning?
6. What do you think your students will learn from service-learning?

Case Example

This example shows how I used service-learning to measure learning in my psychology of motivation class. As discussed earlier in the chapter, it is vital to connect what the students are learning in the classroom with the actual service-learning project. Therefore, students wrote a reflection paper individually that was turned in for a grade. Then, in class they worked in small groups to discuss their observations. A report on this service-learning activity was published in the Faculty Forum section of the journal *Teaching of Psychology* (Clanton Harpine 2007).

Reflection assignment: Students wrote a reflection paper using the motivational terms studied from the textbook and as a follow-up to their week at *Camp Sharigan*.

1. List 10 intrinsic motivators from *Camp Sharigan* that you think worked well.
2. Were any extrinsic motivators used? What was the cost factor involved? Do you think these extrinsic motivators will help or hinder intrinsic motivation?
3. Were there any motivators that you think did not work well?
4. Were there any extrinsic regulators? What kind: external, introjected, identified, or integrated? Did these regulators help or hinder intrinsic motivation?
5. List any positive or negative incentives that you observed being used. Did these contribute to or hinder intrinsic motivation and self-efficacy?
6. List any positive or negative reinforcers that you observed being used? Did these contribute to or hinder intrinsic motivation and self-efficacy?
7. List any positive or negative punishers that you observed being used. Did these contribute to or hinder intrinsic motivation and self-efficacy?
8. Describe 10 changes that you would make in order to increase intrinsic motivation and self-efficacy with the children. Remember to explain the reasons for your suggestions. Unsupported opinions are not accepted. We are looking for textbook knowledge and reasoning. This is to be completed and turned in at the beginning of our next class session (Clanton Harpine 2007).

   Application to real world. The students returned to class after their service-learning project eager to discuss what they had observed. Discussion began with a review of the eight questions on observed motivational strategies. Students commented on how much easier it was to understand why extrinsic regulators and punishers could be harmful when they saw motivation in action in the real-world rather than just reading through examples in the text.

   Evaluation of learning from the service-learning project and reflection assignment. In class, teams were organized to evaluate the lists of motivators that worked, and the changes proposed by each person. Teams were given fifteen minutes to compile a combined list of 3 changes that they wanted to propose. The class had developed criteria for evaluation.

Group discussion and analysis became a teaching tool. Teams were consolidated into small groups. Each small group was to compile a final list of 5 changes. Each small group was given 30 minutes to compile their list. The small group had to identify the type of motivation their change would use and tell how that motivator would help or restrict intrinsic motivation and self-efficacy.

Students were allowed to use their textbook to support proposed changes. Each group explained how their proposed change would be better for the children.

Using both small and large group discussion provides an assessment or check on what is being learned. Small groups reported to the total class and each group spoke for adoption of their changes. The proposed changes were placed on the board and evaluated against the problems the students identified in their observations, and finally six changes were agreed upon by the total class.

The key element throughout the class evaluation session was the fact that all students had participated in the same service-learning project, had seen the needs of the children, had seen what worked at *Camp Sharigan*, and returned to class armed with textbook knowledge and a real-world situation in which to apply that knowledge. The service-learning project worked as the catalyst for applying textbook theories to real life. The classroom activity was much more meaningful than if I had merely given the students an example in class.

References

Arum, R., & Roksa, J. (2011). *Academically adrift: Limited learning on college campuses.* Chicago: University of Chicago Press.

Ash, S. L., & Clayton, P. H. (2004). The articulated learning: An approach to guided reflection and assessment. *Innovative Higher Education, 29*, 137–154. https://doi.org/10.1023/B:IHIE.0000048795.84634.4a

Baird, L.L. (1985). Do grades and tests predict adult accomplishment? *Research in Higher Education, 23*, 3–85. https://doi.org/10.1007/BF00974070

Blight, D. W. (2002). *Race and Reunion: The Civil War in American memory*. Belknap Press: Cambridge, MA.

Bohyun, K. (2015). Designing gamification in the right way. *Library Technology Reports, 51*, 29–35.

Butler, A. C. (2018). Multiple-choice testing in education: Are the best practices for assessment also good for learning? *Journal of Applied Research in Memory and Cognition, 7*, 323-331. https://doi.org/10.1016/j.jarmac.2018.07.002

Clanton Harpine, E. (2007). Applying motivation theory to real-world problems. *Teaching of Psychology, 34,* 111–113.

Clanton Harpine, E. (2015). *Group-centered prevention in mental health: Theory, training, and practice*. New York: Springer.

Clanton Harpine, E. (2024). *Camp Sharigan: A ready-to-use group-centered intervention for grades 1-3* (3rd ed.). Corpus Christi, TX: Group-Centered Learning.

Couch, B. A., Hubbard, J. K., & Brassil, C. E. (2018). Multiple-true-false questions reveal the limits of the multiple-choice format for detecting students with incomplete understandings. *BioScience, 68,* 455–463. https://doi.org/10.1093/biosci/biy037

Deslauriers, L., & Wieman, C. (2011). Learning and retention of quantum concepts with different teaching methods. *Physical Review Special Topics - Physics Education Research. 7*, 010101-1-010101-2. https://doi.org/10.1103/PhysRevSTPER.7.010101

Deslauriers, L., McCarty, L. S., Miller, K., Callaghan, K., & Kestin, G. (2019). Measuring actual learning versus feeling of learning in response to being actively engaged in the classroom. *Proceedings of the National Academy of Sciences, 116*, 19251–19257. https://doi.org/10.1073/pnas.1821936116

Deci, E. L., & Ryan, R. M. (1985). *Intrinsic motivation and self-determination in human behavior*. New York, NY: Plenum Press.

Eyler, J. (2002). Reflection: Linking service and learning -- linking students and communities. *Journal of Social Issues, 58,* 517–534. https://doi.org/10.1111/1540-4560.00274

Eyler, J., & Giles, Jr., D. E. (1999). *Where's the learning in service-learning?* San Francisco, CA: Jossey-Bass.

Fink, L. D. (2013). *Creating significant learning experiences: An integrated approach to designing college courses* (2nd ed.). San Francisco, CA: Jossey-Bass.

Freeman, S., Eddy, S. L., McDonough, M., Smith, Nnadozie Okoroafor, M. K., Jordt, H., & Wenderoth, M. P. (2014). Active learning increases student performance in science, engineering, and mathematics. *Proceedings of the National Academy of Sciences (PNAS), 111,* 8410–8415. https://doi.org/10.1073/pnas.1319030111

Gernsbacher, M. A., Soicher, R. N., & Becker-Blease, K. A. (2020). Four empirically based reasons not to administer time-limited tests. *Translational Issues in Psychological Science, 6,* 175–190. https://doi.org/10.1037/tps0000232

Hart, S. M., & King, J. R. (2007). Service learning and literacy tutoring: Academic impact on pre-service teachers. *Teaching and Teacher Education, 23,* 323–328. https://doi.org/10.1016/j.tate.2006.12.004

Jacoby, B. (2015). *Service-learning essentials: Questions, answers, and lessons learned.* San Francisco, CA: Jossey-Bass.

Kamuche, F. U. (2006). Service learning and student performance. *Academic Exchange Quarterly, 10*, 187–192.

Kim, B. (2015). Understanding gamification. *Library Technology Reports 51*, 29–35.

Knight, J. K., & Wood, W. B. (2005). Teaching more by lecturing less. *Cell Biology Education, 4,* 298–310. https://doi.org/10.1187/05-06-0082

Krsmanovic, M. (2021). Course redesign: Implementing project-based learning to improve students' self-efficacy. *Journal of the Scholarship of Teaching and Learning, 21,* 93–106. https://doi.org/10.5206/cjsotl-rcacea.2014.1.2

Lovett, M. C., Bridges, M. W., DiPietro, M., Ambrose, S., & Norman, M. K. (2023). *How learning works: 8 research-based principles for smart teaching*. Hoboken, NJ: Jossey-Bass.

McKenna, P. (2019). Multiple choice questions: Answering correctly and knowing the answer. *Interactive Technology and Smart Education, 16*, 59–73. https://doi.org/10.1108/ITSE-09-2018-0071

Miller, R., & Leskes, A. (2005). *Levels of assessment: From the student to the institution.* Washington, D. C.: Association of American Colleges and Universities.

Nilson, L. B. (2015). *Specifications grading: Restoring rigor, motivating students, and saving faculty time*. Sterling, VA: Stylus Publishing.

Nomme, K., & Birol, G. (2014). Course redesign: An evidence-based approach, *The Canadian Journal for the Scholarship of Teaching and Learning, 5,* 1–26. https://doi.org/10.5206/cjsotl-rcacea.2014.1.2

Reeve, J., Ryan, R. M., & Deci, E. L. (2018). Sociocultural influences on student motivation as viewed through the lens of self-determination theory. In G. A. Liem & D. M. McInerney (Eds.) *Big theories revisited 2*, (pp. 31-60). Charlotte, NC: Information Age Press.

Richmond, A. S., Fleck, B., Heath, T., Broussard, K., & Skarda, B. (2015). Can inquiry-based instruction promote higher-level learning? *Scholarship of Teaching and Learning in Psychology, 1*, 208–218. https://doi.org/10.1037/stl0000032

Roediger, H. L. III, & Marsh, E. J. (2005). The positive and negative consequences of multiple-choice testing. *Journal of Experimental Psychology: Learning, Memory, and Cognition, 31*, 1155–1159. https://doi.org/10.1037/0278-7393.31.5.1155

Spence, L. (2001). The case against teaching. *Change: The Magazine of Higher Learning, 33*, 10–19. https://doi.org/10.1080/00091380109601822

Stassen, M., Doherty, K., & Poe, M. (2001). *Course-based review and assessment: Methods for understanding student learning*. Amherst, MA: University of Massachusetts Amherst.

Tomlinson, M. (2012). Graduate employability: A review of conceptual and empirical themes. *Higher Educational Policy 25*, 407–431. https://doi.org/10.1057/hep.2011.26

Valtonen, T., Leppänen, U., Hyypiä, M., Kokko, A., Manninen, J., Vartiaainen, H., Sointu, E., & Hirsto, L. (2021). Learning environments preferred by university students: A shift toward informal and flexible learning environments. *Learning Environments Research, 24*, 371–388. https://doi.org/10.1007/s10984-020-09339-6

Veletsianos, G. (2020) *Learning online: The student experience*. Baltimore, MD: Johns Hopkins University Press.

Vlachopoulos, D., & Makri, A. (2017). The effect of games and simulations on higher education: A systematic literature review. *International Journal of Educational Technology in Higher Education 14*, 1–33. https://doi.org/10.1186/s41239-017-0062-1

Warren, J. L., & Sellnow, T. L. (2010). Learning through service: The contributions of service learning to the communication discipline. In D. L. Fassett & J. T. Warren (Eds.), *Handbook of communication and instruction* (pp. 129–145). Thousand Oaks, CA: Sage Publications.

Whetten, D. A. (2007). Principles of effective course design: What I wish I had known about learning-centered teaching 30 years ago. *Journal of Management Education, 31*, 339–357. https://doi.org/10.1177/1052562906298445

Chapter 8
What Should an Academic Service-Learning Syllabus Include?

One semester I agreed to conduct Camp Sharigan at a new community worksite. Everything was set, checked, and rechecked. The night before Camp Sharigan was scheduled to begin, the community organization informed me that they would no longer be able to host Camp Sharigan. No, I did not even think about rescheduling. All of my students had worked out their family and work schedules and arranged to be available for the afterschool hours when Camp Sharigan was to be held. We also had four other university classes planning to participate. Furthermore, we had 30 children scheduled to show up after school. The reading camp had been publicized along with its location and time, and the local newspaper was coming to take pictures on the first day. My students had also arranged to go in early in the morning to help me set up the make-believe camp with its 10 workstations and banners. Everything was working as planned, except for the worksite location. Fortunately, there was another community organization directly across the street. I called. They said yes. I stationed students at the original site to direct children and parents across the street. Greeters at the door and footprints inside the building led to our new location. The week was fabulous. Camp Sharigan went off without a hitch, and I continued to work at this new community worksite for the next eight years.

Academic service-learning involves working with others, and sometimes, when we work with others, even the best laid plans go awry. The way you help students deal with and conquer problems is part of the learning experience with academic service-learning (Howard 1998; Jacoby 2015). It is also why academic service-learning falls under the classification—*high impact learning experience* (Association of American Colleges and Universities 2007; Kuh 2013). Academic service-learning is *high impact* because students demonstrate improvement in problem-solving, critical thinking, higher levels of cognitive development (including remembering and decision making), and application of knowledge (Barnett et al. 2009). Therefore, your syllabus must also be of high quality (Ballard and Elmore 2009; Kieran and Haack 2018). An

E. Clanton Harpine, *Service Learning in Higher Education*,
https://doi.org/10.1007/978-3-031-51378-7_8

academic service-learning syllabus should be detailed, clear, concise, and definitely accurate. When you hand students a syllabus on the first day, you have taken a step toward reshaping the knowledge students possess. An academic service-learning syllabus is an invitation to learn about life. Be sure to make your invitation inviting.

Why Is an Academic Service-Learning Syllabus So Important?

An academic service-learning syllabus is not the same as a syllabus that you write for a lecture class. Academic service-learning needs a syllabus with accurate scheduling, a link between service and learning, and a focus on student engagement (Howard 1998; Jacoby 2015). Writing a syllabus takes careful planning because an academic service-learning syllabus is more than just a list of assignments and due dates.

An academic service-learning syllabus guides the course. As students read the syllabus on the first day, you want students to trust that you have organized every detail of the service-learning project to the extent that they can now confidently go and make family, work, childcare, or other arrangements based on your plans. Even though many professors believe that students lose, throw in the trash, or never look at their syllabus, research illustrates that students do actually read and use their syllabus to organize and plan throughout the course, especially when the syllabus contains "important details" (Calhoon and Becker 2008). Therefore, it becomes essential to design a syllabus that guides students through the academic service-learning course and is filled with important details.

An academic service-learning syllabus sets the schedule. The syllabus must synchronize student schedules, coordinate multiple classes (if collaborating with others), and match the needs of the community organization and the beneficiaries of your service. Scheduling will always be challenging, but think twice before making changes to a schedule. As illustrated in the opening story, problems do arise. Consider the disaster that would have resulted if I had said, "we must reschedule."

> I had over 100 people (university students, children, parents, community workers) arriving on the first day for *Camp Sharigan*. Students had rearranged their agendas at work, home, and even organized childcare as needed. Parents had also arranged their child and family plans to accommodate *Camp Sharigan*. Yes, changes had to be made, but when coordinating that many people, make the least number of changes possible.

Scheduling becomes extremely important and is one of the key elements for success with an academic service-learning community project (Howard 1998; Salam et al. 2019). As you write your syllabus, double check the details so that as you introduce this new academic service-learning adventure to your students, they will become excited but confident of the schedule and thereby eager to get involved.

An academic service-learning syllabus provides structure for the course. Research shows that it is better to write a detailed syllabus rather than a brief, generalized overview because details provide structure and organization for the course

(Parkes and Harris 2002; Saville et al. 2010; Wasley 2008). An academic service-learning syllabus should give a clear description of each assignment, what the student is expected to learn, requirements for fulfilling the assignment, how the assignment will be evaluated or graded, and how each assignment relates to the service-learning project (Cullen and Harris 2009; Richmond 2016). The quality of the syllabus is one of the determinants of whether an academic service-learning course will be successful or not (Woolcock 2006).

What Should a Syllabus Include to Support Academic Service-Learning?

A syllabus is an invitation to learn (Bain 2004). An academic service-learning syllabus should invite students to engage in a learning experience, not just attend class.

An academic service-learning syllabus focuses on student learning.

An academic service-learning syllabus should define and explain the course expectations. As explained in Chapter 1, many students have preconceived ideas about service learning. You must confront these ideas and clarify that academic service-learning is different from community service. Therefore, the syllabus should include a definition of academic service-learning and an explanation of academic service-learning as a teaching method using active learning instructional techniques.

An academic service-learning syllabus should describe your teaching methods. Emphasize that research shows academic service-learning to be one of the most effective teaching methods (Mottner 2010) because of the transferability of the skills and knowledge learned in the course to real life (Felten and Clayton 2011). Reassure students that they will be covering the same material as they would in a lecture class. Then, explain that research demonstrates that academic service-learning yields higher student grades and stronger student engagement, while helping students remember and understand what they are learning better than traditional lecturing (Freeman et al. 2014; Hart and King 2007; Kamuche 2006; Stains et al. 2018). The way you teach matters, especially when it leads to stronger student outcomes and learning (Bain 2004).

An academic service-learning syllabus should include all university requirements. Does your department require that a statement be added for academic honesty, disability, or inclusion for diversity? How many assignments? Midterm or final exam? Is there a grading policy? Are there course content requirements? Prerequisites? Requirements for service-learning projects? Check with the department chair or faculty resource center to discover what is required before designing your syllabus.

An academic service-learning syllabus should set the mood for the course. In 2011, researchers decided to study the effect of a syllabus written in a friendly tone as contrasted with one written with more formal language. The students responded more favorably to the friendly tone. The students said that they thought the instructor who used a syllabus with a friendly tone would be more "approachable and motivated" (Harnish and Bridges 2011). Other researchers also found that syllabi written with a friendlier tone encouraged student engagement (Amerstorfer and Freiin von Münster-Kistner 2021; Cullen and Harris 2009). Since academic service-learning strives to generate student engagement as well as create an intrinsically motivating learning environment (see Chapter 5), writing a syllabus in a friendly tone fits perfectly with our needs. Use a friendly tone as the first step in creating an intrinsic atmosphere. Let's look at an example. First, we will look at a more traditional approach.

> This course is taught as an academic service-learning experience. The course content is applied to a community service-learning project. The service project is required. All students will work on the same service-learning project near campus. You do not need to set up your own service project. This is a class project. Each student is required to spend a minimum of two hours of service at the worksite. If needed, an alternative project may be arranged. Learning through experience at a community service worksite will allow application of the academic knowledge acquired from the classroom to be applied to real world needs in the community. The service-learning project will be an integral part of the course throughout the semester through planning, evaluation, and reflection. Application of textbook knowledge is stressed. Using an academic service-learning teaching approach will enhance the curriculum and learning experience for this course by extending learning beyond the textbook and classroom.

Now, let's provide the same information to the students, but use a friendlier tone.

> Welcome! I am glad you are joining us for our academic service-learning section of psychology of motivation. This semester, we will be learning about motivation and how it can be applied in the real world as we build a motivational reading clinic. The children we will be working with are struggling or failing in reading. Reading failure has been shown to be one of the root causes of violence and dropping out of school before graduation. We want to help these children succeed and overcome reading failure. Motivation is the key. We will all be working on the service project together. The project and worksite have been selected, and you will learn in class how you can best help the children overcome reading failure as you learn how to use the principles of motivation. You are required to spend a minimum of two hours at the reading clinic, but, if you get excited and enjoy working with the children, you are welcome to work all week. The program is called *Camp Sharigan.* It is a 10-hour, one week reading clinic that meets for two hours a day after school. During class, we will look at research showing how effective this program has been. You will help with the planning and organizing as well as working at the reading clinic. *Camp Sharigan* will be held the week of __(date)__ at ____(address)_____, a location near campus. If you foresee any problems or conflicts, talk with me. I am always happy to help. There is never a problem so big that we cannot solve it together.

A syllabus with a friendlier tone helps encourage interaction on the first day. When the tone is retained throughout the syllabus, a friendly tone also stimulates teamwork.

An academic service-learning syllabus should describe the service-learning project. Give a detailed but brief description of the service project. Students will have many questions. The syllabus should provide as many answers as possible.

How many hours of service are required? Check first with your department. Some universities have set requirements for service-learning courses. Then, make sure the required service hours are listed and explained on the syllabus. As we discussed in Chapter 3, there is no magic number for how many service hours to require. With community service, some faculty state that you need 20 or 30 hours for students to have a meaningful experience. That is not true with academic service-learning. Remember, community service and academic service-learning are very different [review Chapter 1 for details]. With academic service-learning, you are linking service and learning together in the classroom as well as at the service project worksite. Therefore, the in-class work done by the students to prepare for the community service project is part of the service-learning experience.

Service begins on the first day of class. As discussed in Chapters 6 and 7, every class session relates the text and course content to the service project. So, before students ever arrive at the community worksite, they have applied many hours of effort toward the service-learning project. Therefore, the number of hours spent at the community worksite happens to be just one aspect of the learning that takes place with academic service-learning. You may require more service hours as your project dictates or your university requires, but the advantages of academic service-learning lie in how you link service and learning together, not in a certain number of service hours. I require two hours because I prefer giving my students the opportunity to choose to work with others. By not demanding a high number of service hours (a full 10 hours), the stress on students is reduced and instead gives students the opportunity to volunteer. After all, part of what we want to teach is the desire to help others.

When should the service project be scheduled—at the beginning or at the end? With academic service-learning, the service-learning experience begins on the first day of class. The service project is not tacked-on nor are students sent out to find their own service project, as is often the case with community service. Academic service-learning is a class project. All students work on the same type of service project. Even if students go to different schools to do tutoring, everyone is doing tutoring. With academic service-learning, the emphasis is on learning. Students start evaluating, planning, analyzing, or problem-solving in relation to the project on the first day.

> I use *Camp Sharigan* (Clanton Harpine 2024) to teach my students how to use motivation in a real-world setting. Each class session talks about how to apply the theory and knowledge from the text to *Camp Sharigan*. I schedule *Camp Sharigan* before midterm, so students can plan, organize, problem-solve, and apply theory through class discussion before *Camp Sharigan* begins. Then, we have time for reflection and continued analysis after the *Camp Sharigan* project. I only require two hours of service. Yet, most of my students volunteer for the week (a total of 10 hours). The students work in class to get ready for *Camp Sharigan* and become as motivated as the children to participate throughout the week. Students rearrange their work schedules, organize childcare, and some even work out carpooling. I had one student who could not arrange childcare beg to allow her child to participate. Afterwards, she stated that she could not believe how much her child's reading skills improved in just one week. I have also had students (after they were no longer in my class) ask to volunteer. Providing students with an opportunity to volunteer is a wonderful way to teach civic responsibility. If we instill a yearning in our students to help others and to care about others in need, then we have truly taught civic mindedness.

Time spent at the worksite is not the critical learning element in academic service-learning, the way it is with community service. For academic service-learning, it is the way you link course content and service together that determines what students learn from the service-learning project. The important element in academic service-learning is learning, and a lot of learning occurs in the classroom before going to the worksite.

What kind of alternative options will you offer for those with schedule conflicts? I have never had a request for an alternative option, but for anyone who needs an alternative, I have a one-on-one reading tutoring packet (Clanton Harpine 2022), and I make arrangements in advance with a community organization that meets on Saturday.

Should alternative service options be related? If I am teaching reading as my service project, then my alternative needs to also be about teaching reading. Otherwise, the in-class discussions, problem-solving activities, and projects would be totally unrelated. As I stated in Chapter 3, for academic service-learning, alternative service projects need to be as similar as possible to the primary class service project. As one professor said, it's not the same when one student goes and helps others in the community while another student sits in the library writing a research paper. So, make your alternative option related to your community service-learning project.

An academic service-learning syllabus should explain how the service project is to be evaluated. Most academic service-learning professors agree that the service project itself should never be graded. As many have said, you don't give extra points for reading the chapter. Therefore, students should not be given a grade for service hours performed or extra credit for service. We are trying to teach civic responsibility, caring for the needs of others as well as applying course content to the real world.

An academic service-learning syllabus should be trustworthy. Students must be able to trust your syllabus and make plans based on the syllabus. The syllabus is everyone's schedule and guide. Every detail must be included. An academic service-learning syllabus cannot be vague. Predictable expectations are essential. The syllabus becomes an instructional tool, but is only useful if reliable.

How Will You Describe Assignments and Assessments on the Syllabus?

Many syllabi workshops and websites start by discussing how to organize assignments. However, if you want your syllabus to focus on learning, start by talking about what the students will be learning (Grunert O'Brien et al. 2008).

An academic service-learning syllabus should focus on learning, not grades. Grades generate negative stress for most students. When planning assignments, faculty should try to reduce stress through the way they describe assignments on the syllabus.

Clarity reduces stress. A more detailed description of the assignment on the syllabus will reduce stress for students. Rubrics often help. We cannot avoid grades, but grades should not be punishing or a negative distractor. We want an intrinsically motivating learning environment. Keep the learning process positive, but assignments should always show evidence of what students have learned.

Allowing improvement reduces stress. As one professor stated, most of us revise and resubmit our journal articles. The peer review process may be stressful, but in the end, it usually helps us produce a better article. The same is true for students. To enhance student improvement, allow rewrites and revisions. Research supports that when students are allowed to rewrite assignments, the rewrite produces higher quality and even increases student understanding of alternative perspectives (Song and Ferretti 2013). When students see that they have an opportunity to rework an assignment, stress is reduced, learning is strengthened. You may allow students to rewrite and resubmit on all or only certain assignments. Identify which assignments qualify for a revise and resubmit. Explain your policy clearly on the syllabus.

An academic service-learning syllabus should tell how service and learning are integrated. Your syllabus needs to make it clear to students from day one that with academic service-learning the service project is interwoven into the course content and learning process (Howard 1998). Academic service-learning is the teaching method. For academic service-learning to be successful, the syllabus needs to explain the connection between the academic content in the course and the service-leaning project. The syllabus must also explain how assignments fit into this new teaching method. Assignments cannot just be tacked on. They must be integrated into the course. Assignments must further student learning and link service and learning together.

What Kind of Written Assignments Will Build a Link Between Service and Learning?

In class, service and learning are linked together through how you teach: problem-solving discussions, critical thinking, analytical reasoning, planning, organizing, case study evaluations, leadership training, and teamwork. For written assignments, the link between service and learning must be built into the assignment. This is accomplished through the types of written projects and work assigned. Also, by asking: What will my students learn? Our goal is to always enhance learning. Let's look at three examples to show how graded assignments can be used with academic service-learning to enhance learning. The case example at the end of the chapter shows how each can be presented on the syllabus. Your assignments will naturally differ because of the requirements of your course, but each type of assignment presented can be used by any college professor for any course. Fine-tune to fit your course's needs.

An academic service-learning syllabus should show how service and learning are linked through reflection. Reflection is one of the main methods used to link service and learning together in academic service-learning. To reflect means to think critically, to analyze, and to evaluate the success of the service project in relationship to the criteria and goals that were set in class before the service project began.

The syllabus should explain the purpose of reflection assignments. Learning can be measured through reflection, but the syllabus must describe the details on which you are evaluating. Reflection assignments provide an in-depth evaluation when reflection assignments do more than just describe what happened or the student's opinion.

The syllabus should describe the requirements for the reflection assignments. When using reflection as one of your methods for measuring learning, make sure that reflection is used throughout the semester, even before students go to the service worksite. Not every reflection paper needs to be graded. Reflections may simply be used to give you a sense of how well students are understanding the text. [For reflection guidelines for written assignments, see Chapter 7.]

Make sure all reflection assignments are quality assignments. If you want reflection to help students learn, the reflection assignments must be quality assignments. Reflection assignments must connect service and learning together. Mere opinions do not strengthen the learning process. Quality assignments include analysis and reference to the text and theories being taught. Quality matters for reflection (Eyler 2002).

> My students keep an observation journal. I give a reflection assignment for the journal at the end of each class. These may be very simple assignments, observations, and reflections, but each assignment relates back to the text and what is being taught that day in class. Many of the journal assignments also connect directly to the service-learning project.

[For an example of a reflection assignment, look at the end of Chapter 7, and for an example of how to describe reflection on the syllabus, see #4 at the end of this chapter.]

An academic service-learning syllabus should show how service and learning are linked through testing. While reflection is one of the most popular means for measuring learning with academic service-learning, it is not the only method. Testing and exams are an integral part of most college courses. What kind of test will you use?

Multiple-choice tests. Research shows that multiple-choice testing is the most prevalent means of assessment used by faculty (Butler 2018). As two different research studies discovered, students often select the correct answer on a multiple-choice test while maintaining incorrect knowledge on the subject they were tested on (Couch et al. 2018; McKenna 2019). They simply guessed correctly. Students even admit that they often guess at the answers. Another study found that while students could answer multiple choice test questions, they actually only knew 8%

more after completing an introductory course than students who had not even taken the course (Rickard et al. 1988). Students memorize for the test. Then, they forget. Research also demonstrates that multiple-choice tests expose students to incorrect options and thereby lead to "false knowledge" or confusion (Roediger and Marsh 2005). So yes, multiple-choice tests are easier, but they do not create a learning experience that stresses higher-order thinking or that is linked with the community or service to the real world.

The syllabus should tell how your exams improve learning. Analysis and critical thinking were two of the skills that businesses were looking for in college graduates (Arum and Roksa 2011). Research substantiates that multiple choice tests do not encourage higher-order thinking, critical analysis, or application to the real world (Weiss 2003). Multiple choice tests also do not help students develop writing skills. Writing skills are another one of the most sought-after skills by employers (Arum and Roksa 2011). Therefore, before you add multiple-choice tests to your syllabus, consider other test options. All assessments should improve learning.

Essay exams. An essay exam encourages critical thinking, analysis, and writing. An essay exam allows concepts to be interrelated and applied to real-life situations. Essay exams need not be long. You can set length restrictions. A take home exam reduces stress and allows students to work on the exam throughout the semester. My take home exams have 12 sub questions. Each of the twelve interrelated sub questions is answered in the textbook and was discussed in class. Unsupported opinions are never accepted on exams. Here is a sample question from my motivation class.

> Test question: Define motivation. How does achievement influence motivation? What are the positive and negative environmental influences associated with motivation? What is the role of self-determination in motivation? Does an individual's self-concept or self-efficacy increase or decrease motivation? Explain. What role does feedback play in motivation? How does motivation affect the cognitive learning process? How do stress and anxiety affect motivation? If you were working at a community service worksite (any age), how would you create a motivational learning environment for the group? Yes, you may use *Camp Sharigan* as an example. How would you accommodate for individual differences in ability, IQ, or gender? Give examples of the motivators that you would use. Would these have positive or negative consequences?

The question is an integrated essay, not 12 short answers [see sample syllabus].

The syllabus should explain if you allow students to rewrite and resubmit for exams. My purpose for giving an exam is to make sure that students are learning the material and know how to apply it. If the student turns the exam in early, I allow rewrites on the exam. Rewriting to correct an exam question is an excellent learning strategy.

An academic service-learning syllabus should show how service and learning are linked through research. A research paper plays a vital role in academic service-learning because research can directly tie the course and service project together. If you orient the research paper to the service project, then it helps to tie textbook theory and application to the real world together. A research paper teaches research and writing skills and becomes more than just an assignment or a way to fulfill a grade requirement.

The syllabus should explain how the research paper is a teaching tool. I request a short (approximately five page) research paper. I believe students can learn more from a short research paper than they can from a 20- or 30-page paper that may be beyond their ability. Again, I am teaching research and writing skills. Yes, I do allow rewrites. I sit down with students, go over their papers individually, and then allow them to rewrite and resubmit. Again, my primary purpose is to improve their research and writing skills.

The syllabus should be written so that it reduces stress. I reverse the order for the research paper. Most courses require the research paper to be due at the end of the semester. For my classes, it is due before the midterm, which enables students to use the information that they learn from their research throughout the rest of the semester. Students will often refer to their research in their reflection assignments. This also reduces stress, since the end of the semester is always extremely stressful for students.

An Academic Service-Learning Syllabus Should Focus on Learning.

It is important to explain on the syllabus what the students will learn and be able to do as a result of participating in an academic service-learning course. Link the course content and the service-learning project together. Review your goals and objectives from Chapter 7, but for the syllabus, remember that all goals and objectives are written to focus on what the students will be learning, not what you will be teaching. The syllabus should also describe in detail all assignments, state the service requirements, how the service project will be evaluated, and other information students need to be successful in the course. The syllabus is a student's guide to success.

Summary

An effective syllabus serves as an effective reference guide for students throughout the semester. It should tell students exactly what they can expect throughout the semester. Scheduling is essential with academic service-learning. The syllabus should be written in a friendly tone and focused on student learning, not what the teacher is teaching. All assessment and evaluation measures should also be focused on learning. An academic service-learning syllabus ties learning and service together.

Building a Service-Learning Pedagogy

Questions to Help in Course Planning

1. Review the goals and objectives that you wrote in Chapter 7.
2. Are these goals and objectives exemplified through your syllabus?
3. How do you describe the service project on the syllabus?
4. Do your assignments include higher-order thinking strategies? Give examples. How do these assignments relate to your course goals and course objectives?
5. How are you working active learning, an intrinsically motivating learning environment, and the service-learning project into your course syllabus?

Troubleshooting Checklist

1. How many hours of service will you require of students?
2. Have you figured in travel time to the worksite? Will students carpool? Is the worksite on a bus route for those who do not have transportation?
3. How will you help students who have schedule conflicts?
4. What should students know before service begins at the worksite?
5. What problems do you think will arise at the service worksite? How will you minimize these problems?

Planning Guide Sheet

1. Do you need to have your syllabus approved by the department chair?
2. Do you have a reflection paper assignment from the service project? Do you ask for details, not generalities? Do you request that students support their reflection and evaluation with theory from the text?
3. Does your syllabus show how service and learning are linked?
4. What do you think your students will learn this semester from the service-learning experience? From the assignments that you have planned?

Case Example

For this syllabus example, I have left some sections blank because the required statements would be different for your university. I have also not listed the reading assignments or due dates because everyone is familiar with them. My purpose is to show how academic service-learning can be interwoven into the course description.

PSYCHOLOGY OF MOTIVATION

Semester, Year, Section

Time

Building and Classroom Location

Dr. Elaine Clanton Harpine
Office:
Office Phone:
E-mail:
Office Hours:

Welcome! I am glad you are joining us this semester for our academic service-learning section of psychology of motivation. This semester we will be learning about motivation and how it can be applied in the real world as we build a motivational reading clinic for at-risk children. The children we will be working with are struggling or failing in reading in school. Reading failure has been shown to be one of the root causes of violence and dropping out of school before graduation. We want to help these children succeed. Motivation is the key. We will all be working on the service project together. The project and worksite have been selected, and you will learn in class how you can best help these children overcome reading failure as you learn how to use the principles of motivation. You are required to spend a minimum of two hours at the reading clinic, but if you get excited and enjoy working with the children, you are welcome to work all week. The program is called, *Camp Sharigan.* It is a 10-hour, one week reading clinic that meets for two hours a day after school. During class, we will look at research showing how effective this program has been. You will help with the planning and organizing as well as helping to run the reading clinic. *Camp Sharigan* will be held the week of _____ (date)_______ at ______(address)_________, a location near campus. If you foresee any problems or conflicts, talk with me. I am always happy to help. There is never a problem so big that we cannot solve it together.

Required Text: *Understanding Motivation and Emotion* by Johnmarshall Reeve
Recommended Supplemental Text: *Writing with Style: APA Style Made Easy* by Lenore T. Szuchman (available in the library)
Service-learning Program Packet: A free copy of the *Camp Sharigan* program is available at the library.
Required Classroom Materials: 3-ring notebook to be brought to class each day.

COURSE GOALS

At the end of this semester, you will be able to:

- Distinguish between intrinsic and extrinsic motivation and demonstrate how to use intrinsic motivation at the service project worksite with the children.
- Identify positive and negative incentives often found in everyday life on campus and on the job and analyze whether these incentives contributed to or hindered intrinsic motivation and self-efficacy.
- Analyze real-world case studies involving positive and negative motivational "punishers" and demonstrate how to implement motivational adjustments that can bring about a positive, intrinsically motivating change.
- Apply motivational strategies to a real-world service-learning project.
- Reflect on your experiences at the worksite and explain what you have learned.
- Communicate effectively through both oral presentation and written projects, which is an important career goal for all psychologists.

INSTRUCTIONAL METHODS

Our classroom sessions will be active. You need to come to class each day prepared to participate in an interactive class. I never lecture. This academic service-learning course links course content from the textbook with real-world service at the reading clinic. Academic service-learning is a teaching method that will help you apply what you are learning in the classroom to a specific community problem. Research shows that academic service-learning is the most effective teaching approach. Students also make higher grades and understand textbook information better through academic service-learning. We cover the exact same amount of material covered in a lecture class, but we use discussion, analysis, critical thinking, problem-solving, and application to a real-world service project. In this way, you get more than just theory and textbook information. You will learn how to relate the concepts that we study to real life. Such knowledge will help you with your campus life and as you prepare for a professional career. You need to always bring your observation notebook with you to class. You may or may not choose to bring your textbook. We will be using the textbook assigned reading each class session in our problem-solving discussions, analysis of case studies, and as we plan and organize the reading clinic for the children. We will spend class time dissecting the material in the text and applying the textbook material to real-life. So, as you can see, attendance and class participation are very important.

SERVICE PROJECT

Camp Sharigan is a motivational reading clinic for first through third grade children who are struggling or failing in reading in school. We will work with 30 children (first through third grade). The ready-to-use program packet has instructions, curriculum, and every detail that we need for an effective reading clinic. The community site where we will be working is approximately five minutes from campus. The purpose of the service project is to link the coursework and theories of motivation that we will be studying with a real-world setting where you can apply these theories. Furthermore, through our work at the reading clinic, we will have the opportunity to change the lives of 30 children. As I like to say, if you teach a child to read, you can change the world.

The service project is required, but there is also an alternative option available. If you have any scheduling problems or concerns, speak with me. Together, we can work out any problem that arises. I'm looking forward to working with you this semester.

COURSE POLICIES

Absences: Participation is essential. Attendance is mandatory and recorded. Obviously since this is an interactive, participatory class, when you skip class you miss out on important analysis and critical thinking that simply cannot be included in class notes. If you are sick, talk with me. I will help you catch up.

Plagiarism is not tolerated. If you use more than 3 words from any source without using quotation marks and a source citation, it is plagiarism. Ideas paraphrased from another author must include source citation as well. If something is not your original idea, then you need to site the source and give credit to the author.

I do not consider plagiarism a minor problem, and I do not take plagiarism lightly. Plagiarism will earn you an "F" for the semester, not just the assignment.

Statement of academic honesty. (Check with your department chair.)

Statement of inclusion and diversity. (Check with your department chair.)

ASSIGNMENTS

Yes, even though this is an interactive class, I do follow university policies and require graded assignments. Don't panic. I'm always happy to help. If you do not understand an assignment or concept, ask me. I'll sit down and explain it to you. I allow you to rewrite and resubmit written assignments (see details for each assignment). I also treat all assignments equally. If you are worried about grades, this can be a big benefit for you. For example, the observation notebook, which is graded on completeness, counts for the same amount as the research paper and take-home exam. So, go for it. You can do this, and I'm always here ready to help you any way that I can.

Grades: While I do want the course to be exciting and enjoyable, there is always work to be done. I do not believe in grading group discussions, group projects, or class participation. We will strive to become a cooperative team who works together to learn about motivation and to go out into the community to provide the best reading clinic possible. As for grades, I only grade you on your own individual work. You will have four graded assignments of equal value. I believe that each assignment is of equal importance. Because my goal is to help you improve your writing skills, you will have the option to revise and resubmit written assignments for regrading. If the written assignment does not improve, obviously the grade cannot improve. I grade resubmitted assignments as to your improvement and completion of the requirements. When you submit a revised written assignment, the first graded copy must be attached. Resubmits cannot be accepted without the original assignment attached. Yes, I do reread your original assignment to look for improvement. Letter grades are determined as follows:

A	90–100
B	80–89
C	70–79
D	60–69
F	below 60

Assignment #1: Observation Notebook

Purpose of assignment: To apply textbook theories to real world observations. Learning to observe and analyze behavior in real-world settings is essential in psychology. You will keep a 3-ring notebook for in-class observation assignments. This notebook must be brought to each class session and will be due on _(date)_. Your notebook will be graded and returned during the final exam period. Observation assignments will be given at the end of each class session and will correlate with the theory being discussed that day in class. Your notebook will be graded on completeness, quality and detail of observation, and application of textbook theory to the observation. Opinions will not be accepted for this assignment. All assignments must be dated and typed. Sorry but untyped assignments will not be graded. Since this assignment is due on the final day of class, it does not qualify for revise and resubmit. If you have questions or concerns about your journal entries, speak to me any time throughout the semester. I am always happy to sit down and go over your journal entries with you. Organize journal assignments by date assigned, please.

For an A on this assignment:

- Must fulfill all requirements listed above.
- Must be an in-depth observation and correctly answer the observation question given at the end of each class.
- Must apply textbook theories from the assigned reading to the written observational report.
- Must follow APA style guide.

Assignment #2: Research Paper

Purpose of assignment: Learning to write concise and accurate research reports is very important in psychology. Many employers hire on the basis of writing skills; therefore, you are being asked to undertake in-depth research on a motivational problem (topic must be approved). This is not a long paper, and you may revise and resubmit if desired. The goal is to enhance your abilities to write research papers using APA style.

I am always happy to work with anyone wanting help.

> The paper will be 1000 words (double spaced, 12-point font, normal one-inch margins). Must be typed. Check with me to get approval on your topic before you start researching and writing. You must have five current (within last five years) sources (peer reviewed psychology journal articles), which must be cited in the paper. You may have more than five sources; books are acceptable as additional sources. Use APA style guide, 7th ed. Complete bibliographic citations must be included. Do not quote from the textbook. Paper is due on _date_, at the beginning of class. Papers turned in after class session has begun are late.

For an A on this assignment:

- Must fulfill all requirements listed above.
- Must use quality references and current sources.
- Must use APA style correctly for writing a research paper and for citing references.
- Must quote five, current (in last 5 years) peer-reviewed psychology journal articles on topic being researched.
- Must demonstrate correct spelling and be free of grammar errors—street slang is not allowed in a research paper.

Assignment #3: Take Home Final Exam

Purpose of assignment: Psychology requires very clear and concise writing. Psychologists are often required to write short but very in-depth reports. The purpose of this exam is to prove that you have read, understand, and can apply theoretical material from the textbook to real life situations.

> There is one take-home exam distributed on the first day of class. The exam must be typed. There are two questions on the exam. Each question will have twelve parts to answer. The answers will be written essays, not just short answer. Each of your essay style answers for the two exam questions will be NOT MORE THAN 250 WORDS MAXIMUM—typed, one page, 12-point font, double spaced. The exam is due during the designated final exam period and may only be turned in at the beginning of class. Late exams will not be accepted, unless circumstances dictate, and arrangements have been made in advance. You are allowed to turn in the exam early. If your exam is turned in early, I am also happy to sit down and read over your exam with you. Unfortunately, I cannot review exams turned in on the due date or at the last minute. Each question will cover material from the text and from class discussions. All quotations and bibliographic citations must be complete and use APA style.

For an A on this assignment:

- Must fulfill all requirements listed above.
- Must give complete answers. All 12 sub questions must be answered correctly.
- Answers must be taken from the textbook, no opinions.

Assignment #4: Reflection Paper and Oral Presentation

Purpose of assignment: Critical thinking is one of the most sought-after skills in psychology and almost any other field. Employers want graduates who can analyze and evaluate the needs of a situation. This assignment will help you apply textbook theories to a hands-on, real-world community-based field experience. Working with children in a service-learning environment will enable you to identify and understand textbook theories as they appear in real life. Reflecting on what you learned from the service project about motivation will allow you to analyze and apply what you have learned this semester to your future career goals.

> This is a two-part assignment: (1) a written reflection assignment following the service project that answers each of the 8 questions on the handout presented in class before the service project and (2) an oral 5-minute presentation during the final exam period answering the question—What I learned this semester? The written assignment will follow an essay format. Your reflection paper will be NOT MORE THAN 250 WORDS MAXIMUM—typed, one page, 12-point font, double spaced. Your reflection paper will be graded on completeness, quality and detail, and application of textbook theory to the service project. The oral presentation will give you an opportunity to demonstrate your creative skills and to practice giving oral reports. Refer to the handout given in class on oral presentation guidelines. Oral presentations are a very real part of being a psychologist. You may not read from your paper or from notes. Developing skills in giving good oral presentations takes practice. Talk with me if you have concerns or need assistance. I am always happy to help.

For an A on this assignment:

- Must fulfill all requirements listed above.
- Reflection paper must relate service experience to textbook theory.
- Reflection paper must be typed and follow APA style guide.

- The presentation will be graded on creativity. Reading from notes will not be accepted.
- Each component must be completed in order to receive an A.

READING ASSIGNMENTS

Please be prepared to discuss assigned pages on the day listed. We will actually be talking, analyzing, and evaluating your reading assignment in class. You will be working in groups, and your group members are counting on you. Therefore, it is very important that you keep up with the reading. The assigned pages are not lengthy. Please read assigned textbook chapters before coming to class. We will spend class time applying the textbook reading to the service-learning project and other real-life situations on campus. You may bring your text to class if desired. If you fall behind on the reading assignment, it is hard to catch up. So, set aside reading time. I look forward to working with you this semester. If you have any concerns or problems, do not hesitate to talk with me. This is going to be a fun semester. Let's go.

References

Amerstorfer, C. M., & Freiin von Münster-Kistner, C. (2021). Student perceptions of academic engagement and student-teacher relationships in problem-based learning. *Frontiers in Psychology, 12,* 713057. https://doi.org/10.3389/fpsyg.2021.713057

Arum, R., & Roksa, J. (2011). *Academically adrift: Limited learning on college campuses.* Chicago: University of Chicago press.

Association of American Colleges and Universities. (2007). *College learning for a new global century.* Washington, D. C.: Association of American Colleges and Universities.

Bain, K. (2004). *What the best college teachers do.* Cambridge, MA: Harvard University Press.

Barnett, M., Silver, P. T., & Grund, T. S. (2009). Implementing service-learning pedagogy: A case example. *Journal of Higher Education Outreach and Engagement, 13,* 117–134.

Ballard, S. M., & Elmore, B. (2009). A labor of love: Constructing a service-learning syllabus. *The Journal of Effective Teaching, 9,* 70–76.

Butler, A. C. (2018). Multiple-choice testing in education: Are the best practices for assessment also good for learning? *Journal of Applied Research in Memory and Cognition, 7,* 323–331. https://doi.org/10.1016/j.jarmac.2018.07.002

Calhoon, S., & Becker, A. (2008). How students use the course syllabus. *International Journal for the Scholarship of Teaching and Learning, 2,* 1–12. https://doi.org/10.20429/ijsotl.2008.02010

Clanton Harpine, E. (2022). *Why can't we teach children to read: Oh, but wait, we can: A step-by-step plan for teaching your child to read.* Corpus Christi, TX: Group-Centered Learning.

Clanton Harpine, E. (2024). *Camp Sharigan: A ready-to-use group-centered intervention for grades 1–3* (3rd ed.). Corpus Christi, TX: Group-Centered Learning.

Couch, B. A., Hubbard, J. K., & Brassil, C. E. (2018). Multiple-true-false questions reveal the limits of the multiple-choice format for detecting students with incomplete understandings. *BioScience, 68,* 455–463. https://doi.org/10.1093/biosci/biy037

Cullen, R., & Harris, M. (2009). Assessing learner-centeredness through course syllabi. *Assessment & Evaluation in Higher Education, 34*, 115–125. https://doi.org/10.1080/02602930801956018

Eyler, J. (2002). Reflection: Linking service and learning – linking students and communities. *Journal of Social Issues, 58*, 517–534. https://doi.org/10.1111/1540-4560.00274

Felten, D., & Clayton, P. H. (2011). Service-learning. *New Directions Teaching and Learning, 128*, 75–84. https://doi.org/10.1002/tl.470

Freeman, S., Eddy, S. L., McDonough, M., Smith, M. K., Nnadozie Okoroafor, Jordt, H., & Wenderoth, M. P. (2014). Active learning increases student performance in science, engineering, and mathematics. *Proceedings of the National Academy of Sciences (PNAS), 111*, 8410–8415. https://doi.org/10.1073/pnas.1319030111

Grunert O'Brien, J., Millis, B. J., & Cohen, M. W. (2008). *The course syllabus: A learning-centered approach* (2nd ed.). San Francisco, CA: Jossey-Bass.

Harnish, R. J., & Bridges, K. R. (2011). Effect of syllabus tone: Students' perceptions of instructor and course. *Social Psychology of Education, 14*, 319–330. https://doi.org/10.1007/s11218-011-9152-4

Hart, S. M., & King, J. R. (2007). Service learning and literacy tutoring: Academic impact on pre-service teachers. *Teaching and Teacher Education, 23*, 323–328. https://doi.org/10.1016/j.tate.2006.12.004

Howard, J. P. F. (1998). Academic service learning: A counternormative pedagogy. *New Directions for Teaching and Learning, 73*, 21–29.

Jacoby, B. (2015). *Service-learning essentials: Questions, answers, and lessons learned.* San Francisco, CA: Jossey-Bass.

Kamuche, F. U. (2006). Service learning and student performance. *Academic Exchange Quarterly, 10*, 187–192.

Kieran, L., & Haack, S. (2018). PRELOAD: A rubric to evaluate course syllabi for quality indicators of community engagement and service-learning components. *Journal of Community Engagement and Higher Education, 10*, 39–47.

Kuh, G. D. (2013). Taking HIPs to the next level. In G. D. Kuh & K. O'Donnell (Eds.) pp. 1–14, *Ensuring quality and taking high-impact practices to scale*. Washington, DC: Association of American Colleges and Universities.

McKenna, P. (2019). Multiple choice questions: Answering correctly and knowing the answer. *Interactive Technology and Smart Education, 16*, 59–73. https://doi.org/10.1108/ITSE-09-2018-0071

Mottner, S. (2010). Service-learning in a nonprofit marketing course: A comparative case of pedagogical tools. *Journal of Nonprofit & Public Sector Marketing, 22*, 231–245. https://doi.org/10.1080/10495142.2010.483274

Parkes, J., & Harris, M. B. (2002). The purposes of a syllabus. *College Teaching, 50*, 55–61. https://doi.org/10.1080/87567550209595875

Richmond, A. S. (2016). Constructing a learner-centered syllabus: One professor's journey. *Idea, 60*, 1–11.

Rickard, H. C., Rogers, R., Ellis, N. R., & Beidleman, W. B. (1988). Some retention, but not enough. *Teaching of Psychology, 15*, 151–152. https://doi.org/10.1207/s15328023top1503_14

Roediger, H. L. III, & Marsh, E. J. (2005). The positive and negative consequences of multiple-choice testing. *Journal of Experimental Psychology: Learning, Memory, and Cognition, 31*, 1155–1159. https://doi.org/10.1037/0278-7393.31.5.1155

Salam, M., Awang Iskandar, D.N., Ibrahim, D.H.A., & Farooq, M. S. (2019). Service learning in higher education: A systematic literature review. *Asia Pacific Education Review, 20*, 573–593. https://doi.org/10.1007/s12564-019-09580-6

Saville, B. K., Zinn, T. E., Brown, A. R., & Marchuk, K. A. (2010). Syllabus detail and students' perceptions of teacher effectiveness. *Teaching of Psychology, 37*, 186–189. https://doi.org/10.1080/00986283.2010.488523

Song, Y., & Ferretti, R. P. (2013). Teaching critical questions about argumentation through the revising process: Effects of strategy instruction on college students' argumentative essays. *Reading and Writing: An Interdisciplinary Journal, 26*, 67–90. https://doi.org/10.1007/s11145-012-9381-8

Stains, M., Harshman, J., Barkers, M. K., Chasteen, S. V., Coles, R., Dechenne-Peters, S. E., … Young, A. M. (2018). Anatomy of STEM teaching in North American Universities. Science, 359, 1468–1470. https://doi.org/10.1126/science.aap8892

Wasley, P. (2008). The syllabus becomes a repository of legalese. *Chronicles of Higher Education, 54,* 1–6.

Weiss, R. E. (2003). Designing problems to promote higher-order thinking. *New Directions for Teaching and Learning, 95,* 25–31. https://doi.org/10.1002/tl.109

Woolcock, M. J. V. (2006). *Constructing a syllabus*. Providence, RI: Brown University, Harriet W. Sheridan Center for Teaching and Learning.

Chapter 9
Applying the Principles of Change: What Type of Leadership Should I Provide?

But I don't want to change. I like things the way they are.

How many times have you heard someone say that they do not want to change? Too many to count. Yet, change is inevitable. Each new day brings something different than the day before. Executive leaders contend that if organizations and companies do not change, they will not survive (Rehman et al. 2021). The same is true for universities (Moser and Fazey 2021). Students, faculty, and even administrators are being asked to change. From the first page of this book to the last, we have been talking about change. Will colleges and universities embrace change? You, the faculty, hold the key.

What Kind of Change Do Colleges and Universities Need?

Universities and colleges make changes every year to be responsive to student needs and the requirements of businesses hiring graduates. Yet, there is one problem that has not given way to change. Major leaders in the field of higher education have been calling for this change for over 20 years (Bok 2020; Fink 2013; Halpern and Hakel 2003; Ramsden 2003; Spence 2001; Whetten 2007). Throughout every chapter, we have documented this call for change. The change being sought is improving student learning by changing the method through which students are taught in the classroom.

The call for change. Paul Ramsden (2003), international expert on improving the quality of teaching, says the college classroom is not the same as it was in the past; therefore, the way we teach must change as well. Derek Bok, former president of Harvard, goes one step further and says that the most important change for universities and colleges to make is improving student learning outcomes (knowledge students learn and how to use that knowledge in life). In his book *Higher*

E. Clanton Harpine, *Service Learning in Higher Education*,
https://doi.org/10.1007/978-3-031-51378-7_9

Expectations: Can Colleges Teach Students What They Need to Know in the 21st Century (2020), he asks,

> "What adjustments would colleges need to make in their curriculum and instructional methods to respond to society's demands? Can their faculties be persuaded to make the necessary changes?" (3)

The change being called for is a completely new way of teaching. The call is for a deep learning approach that concentrates on the meaning of information learned and high-impact transfer of knowledge to the real world (Jackson 2012). Academic service-learning answers this call for change and relates knowledge to real-world settings.

What kind of faculty leadership is needed to bring about change? Instead of just conveying information, professors must undertake a leadership role that leads students to a deeper level of learning. This would include higher-order thinking, group and collaboration skills, transference of knowledge to the real world, and concentrating on the value and usability of what is learned (Jackson 2012). To bring about this change, faculty leadership must be focused on how students learn best [see Chapter 4].

Professors can become the leaders of this change by transforming how they teach. Many professors are already leading the way. Some are serving as leaders in their field and changing entire departments, such as the team working for pedagogical change in introductory biology (Cooke et al. 2023). They are bringing interaction into what once was a mere lecture hall. Still others are working to improve teaching methods with just their students. Regardless of whether you work with only the courses you teach or are leading a movement to change teaching across your university or throughout your entire field, effective leadership is required.

Effective leaders stay focused on helping students learn. The call is for an interactive style of leadership that is innovative, focused on improving student outcomes, and concerned with connections to the community (Bok 2020; Freitas et al. 2021; Hattie 2015). This kind of leadership encourages faculty and students to interactively work together as they analyze and construct meaning from their studies (Okinyi et al. 2015).

Good leaders empower students to work up to their best ability. Your leadership style needs to be energetic, enthusiastic, and passionate. You need to be enthusiastic about improving learning outcomes and focused on helping students succeed (Caldwell and Anderson 2021). Faculty should also become involved in the learning process with their students (Freitas et al. 2021). Academic service-learning can help faculty achieve this higher level of learning.

Professors can become the leaders of change. The strongest faculty leadership effect on student outcomes transpires from selecting a more effective teaching pedagogy (Fink 2013). For some, this will entail undertaking a new leadership role in the classroom. Others have already stepped forward to embrace this change. Still others may choose to use this chapter to encourage peers to make the change. Leadership is action, being an agent of change is part of that action. To lead means to guide, give direction. Academic service-learning helps professors make these necessary changes and enables students to tackle careers and jobs that require a more interactive style of learning, as well as to develop critical thinking, problem-solving, team-building, motivation, and analytical writing.

Applying the Principles of Change

There are many different approaches to implementing change. We will refer to six basic principles of change: identify the problem, develop a criterion for evaluation, create a plan, evaluate the plan against the criteria, implement change, and evaluate the effectiveness of the change.

Step 1: Identify the Problem, Exactly What Are We Seeking to Change?

In 2020, 96% of academic leaders surveyed said they believed that their college or university was doing a good job preparing students for jobs and careers (Jaschik and Lederman 2020). Sadly, when 43 randomly selected 4-year universities were surveyed, only 41% of the students agreed and only 11% of the business leaders concurred (Strata Educational Network 2017). [It should be noted that the Strata survey was before the pandemic; therefore, the problem existed prior to the lockdown]. This is important because the desire to get a better job is one of the primary reasons students give for going to college. What kind of change are students and business leaders seeking?

Universities and colleges need to change to meet the demands of the modern job market. In the survey above, business leaders were very dissatisfied with lecture style teaching because lectures were not producing graduates who could adapt to the needs of today's businesses. As Derek Bok (2020) explained:

> "Employers seek graduates who can adapt successfully to rapid changes in the nature of their jobs, solve problems creatively, work adaptly in teams, interact effectively with diverse groups of colleagues, subordinates, and customers, and be resilient enough to overcome the challenges and risk created by constant economic change." (2)

Lectures and multiple-choice tests do not prepare students for this type of employment.

Universities and colleges need to focus on stronger student engagement and participation. Experts are calling for professors to focus on teaching techniques that engage students and help them learn. To increase student engagement, faculty must not simply convey information and theories from the textbook; professors must also find ways to show students how to put such knowledge into practice (Freeland 2019). Students are also calling for a more participatory role in the learning process (Heffernan 2001). Learning is active, not passive (reread Chapter 4 on best ways for students to learn). Students need to be able to apply knowledge, not just sit and listen. Academic service-learning teaches long-term retention, transfer of knowledge to real-world settings, critical thinking, teamwork, leadership, and analytical writing.

Universities and colleges need to stress a "deeper approach to learning." One of the first big changes that many researchers are calling for is for faculty to teach for long-term retention and transfer of knowledge rather than just for results on the end of the semester exam (Halpern and Hakel 2003). A deeper approach to learning requires that students be able to transform information and theories from the textbook into usable knowledge that can be transferred to the real world. A deeper level of learning and transfer of what was learned requires that students actively participate in the learning process (Halpern and Hakel 2003).

Universities and colleges need to stop relying on retention-based tests as an indicator of what students have learned. It is possible that students can do very well on a multiple-choice test yet have no idea how to apply the information from the test to real-world problems. Just recognizing the correct answer is not true learning. Students need to be able to use the information they are learning in class and be able to apply it to the real world (Halpren and Hakel 2003). Life in today's society and job market also requires that students be skilled in critical thinking (Butler and Halpern 2020).

Universities and colleges need to teach analytical reasoning. When you teach problem solving, you help students engage in analytical thinking. Analytical thinking is more than just figuring out the correct multiple-choice answer on a test (Halpren and Hakel 2003). By definition, when students engage in analytical thinking and reasoning, they break down information from data, a situation, or a problem. Filtering out facts and then reconstructing a workable action for the real world (Halpern and Dunn 2021). Analytical thinking involves perception, awareness, and the ability to organize and interpret new experiences (see Chapter 4). Analytical reasoning relies on facts and verifiable information not opinions. Employers are also seeking graduates who can do analytical writing, while evaluating and interpreting the significance of the information learned. Approximately 90% of employers are asking for graduates who can perform analytical reasoning, writing, problem-solving, and critical thinking (Arum and Roksa 2011). The way one teaches in the classroom can make a difference (Nickerson 2020).

Universities and colleges need to emphasize critical thinking. Critical thinking is the process of evaluating thoughts, information, or ideas. Critical thinking looks for loopholes, incorrect ideas, or false information. Critical thinking dissects information in order to prove it right or wrong. Lecturing and multiple-choice testing do not prepare graduates to go out in the world and employ analytical reasoning or critical thinking (Halpern and Dunn 2021). Students no longer need a Rolodex of memorized facts; instead, they need the ability to analyze, solve problems, and critically dissect facts from opinions or false information. Learning in the university classroom must be more than just the accumulation of textbook knowledge (Southworth 2022). Academic service-learning teaches critical thinking, problem-solving, and analytical reasoning as well as teaching students how to apply what they are learning in a real-world setting.

Step 2: Developing a Criteria for Evaluation, What Should the Criteria Include?

The effectiveness of any teaching pedagogy is the impact that it has on student learning (Pribbenow 2005). According to the list of needs in Step 1, an effective pedagogy should use teaching strategies that provide a deeper level of learning and higher-order thinking skills. Deeper learning includes critical thinking, analytical reasoning, communication, teamwork, motivation, leadership skills, and application to real-world problems. Students have also stated that they would like a more interactive teaching approach (Valtonen et al. 2021). Therefore, the criteria should include:

- a deeper level of learning—critical thinking and analytical reasoning
- intrinsic motivation, perspective taking, and helping others
- teaching teamwork and working with others
- analytical writing skills
- problem-solving, especially in the real world
- experience working in groups with real world significance
- leadership training in real world settings
- applying knowledge to real-world situations
- a more interactive classroom teaching method
- an emphasis on student engagement in the classroom

Step 3: Creating a Plan for Change: Is This a Plan that Faculty can Implement?

The plan is to adopt an academic service-learning pedagogy for teaching university and college courses. Research shows that academic service-learning is the most effective teaching method for the college classroom (Hart and King 2007; Mottner 2010), and that intrinsic motivation is one of the key elements surrounding the success of service-learning (Lo et al. 2022). Academic service-learning introduces students to hands-on learning experiences (learning by doing), real-world problem solving, group discussion and decision making, observing change in action, as well as reflecting on what has been learned. Academic service-learning allows students to put theory into practice (Forsberg et al. 2019). Research has repeatedly shown that students who are actively engaged in the learning process learn more (Bringle and Hatcher 2017). With academic service-learning, service-learning becomes the method through which the professor teaches the course. With academic service-learning, learning takes place in both the classroom and at the community worksite. Research shows that the benefits of academic service-learning are the same regardless of the size of the institution—community college, 4-year, private, or research university (Cronley et al. 2015; Sandy and Holland 2006; Taggart and Crisp 2011). Academic service-learning integrates the service project into the course content. It is this linking of service and learning that makes academic service-learning so successful. Throughout the book we have been developing a pedagogy for this teaching approach.

Step 4: Does the Plan Meet the Criteria?

Derek Bok (2020) says that instruction must be creative and focused on problem solving. It must also teach teamwork, working with others, build resilience, be adaptable, follow "high ethical standards," emphasize interdisciplinary education, and be responsive to the real world. Academic service-learning fulfills this need.

Academic service-learning provides in-depth learning. Academic service-learning produces higher student outcomes (GPA, test scores, and knowledge learned), better long-term retention and transfer of knowledge, stronger student engagement, critical thinking, motivation, problem-solving skills, and persistence (Bringle and Hatcher 2017; Krsmanovic 2022; Warren and Sellnow 2010). Academic service-learning emphasizes helping students apply knowledge from the textbook to real-world problems. The feature that makes academic service-learning so effective is *connecting the course material and the service project* (Howard 2001; Kuh et al. 2008; Warren 2012).

Academic service-learning uses an interactive teaching style. When faculty and students interact in the classroom, they generate new ideas and knowledge. Faculty and students add to this knowledge through reflection on how such knowledge is important in the real world. Academic service-learning becomes the teaching method and provides interaction, analysis, and reflection for the classroom. (see Chapter 6).

Academic service-learning teaches real life problem-solving. Academic service-learning teaches students how to apply the course's content to real-life problems and encourages students to problem-solve to find solutions to those problems. This is exactly what the business community is seeking from colleges and universities.

Academic service-learning helps students learn to work with others. Students work in class and at the service worksite in groups. Academic service-learning gives students the opportunity to practice teamwork, leadership skills, and to work as a group constructively. Students transfer these skills to their career and jobs.

Academic service-learning teaches for today's job market. Academic service-learning uses problem solving, analytical writing, critical thinking, and application to the real world. As several studies have demonstrated, faculty who support academic service-learning do so because they want to improve student learning in the courses they teach (Carberry et al. 2013; Hart and King 2007; Hou and Wilder 2015; Kennedy and Gruber 2020; Krsmanovic 2022; O'Meara et al. 2011; Shin et al. 2018; Warren 2012).

Step 5: Implement Change

In my own classes, responses were supportive of the interactive style of teaching that I use with academic service-learning. When I asked which they preferred—interactive or lecture, students made the following end of the semester comments:

"Interactive. It helps you to better understand the material and is more interesting than traditional lecture."
"Interactive. It teaches me more, helps me understand."
"Interactive because it makes you wanna go to class. Traditional lecture keeps me uninterested and wanting to go to sleep."
"Interactive because it relates the subject to us and makes it easier to understand."
"Interactive. It forces you to pay attention and interact with the professor. You learn so much more."
"Interactive because it is easier to grasp concepts when you are a part of them."
"Interactive. I learn more. I am more interested, and I stay focused more."
"Interactive, it involves student participation and gives hands on training."

Step 6: Does Academic Service-Learning Effectively Meet the Identified Needs?

When professors adopt academic service-learning, they take on a leadership role that can bring about change for their students and for the community. This leadership role involves a higher level of learning. Academic service-learning can bring these learning opportunities to the classroom but only when professors believe in the underlying principles and pedagogy that makes academic-service learning successful.

Evaluation from the faculty perspective. As research from two economics professors documents, academic service-learning is more than just community service:

> "Service-learning is an experiential learning pedagogy that promotes deep learning because of what occurs when students integrate their classroom studies with service activities in their communities. For example, when undergraduate economics students volunteer at a homeless shelter, distributing services or tutoring homeless children, they are providing a needed and valuable SERVICE to their communities. But when those same students use their experiences at the shelter to better understand the economics of poverty and the shortage of low-income housing, they are LEARNING about the economics of their communities. Service-learning combines SERVICE with LEARNING in intentional ways that benefits both the community and the student-learner. Service activities are not just add-ons,

> but are closely linked to the academic content and learning objectives of a class. Students use the theories of economics within the context of the world in which they will ultimately participate.." (Ziegert and McGoldrick 2008 p. 40)

Every course in every department at every university can use academic service-learning. Instead of lecturing, academic service-learning becomes the teaching method that helps students use what they are learning in the classroom in a real-world setting (reread Chapter 6). The key to making this change lies in the hands of the faculty.

Evaluation from the Student Perspective. As one student described her experience with academic service-learning, she said,

> "I do not have the words to describe how amazing my experience was at the prenatal clinic. I'm studying nursing and Spanish and my experience in this clinic has helped me learn more about both. I've learned lots of medical information that will be useful in my future nursing courses. The best part is that while I was learning this information, I had the opportunity to practice speaking Spanish at the same time. I am so excited that I have the opportunity to continue translating in this clinic the next semester.." (Adams 2015, p. 12)

When students see the usefulness of what they are learning from their textbook and truly believe that what they are learning in class can make the world a better place to live, then they are motivated to become fully engaged in the learning process.

Taking action—the leadership role. Everything a professor does in class must lead to actual learning. The way professors approach changing the teaching method used in the classroom will influence student acceptance and enthusiasm for working with academic service-learning. Change takes preparation, planning, and commitment, but most of all, it takes the willingness to take action. College and university faculty are the key to change. Turn the classroom into a learning laboratory where students are challenged to think, to evaluate, and to solve problems. As one of my students said, "Very interesting teaching style, it brought the real world into the class."

What Type of Leadership Should I Provide?

You may be saying, okay I agree academic service-learning would be a good idea, but I have no idea how to get my university to change. I don't even know where to start. Start small. Instead of walking into the Dean's office and declaring that everything has to change, lead by example. If you only teach one class, that is a beginning. Be a leader in your department. Provide leadership that is focused on learning and how students learn best (reread Chapter 4).

Lead by teaching students to analyze critically. An entire academic service-learning project could be developed around problem solving and critical thinking.

For example, after the pandemic, a brewing problem developed over whether vaccines are or are not good for children and adults. This is definitely a topic that health and education majors should be concerned about, but it could also be appropriate for every course taught at any university. This problem affects life, our economy, and the future health and prosperity of our nation. Every teacher could apply this topic to their course. Again, students could research the topic. Look for facts, not opinions. With my own students, I tell them I do not want to know what the Internet says. I want factual, verifiable research, not political opinions. It's what business leaders are asking of the university: teach students to look beyond popular opinion and find the truth. Again, the service project could be preparing campus and community programs that would share this information with parents, teachers, and the community as a whole. Presenting a factual community program is service in and to the community. The world is overrun with opinions. It's time to search for the truth.

Lead by being in favor of change. Some people see change as a threat. Stress and fear keep people from changing. It's called the *status quo bias*. If we are always fighting to keep things the way they are or have always been, then we are less likely to accept or want to change. Before we can bring change to a university, we must first overcome persistent resistance to change. One way to encourage change is to form concrete plans, as we have done in this book. We've talked about why academic service-learning is more effective and how to develop an academic service-learning pedagogy. Yet, there will still be professors who turn away and go back to lecturing. Why?

Fear: Some professors worry that academic service-learning will not relate to what they are teaching. Converting a course to academic service-learning does not take away from the content of what should be taught in the course. It also does not make the course less rigorous. Academic service-learning can fit with any course at a large or small college as well as at a research university. For example, select a topic for your service project that allows students to utilize analytical reasoning.

> One suggestion might be to ask if a power plant that burns coal, gas, one that uses nuclear energy, or a solar and wind power station, would be more cost-efficient, better for the environment, and more sustainable in the long term.

This is a topic that could apply to almost any course because it's a real problem that we are facing right now in our country. Since one of the jobs of the university is to train tomorrow's leaders, this is a question that all students need to think about. If you are teaching economics, look at the cost factor. History, communication, environmental studies, and science can stress the effects on people and the environment. Nursing, psychology, and social work students can explore the health problems and benefits. Engineering majors can look at the feasibility of each proposal. English language majors or foreign language students, especially in Spanish, could definitely identify with this project as they work in the community to help others understand the best solution. Use class time to analyze the problem. Students could even do a research paper. Then, for the community service project, students could develop and present a campus-community program to explain what they have learned. There is so much misinformation and, in some cases, just out and out lies on the Internet that this kind of academic service-learning project could be very valuable for students, the community, and the nation. Set politics and personal opinion aside. The key ingredient of analytical thinking is searching for facts, not opinions or personal beliefs.

Tenure. Another reason given by universities where tenure is a consideration is that tenure hinges on research, not teaching. As John Tagg explains in his article *Why Does the Faculty Resist Change*? (2012), as long as universities link hiring, promotions, and tenure to research, then the emphasis on research will devalue teaching and learning. Lectures are seen as easy, economical, and less time-consuming, which allows more time for research. However, the businesses who hire graduates are asking for a change. Academic service-learning provides the teaching method. You provide the leadership.

Research. There are professors at large research institutions who claim that they cannot afford to switch away from lecturing because of the number of students in their classes. Even though universities say that service, teaching, and research are all important, the emphasis is on research at many large universities, and as long as research is given a higher level of importance, professors will resist change. Even journals place more importance on traditional research rather than field studies. One suggestion is to link academic service-learning with your research (Furco 2001).

> That's exactly what I did. As a psychologist I got involved with reading because of the impact reading failure had on mental development and psychological well-being. I started with *Camp Sharigan* (Clanton Harpine 2024). My service team and I traveled to many states conducting *Camp Sharigan*. Even though our post-tests showed strong evidence of improvement (Clanton Harpine and Reid 2009; Clanton Harpine and Pazda 2019), some children needed more than just a one-week reading clinic. To answer that need, I created a year-long program and incorporated it into my academic service-learning courses. Preventing reading failure became my research emphasis, and I began to develop and test the effectiveness of several reading programs. My university students participated in this research. We published the results of an eight-year study with some of my undergraduate students assuming lead authorship on several chapters (Clanton Harpine 2019). My undergraduate students and I presented numerous national conference presentations based on the research and data from the academic service-learning projects that I was using as my teaching method.

Research, service, and teaching really can be combined.

Will the Faculty Lead?

If change comes to universities, it will be because the faculty pushed for change and are leading the way. As Bok (2020) asks, can today's faculty "...be persuaded to make the necessary changes" and lead today's universities and colleges to a new higher level of learning that meets the demands of today's society?

Summary

There is a gap between what the faculty believe students are learning and what students have actually learned. Leaders in higher education have been calling for change for over 20 years. By turning classrooms into interactive learning experiences, faculty can lead by providing direction and guidance. Faculty must become not just teachers, but leaders who lead students through the learning experience. When professors assume an interactive leadership role, they consider themselves responsible for whether students learn or do not learn. Academic service-learning provides the pedagogy for change. The faculty provides the leadership.

Building a Service-Learning Pedagogy

Questions to Help in Course Planning

1. What kind of change do you want to bring to your university?
2. What kind of change do you want to bring to your classroom?
3. Review the goals that you have set for your course.
4. Did you add any new goals? Are there new goals that you would like to add?
5. Are you using only analytical and critical thinking strategies? Give examples.
6. How are you working active learning, an intrinsically motivating learning environment, and the service-learning project into your plans for change?

Troubleshooting Checklist

1. Do all of your plans for change link learning with the service project?
2. What do you think will be the most difficult aspect of changing how you teach? How will you accomplish these changes? How will service-learning help?
3. How will you encourage students who are reluctant to change to an academic service-learning teaching approach?

Planning Guide Sheet

1. What type of changes are you planning for your course? For your students?
2. How will you use an intrinsically motivating learning environment to help bring change to your classroom? (see Chapter 5)
3. How will you use active learning to encourage change? (see Chapter 6)
4. Which teaching strategies will help you facilitate change? How will you make sure that the changes you have planned will work with how students learn best? Refer back to Chapter 4 for help.
5. How does the service-learning project fit into your plan for change?

Case Example: Create a Plan for Change

When I first started teaching as a graduate assistant, I will admit that I taught differently than all of the other graduate assistants. I was a group specialist, so I naturally taught using group discussions. I have long believed in community service. When I later became a believer of the merits of academic service-learning, I combined my focus on teaching through groups with my belief in service. *Camp Sharigan* was no longer just a service project; it was the teaching method that I used in the classroom to bring about a deeper level of learning. Instead of using classroom exercises, I wanted my students to be working on real problems that would bring about actual change in their lives and the lives of those they worked with in the community. *Camp Sharigan* was the key to my plan for change. *Camp Sharigan* has been tested with hundreds of children and proven to be effective in numerous communities in six different states.

As I've stated before, not every service project works. It is essential for you to use a service project that actually works. There is nothing more disheartening for college students than to discover that the project they have worked on all semester has failed. Yes, I know, we learn from our experiences, but this is not the time for that lesson. Pick a service project that you are certain will work. I have used *Camp Sharigan* for over 20 years, and it has never failed.

Step one: I identified a service project, community need, and a project that I had tested with university students and proven to be successful. [see Chapter 3]

Step two: I laid out all of the information that I wanted to teach in my course so that I would know how much content material I wanted to cover. [see Chapter 6]

Step three: I began linking content and service together. I asked myself how can I use *Camp Sharigan* to teach textbook material to the students in class: I decided on a problem-solution format. I start each class with a problem. I use only realistic problems from the actual service project. I use real case studies, nothing fictional or contrived. Students are given a situation or problem and told to: (1) identify the problem, (2) set-up criteria for evaluating the problem (what do you hope for or need—goal(s) or ideal situation), (3) propose solutions to the problem, (4) evaluate proposed solutions through analysis and critical thinking against the criteria that had been established, (5) test the best solution in a real world setting, (6) reflect through analysis and evaluation on the success of the solution, (7) make changes as needed, and (8) reevaluate for improvement.

Use only safe proposals. Since I was working with children, I was always very careful to make sure that any student solutions or proposals for change were safe and in keeping with the group-centered prevention strategies of *Camp Sharigan.* University students were not allowed to change the actual teaching structure, curriculum, or hands-on materials used for *Camp Sharigan.* The reading curriculum came totally from the ready-to-use *Camp Sharigan* program packet.

Undergraduates are not ready to design a workable program. An example of a problem that students were allowed to test is how to use the "treasure hunt maps" to help students move around to the 10 workstations more easily. This does not change either the curriculum, or what the children are learning, but it is a real, ongoing problem that each university class must solve. Obviously, the arrangement of the room(s) changes how the children move from workstation to workstation. Therefore, this gives my students real input, but it also ensures that the program will retain its original curriculum, be successful, and that the children who come to *Camp Sharigan* will learn. As most professional program designers will tell you, it is impossible to design a really good program and test it for effectiveness in only one semester. I spent 10 years designing and testing *Camp Sharigan* (Clanton Harpine 2024) before I could guarantee that *Camp Sharigan* (if used as written) would work every time.

Step four: As we continued to make plans and organize *Camp Sharigan*, students discussed and worked on solving problems. Students also worked on making signs for each workstation, organizing supplies, selecting books, and figuring out how to best set up the room(s) in the community space provided. All discussions were oriented toward applying the textbook information to *Camp Sharigan.* Such questions as: How can we rebuild self-efficacy with the children at *Camp Sharigan*? How can you use intrinsic motivation to help a child who is struggling? What if a child won't participate?

Organization. So, students were both involved with the organizing of *Camp Sharigan* as well as the application of the theories and textbook information. *Camp Sharigan* could be used at the beginning, middle, or even at the end of the semester. It depended on the university course and what I was trying to achieve through the service project. For example, my psychology of motivation students might conduct *Camp Sharigan* in the middle of the semester because they needed to learn a little bit about motivation before they were ready to apply it in a real-world setting. In contrast, my group therapy students might need to start with *Camp Sharigan* because they would be using *Camp Sharigan* to learn about group process, and then they would be comparing it to the therapy groups that they would be working with later in the semester. Still other classes might use *Camp Sharigan* at the end of the semester.

Teach content. The primary focus with academic service-learning is to use your service project to teach the content of your course in a real-world setting. If you have a service project that has been tested with the community, such as *Camp Sharigan*, then you do not need to worry about fulfilling your desire to build civic mindedness. Academic service-learning links service and learning together.

References

Adams, C. E. (2015). Service-learning projects: What students' reflections reveal. *Journal of Service-Learning in Higher Education, 4,* 1–23.

Arum, R., & Roksa, J. (2011). *Academically adrift: Limited learning on college campuses.* Chicago: University of Chicago press.

Bok, D. (2020). *Higher Expectations: Can colleges teach students what they need to know in the twenty-first century?* Princeton, NJ: Princeton University Press.

Bringle, R. G., & Hatcher, J. A. (2017). Innovative practices in service-learning and curricular engagement. *New Directions for Higher Education, 147*, 37–46. https://doi.org/10.1002/he.356
Butler, H. A., & Halpern, D. F. (2020). Critical thinking impacts our everyday lives. In R. J. Sternberg & D. F. Halpern (Eds.), *Critical thinking in psychology* (2nd ed., pp. 152–172). Cambridge, England: Cambridge University Press.
Caldwell, C., & Anderson, V. (2021). "University professors as "transformative leaders". *The Journal of Values-Based Leadership, 14*, 1–12.
Carberry, A. R., Lee, H-S., & Swan, C. W. (2013). Engineering service students' perceptions of service as a source of learning technical and professional skills. *International Journal of Service Learning in Engineering, 8*, 1–17.
Clanton Harpine, E. (ed.) (2019). *After-school programming and intrinsic motivation: Teaching at-risk students to read.* Cham, Switzerland: Springer Nature.
Clanton Harpine, E. (2024). *Camp Sharigan: A ready-to-use group-centered intervention for grades 1–3* (3rd ed.). Corpus Christi, TX: Group-Centered Learning.
Clanton Harpine, E., & Pazda, A. (2019). Is group-centered better than classroom instruction for teaching reading? The need for a group-centered approach. Testing two group methods. In E. Clanton Harpine (Ed.), *Afterschool programming and intrinsic motivation: Teaching at-risk students to read.* (pp. 29–47). Cham, Switzerland: Springer Nature.
Clanton Harpine, E., & Reid, T. (2009). Enhancing academic achievement in a Hispanic immigrant community: The role of reading in academic failure and mental health. *School Mental Health,* 1, 159–170. https://doi.org/10.1007/s12310-009-9011-z
Cooke, T. J., Jensen, J. S., Carleton, K. L., Hall, K. L., Jardine, H. F., Kent, B. W., Redish, E. F., & Schultz, J. W. (2023). Group active engagements for facilitating principles-based learning in introductory organismal biology. *The American Biology Teacher, 85,* 317–326. https://doi.org/10.1525/abt.2023.85.6.317
Cronley, C., Madden, E., & Davis, J. B. (2015). Making service-learning partnerships work: Listening and responding to community partners, *Journal of Community Practice, 23*, 274–289. https://doi.org/10.1080/10705422.2015.1027801
Fink, L. D. (2013). *Creating significant learning experiences: An integrated approach to designing college courses* (2nd ed.). San Francisco, CA: Jossey-Bass.
Forsberg, E., Bäcklund, B., Telhede, E., & Karlsson, S. (2019). Virtual patient cases for active student participation in nursing education—students' learning experiences. *Creative Education,* 10, 1475–1491. https://doi.org/10.4236/ce.2019.107108
Freeland, R. (2019). *Transforming the urban university.* Philadelphia, PA: University of Pennsylvania Press.
Freitas, J. C., Souza, I. R., Cabral, P. M. F., & Bruno, L. V. P. (2021). Leadership: Challenge or need in faculty development of the universities. *Development Studies Research, 8,* 356–364. https://doi.org/10.1080/21665095.2021.1990098
Furco, A. (2001). Advancing service-learning at research universities. *New Directions for Higher Education*, 114, 67–78.
Halpern, D. F., & Dunn, D. S. (2021). Critical thinking: A model of intelligence for solving real-world problems. *Journal of Intelligence, 9*, 22. https://doi.org/10.3390/jintelligence9020022
Halpern, D., & Hakel, M. (2003). Applying the science of learning to the university and beyond: Teaching for long-term retention and transfer. *Change: The Magazine of Higher Learning, 35*, 36–41. https://doi.org/10.1080/00091380309604109
Hart, S. M., & King, J. R. (2007). Service learning and literacy tutoring: Academic impact on pre-service teachers. *Teaching and Teacher Education, 23,* 323–328. https://doi.org/10.1016/j.tate.2006.12.004
Hattie, J. (2015). High-impact leadership. *Educational leadership, 72*, 36–40.
Heffernan, K. (2001). *Fundamentals of service-learning course construction.* Boston, MA: Campus Compact.
Hou, S., & Wilder, S. (2015). Changing Pedagogy: Faculty adoption of service- learning: Motivations, barriers, and strategies among service-learning faculty at a public research institution. *SAGE Open, 5*(1). https://doi.org/10.1177/2158244015572283

Howard, J. (ed.). (2001). *Michigan journal of community service learning: Service-learning course design workbook*. Ann Arbor, MI: OCSL Press.
Jackson, M. (2012). Deep approaches to learning in higher education. In: N. M. Seel (Ed.), *Encyclopedia of the Sciences of Learning* (pp. 913–915). Boston, MA: Springer. https://doi.org/10.1007/978-1-4419-1428-6_1843
Jaschik, S., & Lederman, D. (2020). *Survey of college and university chief academic officers*. Washington, D. C.: Inside Higher Education/Gallup.
Kennedy, H. R., & Gruber, A. H. (2020). Critical thinking in a service-learning course: Impacts of information literacy instruction. *Communications in Information Literacy, 14*, 205–226. https://doi.org/10.15760/comminfolit.2020.14.2.3
Krsmanovic, M. (2022). Fostering service-learning and leadership development through first-year seminar courses. *Journal of Service-Learning in Higher Education, 15,* 54–70.
Kuh, G. D., Cruce, T. M., Shoup, R., & Kinzie, J. (2008). Unmasking the effects of student engagement on first-year college grades and persistence. *Journal of Higher Education, 79,* 540–563. https://doi.org/10.1353/jhe.0.0019
Lo, K. W. K., Ngai, G., Chan, S. C. F., & Kwan, K. P. (2022). How students' motivation and learning experience affect their service-learning outcomes: A structural equation modeling analysis. *Frontiers in Psychology, 13*, 825902. https://doi.org/10.3389/fpsyg.2022.825902
Moser, S. C., & Fazey, I. (2021). If it is life we want: A prayer for the future (of the) university. *Frontiers in Sustainability, 2*, 1–7. https://doi.org/10.3389/frsus.2021.662657
Mottner, S. (2010). Service-learning in a nonprofit marketing course: A comparative case of pedagogical tools. *Journal of Nonprofit & Public Sector Marketing, 22*, 231–245. https://doi.org/10.1080/10495142.2010.483274
Nickerson, R. S. (2020). Developing intelligence through instruction. In: Sternberg R. J., & Kaufman, S. B. (Eds.), *The Cambridge Handbook of Intelligence.* (2nd ed.) (pp. 205–237). Cambridge: Cambridge University Press.
O'Meara, K., Sandmann, L.R., Saltmarsh, J., & Giles, Jr., D. E. (2011). Studying the professional lives and work of faculty involved in community engagement. *Innovative Higher Education 36*, 83–96. https://doi.org/10.1007/s10755-010-9159-3
Okinyi, N. P., Kwaba, J. G., & Nyabuto, N. N. (2015). The role of leaders in transforming learners and learning in the higher learning institutions in Kenya. *Journal of Education and Practice, 6,* 105–116.
Pribbenow, D. A. (2005). The impact of service-learning pedagogy on faculty teaching and learning. *Michigan Journal of Community Service Learning, 11*, 25–38.
Ramsden, P. (2003). *Learning to teach in higher education*, 2nd ed. NY: Routledge Fulmer.
Rehman, N., Mahmood, A., Ibtasam, M., Murtaza, S. A., Iqbal, N., & Molnár, E. (2021). The psychology of resistance to change: The antidotal effect of organizational justice, support and leader-member exchange. *Frontiers in Psychology, 12*, 1–15. https://doi.org/10.3389/fpsyg.2021.678952
Sandy, M., & Holland, B. A. (2006). Different worlds and common ground: Community partner perspectives on campus–community partnerships. *Michigan Journal of Community Service Learning, 13*, 30–43.
Shin, J., Kim, M., Hwang, H., & Lee, B. (2018). Effects of intrinsic motivation and informative feedback in service-learning on the development of college students' life purpose. *Journal of Moral Education, 47*, 159–174. https://doi.org/10.1080/03057240.2017.1419943
Southworth, J. (2022). Bridging critical thinking and transformative learning: The role of perspective-taking. *Theory and Research in Education, 20*, 44–63. https://doi.org/10.1177/14778785221090853
Spence, L. (2001). The case against teaching. *Change: The Magazine of Higher Learning, 33*, 10–19.
Strata Education Network. (2017). *College student survey: A nationally representative survey of currently enrolled students*. Washington, D. C.: Gallup, Inc.
Tagg, J. (2012). Why does the faculty resist change*? Change: The Magazine of Higher Learning, 44,* 6–15. https://doi.org/10.1080/00091383.2012.635987

Taggart, A., & Crisp, G. (2011). Service learning at community colleges: Synthesis, critique, and recommendations for future research. *Journal of College Reading & Learning, 42*, 24–44.

Valtonen, T., Leppänen, U., Hyypiä, M., Kokko, A., Manninen, J., Vartiaainen, H., Sointu, E., & Hirsto, L. (2021). Learning environments preferred by university students: A shift toward informal and flexible learning environments. *Learning Environments Research*, *24,* 371–388. https://doi.org/10.1007/s10984-020-09339-6

Warren, J. L. (2012). Does service-learning increase student learning? A meta-analysis. *Michigan Journal of Community Service Learning, 18,* 56–61.

Warren, J. L., & Sellnow, T. L. (2010). Learning through service: The contributions of service learning to the Communication discipline. In D. L. Fassett & J. T. Warren (Eds.), *Handbook of communication and instruction* (pp. 129–145). Thousand Oaks, CA: Sage Publications.

Whetten, D. A. (2007). Principles of effective course design: What I wish I had known about learning-centered teaching 30 years ago. *Journal of Management Education*, *31*, 339–357. https://doi.org/10.1177/1052562906298445

Ziegert, A., & McGoldrick, K. (2008). When service is good for economics: Linking the classroom and community through service-learning. *International Review of Economics Education, 7,* 39–56. https://doi.org/10.1016/S1477-3880(15)30090-6

Chapter 10
What Impact Will the Academic Service-Learning Project Have on the Community? How Can I Best Prepare My Students to Work at an Off-Campus Community Setting?

> *"I was first introduced to group-centered prevention programs* [*Camp Sharigan*] *as an undergraduate. I was a nursing student who needed to complete a graduation requirement and thought psychology would be a good accompaniment to my major. Before graduation, I became a paid staff member and worked as an Assistant Director* [at the after-school year-long program—*Reading Orienteering Club*]. *Little did I know, I would be using the information I learned and the skills I gained, throughout the next several years. I have been able to utilize group-centered interventions in my work with schools, nonprofit organizations, and university courses."* [taken from first person account from a graduate student] (Clanton Harpine et al. 2019 p. 163)

As expressed in this graduate student reflection, university students benefit from academic service-learning, even years after they have left the university. Research shows that the benefits of academic service-learning are the same regardless of the institution's scope—community college, 4-year, private, or research university (Cronley et al. 2015; Sandy and Holland 2006; Taggart and Crisp 2011). In Chapter 1, we focused on the benefits of academic service-learning for the university, for faculty, and for students. In this final chapter, we continue to look at the benefits for students and faculty, while also looking at the benefits for the community.

E. Clanton Harpine, *Service Learning in Higher Education*,
https://doi.org/10.1007/978-3-031-51378-7_10

What Is the Impact of an Academic Service-Learning Project for the Community?

Community partners are often eager to participate in university-community service projects first and foremost because they need volunteers. Service-learners are a critical part of the workforce of some organizations. As one community partner stated:

> "Our program would probably not survive if we do not have service-learners. It's economics. We couldn't possibly hire the number of people we need to do our programs." (Sandy and Holland 2006 p. 36)

Free volunteers are not the only benefit for community organizations, because a special bond can develop between university students and community workers.

Academic service-learning helps create a bond between the university and the community. When students work, for example, as mentors, tutors, or community organizers, they create a link between the people they are working with and the knowledge that they have gained from the university (Cronley et al. 2015). They take critical thinking into the community. They bridge the gap between textbook theory, new research, and the real world. Students help raise public awareness. As one community partner stated:

> "[Students] come from the university hoping to help us build a house, but with service-learning in context, that same student would understand why there is a lack of affordable housing, what is the impact of a lack of housing on the community, on a low-income family, on a neighborhood." (Sandy and Holland 2006 p. 35)

Academic service-learning educates as well as helping those in need. Academic service-learning is more than just community service. The students are at a community worksite for more than just putting in a certain number of service hours. Students bring new information, new solutions to old problems, and the desire for change. Let's look at *Camp Sharigan* (Clanton Harpine 2024) as an example.

> *Camp Sharigan* began as a summer service project. I tested it in communities in Tampa, Chicago, Dallas, Akron, and the Bronx in New York. Once I was certain that *Camp Sharigan* would work in any community, I brought it back home and based my academic service-learning pedagogy on *Camp Sharigan*. Students and faculty from computer science, math, sociology, criminal justice, education, nursing, communication, biology, history, English, and naturally psychology participated in *Camp Sharigan*. Community organizations that worked with children requested permission to send children to *Camp Sharigan*. Parents, whose children were struggling in school, frequently contacted me seeking help. When I expanded the *Camp Sharigan* project to a year-long program, even the schools were contacting me asking to be allowed to send students. A single academic service-learning project can become a community project that helps hundreds.

What Is the Impact of the Academic Service-Learning Project for Students?

Academic service-learning benefits universities, faculty, and students because it expands and deepens the learning experience as well as increasing the relevance of what is learned in the classroom (Campbell and Oswald 2018). Deeper learning and critical thinking are also beneficial for the community. As Robert J. Sternberg and Diane F. Halpern (2020) stated in the preface to their book, *Critical Thinking in Psychology*,

> "We live in an age in which, frankly, many people have begun to wonder whether our society as a whole and its governing officers have lost their ability to think critically. Officials at the highest levels of government talk about "alternative facts" or argue that "truth isn't truth." (xii)

Critical thinking is important for everyone. If you teach critical thinking, students will take critical thinking into the communities where they work.

Real-world problem-solving. Students need to climb out of the university campus' protective world. They need to work and confront problems in real-world settings (Clanton Harpine and Reid 2009). Academic service-learning provides this real-world contact. Academic service-learning links the real world with course content and what students are learning in the university classroom (Clanton Harpine and Pazda 2019). A real-world experience is the most valuable impact that academic service-learning can provide for university students.

Change. University students become role models; they foster change in a community setting. The community also becomes an agent of change for university students. A student's attitudes and beliefs about poverty and those who live in poverty may be completely and totally changed through an academic service-learning project (Seider et al. 2011). The university can also become known as an avenue of change. As a lady asked me one day in the grocery store, "Are you the lady that works at that place downtown where they teach children to read?" Academic service-learning generates excitement, intrinsic desire, commitment, and engagement. When you combine learning from the classroom with real-world service application, the result is deeper learning outcomes for students as well as benefits to the community.

How Can I Best Prepare My Students to Work at an Off-Campus Community Setting?

Obviously, in-class preparation for students depends on the type of service project being undertaken. Your academic service-learning pedagogy should include training to help students prepare for their service experience. Academic service-learning helps students build confidence, strengthens communication skills, and serves as a change agent. Helping students change the world around them for the better is a powerful lifelong lesson for every university student to learn.

Choose a service project that fits with your students' needs and abilities. The first step in preparing your students to work at an off-campus community service worksite is to select a project that fits with student needs and abilities (reread Chapter 3 for guidelines). Do not choose a project that students simply cannot do. Failure is not constructive. You want to bring about positive change for both the students and the community. As one college student from *Camp Sharigan* said:

> "It is very important that the clinic make an impact on these children and hopefully benefit them for the rest of their lives. I thoroughly enjoyed working at this clinic and it gave me a

> very real insight as to how diverse academically my students will be when I become a teacher and will have to accommodate them." (Clanton Harpine et al. 2019 p. 162)

Select a service project that offers skills and benefits for all of your students.

Match student skills to the task. If you are collaborating with Habitat for Humanity, you need to discuss the type of work they want students to do. Not everyone can climb on a house and lay shingles for a new roof. Yet, you do not want some students working while others merely watch. Preparation includes outlining the types of jobs that need to be done and, then, matching student skills to those jobs.

Teach skills in class before you arrive at the worksite. Build necessary training into your classroom work sessions. Teach critical thinking, problem-solving, and analytical reasoning through examples that come directly from the service project (see case example at the end of this chapter). In this way, the students will have experienced thinking about problems that will arise and have practiced how to solve such problems before they arrive at the service worksite. Three steps to follow in preparation are:

1. **Awareness**: Teach students about the social problem or organization that you are going out into the community to work with. If you're going out to work on voter registration, then teach about the problems of unrepresented voters, gerrymandering, and how low socioeconomic and handicap citizens are kept from voting. Incorporate the community problem into your course content. For example, *Camp Sharigan* is designed to prevent reading failure; therefore, I teach my students about the severity and widespread nature of reading failure by using statistics from the Nation's Report Card. They are shocked to learn that 60% of 4th, 8th, and 12th graders cannot read at grade level. I also teach my students the community outcomes of reading failure by explaining that 85% of juveniles going through the court system are classified as being illiterate because they cannot read (for more on this research, see, Clanton Harpine 2013). Students need to be aware of the problem they are working to correct. I link reading failure to motivational psychology by showing how intrinsic motivation can make a difference in helping children learn to read. Most university students are eager to help others, especially if they feel confident that the service-learning project will actually help.
2. **Problem-solving.** Teach students how to solve problems that they will encounter at the community worksite. As one university student said,

> "One student I worked with could barely write his name. I worked with him, holding his hand, and helping him to shape his letters." (Clanton Harpine et al. 2019 p. 163)

University students need to be able to handle any problem or emergency that arises. For example, my students practice (through case studies) how to handle real problems that have arisen at *Camp Sharigan*. If possible, always use real case studies rather than fictional stories. If you want your service-learning project to succeed, problem-solving training is essential. If you are working with a homeless community, then teach students how to be aware of the needs of homeless people, how to speak in a considerate manner, and why homelessness is such a devastating problem for all citizens.

3. **Take action.** If you have trained your students well and have integrated the theory and knowledge they need into your class sessions, students should be eager

to go out into the community. One of the best ways to support your students and make sure that the service-learning project succeeds is to work alongside your students. Get involved. Instead of just sending students out into the community to do a job, go with them and work with them. Community leaders really appreciate it when faculty are at the site supporting their students, and students really admire professors who believe in service so strongly that they are willing to volunteer and work side-by-side with their students.

Summary

When we increase student and faculty participation in the community through academic service-learning, we enhance and improve university-community relations. We also help prepare students to assume their role as tomorrow's leaders in the real world. The best way to help prepare students for an academic service-learning project is to teach the skills that are needed during classroom sessions.

Building a Service-Learning Pedagogy

Questions to Help in Course Planning

1. Review the goals that you have set for your course.
2. Are there goals that you would like to add after reading this chapter?
3. How will you help prepare your students for working at the community worksite?

Troubleshooting Checklist

1. How will you increase the awareness of your students for the social problem that you are working on?
2. How does the course that you are teaching link with the social problem that you are working to change?
3. What kind of training will your students need to be successful with the service project? How will you provide this training?

Planning Guide Sheet

1. What type of training will you implement during class sessions?
2. How will you use an intrinsically motivating learning environment to help train your students? (see Chapter 5)
3. How will you use active learning to train your students? (see Chapter 6)
4. Which teaching strategies will help you facilitate training?
5. How will you make sure that the training you have planned will work at the service project worksite?

Case Example

I use *Camp Sharigan* as my service-learning project with all my courses. Reading failure is a universal problem. Reading failure relates to every student no matter what subject they are majoring in. To prepare my students to work at *Camp Sharigan*, I use real problem-solving case studies from *Camp Sharigan*. Using real problems and case studies are the best way to train my students. When we arrive at *Camp Sharigan*, the students know what to expect, and they have had an opportunity in class to learn how to respond to problems that frequently arise. In-class training helps students plan how they will respond. Preparation and training are the keys to success.

An example of how I use real case studies comes from a little first grade boy. [I never include names or any identifying information.] First, I have students work individually before class by writing in their journal how they would respond to the case study. This is a take-home assignment, and they are encouraged to use their textbook.

> Case Study: On the first day of *Camp Sharigan*, a little first grade boy arrived about 30 minutes late. He had after-school detention. Upon his arrival, the university student in charge gave him a *treasure hunt* map and showed him how to find the different workstations. As she explained, "All you need to do is match the letters here on the treasure hunt map with the letters on the signs to find your way around the room. Make sure you go to all 10 stations because we are making a very special puppet today, and you will find a piece for your puppet at each workstation. Have fun." [We teach the children to match the letters rather than reading the signs because some of the children cannot read yet.] We were working in the school gymnasium that day. The little boy at first seemed to be going in the right direction. Then, he switched directions, went to the far corner of the gym, plopped down on the floor, and proceeded to roll back and forth across the gymnasium floor. What should the university students do? How would you handle a similar situation if such occurred?

The university students bring their written responses to the next class session. Then in class, they work first in small groups to establish a criterion and evaluate their responses. They collectively decide on a group response to present to the total class. As a class, we evaluate each response in keeping with the criteria established by the class. Then, I tell the students the rest of the case study and how the problem was dealt with at the reading clinic and why. Therefore, this one case study becomes both a training exercise and an example of how textbook theory can be applied in a real-world setting.

Academic service-learning can turn your classroom into a learning laboratory where students challenge themselves to change the world. Academic service-learning will also help you teach more course content than you ever dreamed possible. Academic service-learning has proven to be an excellent way to increase student engagement and academic success. Helping students learn is what academic service-learning is all about.

References

Campbell, C. G., & Oswald, B. R. (2018). Promoting critical thinking through service learning: A home-visiting case study. *Teaching of Psychology, 45*, 193–199. https://doi.org/10.1177/0098628318762933

Clanton Harpine, E. (2013). *After-school prevention programs for at-risk students: Promoting engagement and academic success*. New York: Springer.

Clanton Harpine, E. (2024). *Camp Sharigan: A ready-to-use group-centered intervention for grades 1–3* (3rd ed.). Corpus Christi, TX: Group-Centered Learning.

Clanton Harpine, E., & Pazda, A. (2019). Is group-centered better than classroom instruction for teaching reading? The need for a group-centered approach. Testing two group methods. In E. Clanton Harpine (Ed.), *Afterschool programming and intrinsic motivation: Teaching at-risk students to read.* (pp. 29–47). Cham, Switzerland: Springer Nature.

Clanton Harpine, E., & Reid, T. (2009). Enhancing academic achievement in a Hispanic immigrant community: The role of reading in academic failure and mental health. *School Mental Health,* 1, 159–170. https://doi.org/10.1007/s12310-009-9011-z

Clanton Harpine, E., Weed, K., Stevens, S., Harpine, W. D., Coleman, B., Reid, T., Ingram, S. Thompson, A., Cederstrom, C., & Hamilton, K. (2019). Where do we go from here? Comments from the research team: How can you apply what we learned to your own after-school reading program? In Elaine Clanton Harpine (Ed.) *After-school programming and intrinsic motivation: Teaching at-risk students to read.* (pp. 149–167). Cham, Switzerland: Springer Nature.

Cronley, C., Madden, E., & Davis, J. B. (2015). Making service-learning partnerships work: Listening and responding to community partners, *Journal of Community Practice, 23*, 274–289. https://doi.org/10.1080/10705422.2015.1027801

Sandy, M., & Holland, B. A. (2006). Different worlds and common ground: Community partner perspectives on campus–community partnerships. *Michigan Journal of Community Service Learning, 13*, 30–43.

Seider, S. C., Rabinowicz, S. A., & Gillmor, S. C. (2011). Changing American college students' conceptions of poverty through community service learning. *Analyses of Social Issues and Public Policy (ASAP), 11*, 105–126. https://doi.org/10.1111/j.1530-2415.2010.01224.x

Sternberg, R. J., & Halpern, D. F. (eds). (2020). *Critical thinking in psychology* (2nd ed). Cambridge, United Kingdom: Cambridge University Press.

Taggart, A., & Crisp, G. (2011). Service learning at community colleges: Synthesis, critique, and recommendations for future research. *Journal of College Reading & Learning, 42*, 24–44.

Correction to: Service Learning in Higher Education

Correction to:
Chapters 2, 6 and 7 in: *E. Clanton Harpine, Service Learning in Higher Education*, https://doi.org/10.1007/978-3-031-51378-7

A colon was missed between the two parts of the chapter title in the titles of Chapters 2, 6 and 7. The title of these chapters have been changed as follows after the initial publication:

Chapter 2: from 'The Advantages of Using Academic Service-Learning in a University Classroom What Does the Research Say?' to 'The Advantages of Using Academic Service-Learning in a University Classroom: What Does the Research Say?'

Chapter 6: from 'Building an Academic Service-Learning Pedagogy How Can a Course Incorporate Academic Service-Learning?' to 'Building an Academic Service-Learning Pedagogy: How Can a Course Incorporate Academic Service-Learning?'

Chapter 7: from 'Designing an Academic Service-Learning Course How Can Faculty Members Measure Learning and Student Reflection?' to 'Designing An Academic Service-Learning Course: How Can Faculty Members Measure Learning and Student Reflection?'

Apart from these a few other minor changes have been made, in other chapters which don't change the basic facts.

The updated version of these chapters can be found at
https://doi.org/10.1007/978-3-031-51378-7_2
https://doi.org/10.1007/978-3-031-51378-7_6
https://doi.org/10.1007/978-3-031-51378-7_7

E. Clanton Harpine, *Service Learning in Higher Education*,
https://doi.org/10.1007/978-3-031-51378-7_11

Index

E. Clanton Harpine, *Service Learning in Higher Education*,
https://doi.org/10.1007/978-3-031-51378-7

P

Q

R

S

T

The manufacturer's authorised representative in the EU is Springer Nature Customer Service Centre GmbH, Europaplatz 3, 69115 Heidelberg, Germany. If you have any concerns regarding our products, please contact ProductSafety@springernature.com

Printed and bound by CPI Group (UK) Ltd, Croydon, CR0 4YY
01/10/2026
02225897-0002